CLASSIC

GERMAN COURSE

IN ENGLISH.

BY

WILLIAM CLEAVER WILKINSON.

NEW YORK:
CHAUTAUQUA PRESS,
C. L. S. C. Department,
150 FIFTH AVENUE, COR. 20TH STREET.
1891.

The required books of the C. L. S. C. are recommended by a Council of Six. It must, however, be understood that recommendation does not involve an approval by the Council, or by any member of it, of every principle or doctrine contained in the book recommended.

PREFACE.

THE present volume has an object similar to that of each volume preceding in the AFTER-SCHOOL SERIES to which it belongs. It aims to enable readers knowing English, but not German, to acquire, through the medium of the former language, some satisfactory acquaintance—acquaintance at once general and particular—with the chief classics of German literature.

The method proposed of accomplishing this is—having first premised a rapid summary sketch and characterization of German literature as a whole—to select, with some Spartan hardness of heart, from among German authors no longer living, those generally acknowledged the best, and present these through translation, in specimens from one or more of their respective masterpieces—whether prose or verse—accompanied with such comment, biographical, explanatory, critical, as may be judged desirable in order to securing the fairest and fullest final impression on the reader's mind, primarily, of the true characteristic individual quality of each author treated, and, secondarily, of each author's historic relation and influence.

The limits imposed by the size in which the volume appears were accepted by the writer as on the whole judiciously chosen, but, at any rate, as fixed and unchangeable. His simple problem has been—problem simple, though found far enough from easy—to make the best possible use of the inelastic space at his disposal. Considerate judges will estimate his success with wise respect to the conditions under which he has necessarily worked.

Hitherto, in the present series of books, some regard has steadily been had to the proportion in the study of foreign tongues, living and dead, observed by the average American school of higher education. Modern languages, especially the French and the German, but more especially the German, have of late been encroaching somewhat on the ancient preserves prescriptively belonging to those two great languages of antiquity, the Greek and the Latin, in the courses of study established by our colleges and universities. Thus far, however, their place therein remains, and, as the present writer thinks, properly remains, generally less than that of their elder kindred. The room, therefore, narrow though it be, given, in the pages which follow, to German literature, is after all not so very inadequate—measured in comparison with the quasi-authoritative standard, to which, as now hinted, habitual deference has, throughout this series of volumes, been paid.

It has not been thought necessary, or even desirable, in fulfillment of the purpose of the present volume—more than in the case of the volumes preceding in the series—that the author should frequently either make new translations of his own, or secure such from other hands, for the extracts to be introduced. A fresh version will indeed here and there be found in these pages; but for the most part recourse has been had to translations previously existing in English. In general, for each case as it arose, the writer has compared various translations one with another, as also, of course, with their common original, sufficiently to satisfy himself what rendering was, all things considered, best suited to his purpose; and then, besides, in the particular passages finally selected from considerable works for transfer to his pages, he has collated his chosen version with the corresponding German text, in order to make corrections or improvements observed by him to be needed. In some instances, however —instances in which the authority of the translator, either for scholarship or for literary skill, was great—he has remitted this caution.

Nothing further, perhaps, in the way of explanation, is required—unless to say that the present writer may be understood, acting under a sense of serious responsibility, to have formed independently for himself, though, naturally, not without much comparative study of various discussion by others, the literary, and by occasion the ethical, judgments and opinions which he has here committed himself to express.

On the whole, it is a humble work, for a work so arduous and so full of risk to himself, that the writer herewith submits to the public. He hopes that he shall at least be found to have done no injustice, either to the authors whom he presents, or to the readers to whom he presents them.

CONTENTS.

CLASSIC
GERMAN COURSE IN ENGLISH

———— ◆◆◆ ————

I.

GERMAN LITERATURE.

To Germany may justly be accorded the paradoxical distinction of possessing at once the most voluminous and the least voluminous national literature in the world. Our meaning is, that while the aggregate bulk of books written and printed in the German language would probably be found to exceed, and even vastly exceed, that of those written and printed in any other language whatever, you would certainly look elsewhere in vain for a second example of a national literature in which the proportion of what, judged at once for substance and for form, could be pronounced choice and admirable was equally small. The German genius is prolific in thought, it is eager for expression; but of beauty in expression for thought, it is far, very far, from being correspondingly, we need not say capable, but desirous. The result is, as we have intimated, that, while of literature, in the large, loose sense of the term, the Germans have even an over-supply, of literature in the strict, narrow sense, they possess comparatively little. Little comparatively, we say; for absolutely they possess much. And of this much in quantity, a part at least is in quality very fine.

Our concern, in the present volume, will be chiefly with what is best in German literature. We shall leave to one side, merely mentioning perhaps, as we pass, all that enormous contribution of the German mind to classical scholarship, to sacred hermeneutics, to dogmatic theology, to metaphysic speculation, to exact science, to historical research. This has been, it still is, it always will be, immensely important to the accumulation of intellectual treasure for the human race ; it is even widely and enduringly important to the development of literature—the literature of the world at large, as well as of Germany ; but proper literature itself it is not. In short, literature in the higher sense of that term—polite literature—has never yet been to Germany the favorite, fullest expression of the national genius.

During a certain limited period of time, such did indeed seem almost to be the case. The period which had its long and splendid culmination in Goethe was, no doubt, a predominantly literary period in Germany. Long, we thus suffer ourselves to call the culmination of that period ; yet in truth, accurately considered, the culmination was not long, but short. It seems long only in a kind of illogical, illusive association with the lengthened life-time and lengthened productive activity of Goethe himself, the space between whose birth and whose death spans well-nigh the entire chief literary history of Germany. Klopstock published the beginning of his *Messiah* in 1748 ; in 1749 Goethe was born. What was there in German literature before the *Messiah* of Klopstock ? In 1832 Goethe died; in 1826 Heine had published the first installment of his masterpiece, the *Pictures of Travel.* What has there been in German literature since ?

Of course, we speak broadly, and with only approximate truth. Klopstock was not the earliest, and Heine is not the latest, of German authors. Still, it is one of the chiefly remarkable things about the history of literature in Germany that that literature should first have been so tardy in beginning, and then should have apparently exhausted itself in a development so sudden and so short.

So tardy, however, in beginning, as we shall thus seem to have represented, German literature in reality was not. You have to run back from Klopstock, two centuries, to Luther, to find the true moment from which to date the dawn of a national literature in Germany. *The* national literature *of* Germany, we ought perhaps rather to say. For even before Luther, the German mind had, as it were unconsciously, grown at least one literary product, important enough to be justly called in itself a literature, and racy enough of the soil from which it sprang to be called emphatically a *national* literature. We refer, of course, to the anonymous epic, the *Nibelungen Lied*, so styled. This poem, however, the Iliad of the German-speaking race, belonged, not only in its probable first state of pure oral tradition, but also in the modified written form to which a later age reduced it, to an order of things that had been completely superseded long before Luther appeared. The epic itself, in Luther's day, had been forgotten, or at least lost utterly out of sight. In truth, a catastrophe in literary history had intervened, which separates the age of the *Nibelungen Lied* from the age of Luther as absolutely as classic Greek and Roman antiquity is separated from the times in which we live. Nay, this comparison understates the fact. For with the now living literature of Germany the *Nibelungen Lied* has far less genetic connection than have the foreign and ancient literatures of Greece and Rome. It is proper, accordingly, to treat the current German literature as a growth rooting itself in a national past no more remote than the age of the Reformation. Luther, it deserves to be added, did not in his time stand solitary, though he stood supreme, as founder of modern German letters. Hans Sachs is a late-resuscitated name—a name which should never have been suffered to sink into need of resuscitation—worthy to ride in the same orbit of literary fame with Luther, as a brilliant, though inferior, satellite by his side. Ulrich von Hütten, too, was a knightly man of letters, who, with far less of shrewd, homely popular instinct than characterized either one of these two contemporaries of his, had genius enough and wit enough to have made his part in the *Epistolæ Obscurorum Virorum*, had he, when writing his contribution to that immortal series of pasquinades, written in German instead of in Latin, a permanent classic of the language.

But Luther's was the true vivific literary, as well as religious, mind of the period. The mighty master-spirit of the great Reformation stamped with his foot on his native soil, and forthwith, obedient to the sign, there sprang up, for his "dear Germans," along with a purified Christianity, a new vernacular literature. These two things, but, alas, not these alone. Wars, too, were awakened—dreadful wars, amid which, and in the sequel of which, for whole generations, literature and Christianity alike seemed near going hopelessly down together in Germany. Seldom in the history of the world has it happened that a civilized country, destined after all to survive, and to survive in eventual power, was brought so close to the brink of irrecoverable desolation as was Germany (1618–1648) by the Thirty Years' War. No wonder, if a people almost annihilated did little more than persist, and perhaps somewhat revive, during the first ages succeeding.

Even, however, during the flagrancy itself of the Thirty Years' War, some brilliant flames shot up to show that the German national mind, though deeply smothered, was yet not quenched. It was now that Kepler, the great mathematical philosopher, confidently committed to the keeping of the world his magnificent contributions to the science of astronomy—with that majestic, prophet-like saying of his, never surpassed for sublimity by any uninspired utterance of man's: "My book may well wait a century for a reader, since God has waited six thousand years for an observer." Leibnitz's infancy was rocked by the dying throes of the thirty years' earthquake that shook Germany; but Leibnitz, a peer in intellect of the greatest of philosophers, and naturally, withal, as Kepler was not, a literary man, wrote almost exclusively either in Latin or in French, and so added nothing to the proper wealth of his country in letters. One name alone stands conspicuously forth—though even this one solitary name conspicuously not to the reader, only to the student of literature—as continuer, for those desolate years, of German literary history. Opitz was in letters a great boast, a great authority, and really a great beneficent force, to his contemporaries; but the fact that Opitz's name, the foremost of his day—and his day of renown was long, it outlasted his life—should signify exactly nothing whatever now, except to the specialist, sufficiently illustrates the completeness of the swoon in which the literary mind of Germany was sunk.

This, however, was the time of Paul Gerhardt, that noblest of the Lutheran lyrists, leading a numerous choir of brethren in sacred song. The Christian Church still, and now in many different tongues, sings some of the sweet, pathetic hymns born of that time of trouble in Germany. "O, sacred head, now wounded" (in its German form a translation by Gerhardt from a Latin hymn of the twelfth century, by Bernard of Clairvaux), is one of these. "Give to the winds thy fears," a more heroic strain, also Gerhardt's (John Wesley's paraphrase), is another inheritance to us all from the German psalmody of this period.

If Luther bequeathed to Germany the inestimable advantage of a catholic literary language, thus first making it possible for a catholic German literature to exist, this service of his to letters, creative of unity and conducive to strength, was in part offset by another, an indirect result of his activity, tending, on the contrary, to division and feebleness. For when the tumults of the Thirty Years' War subsided at last, then, in addition to the general death-like exhaustion of national strength produced by the struggle, there was found to have been precipitated in deposit upon Germany a political system of so many petty states and sovereignties, independent of each other, that the German republic of letters had, and could have, no recognized center and capital. The state of things that existed before was like indeed, but less evil. Luther, thus, at the same time that he originated a condition of the language friendly, had in effect originated a political condition, temporarily, at least, more hostile than ever, to the prospect of unity and prosperity for

2

the literature of Germany. The inspiring sentiment of national unity, of national dignity, was lost. Worse: the sentiment of national liberty had expired. For the hundred separate governments under which Germany was left to groan were a hundred separate despotisms, crass, stolid, stupid, and all of them organized to be vexatiously meddlesome in proportion as they were ridiculously small. And, to think of it!—during the time that, on the country which had but lately given its mightiest launch to the modern human mind, this nightmare of literary impotence was resting—during that very time, in England, Milton was chanting his *Paradise Lost;* in France, the clustered glories of the reign of Louis XIV. were filling the heavens with light!

But a great change impended for Germany. A bold, long step forward was now suddenly to be taken in that grand forced march toward national unity for Germans which it was reserved for our own times to see finished at last in triumphant arrival at the goal, when, with far-heard sound of celebration, King William was proudly—too proudly?—crowned at Versailles first Emperor of Germany.

A century had passed after the close of the Thirty Years' War, and Frederick the Great, in 1740, became king of Prussia. In this shaker of kingdoms the German spirit asserted itself once more. It ceased to sleep as if the sleep of death. The fresh impulse felt was military and political, rather than literary or even intellectual; but the law of the conversion, or translation, of force works very widely, and the movement from Frederick, which began in war and in politics, went over also, transposed, into the world of the intellect and of literature. Besides, the new king was, in his way, a man of letters. True, he was, as it were, a foreign man of letters, despising the language to which he was born, and himself writing only in French. But there was at least light now where had been "darkness visible" before; and a ray of light from the throne—much more, when the throne is that of Frederick the Great—becomes "illustrious far and wide." The royal example contributed at first to confirm the wretched tendency already then prevalent among Germans to imitate slavishly in literature the omnipotent French; but it also in the sequel incited some stronger, freer spirits, notably Lessing—that Luther of a literary reformation in Germany—to declare their intellectual independence. Even those German authors themselves, of Frederick's time, whose literary mission it was, as they conceived it, to practice and to teach obedience to French canons in the art of writing, were pricked with patriotic ambition to prove to the disdainful monarch of Prussia that native German genius, uttering itself in native German speech, was not so wholly to be despised. Gottsched was the chief of such; but it is creditable to Frederick that Gellert, a quite different writer, less aggressively French, succeeded better than Gottsched in making a favorable impression on the royal arbiter. As between these two writers, the general verdict has since confirmed the preference of Frederick.

Whether or not it was some spirit breathing in the free air of Switzerland, there arose contemporaneously in the Swiss city of Zurich a German literary school, with Bodmer at their head, who waged open war on the French classicism of Gottsched and his fellows. The Zurich circle, however, in refusing to be French, did not after all become truly independent and German. They were only otherwise, perhaps more judiciously, dependent, and—English. Bodmer published a German translation of Milton's *Paradise Lost.* This was a literary event of prime importance for Germany. It gave her the *Messiah* of Klopstock; and, with the publication of the *Messiah* of Klopstock, the long-arrested development of German literature began fairly to go forward again. Lessing, Herder, Wieland, Goethe, Richter, Schiller, and a score of names only less than these, now follow one another in rapid succession, or jostle each other in crowded simultaneous appearance. The firmament of German literature is suddenly full. It blazes with stars and with constellations.

German literature, considered as a body of recognized classics, remains to this day very much what the great age

of Goethe bequeathed it to the world. We need not therefore bring down our historical sketch to a point lower than
the date here reached.

Briefly now as to the forms or kinds in which the literature
thus sketched has appeared.

Unlike the French, and like the English, German literature
inclines as naturally to assume the form of verse as it does
the form of prose. In epic poetry, however, that is, epic
poetry of the first class, it cannot be reckoned rich. The
two chief German poems which might claim for themselves
the highest epic rank are the *Nibelungen Lied* and the *Messiah* of Klopstock ; of which the former is rather interesting
and remarkable than really great, and of which the latter is
remarkable, perhaps, but hardly either great or interesting.

In dramatic poetry German literature is strong; Schiller's
single name being sufficient to give it beyond cavil that
character. With Schiller's name, however, are to be joined
the names, not far unequal to his, of Goethe and of Lessing,
as representatives of the drama in Germany. It is to
tragedy, rather than to comedy, that the grave German
genius instinctively turns to find its favorite dramatic expression. Still, Lessing was witty enough to be a successful writer of comedy. German Molière, there is none ;
but that he would have liked to be one is a confession of
Lessing's.

In lyric poetry German literature may vie with any other
literature, either of ancient or of modern times. What
battle pæans are finer than Körner's ? What strains of patriotism more spirit-stirring, or more pathetic, than Körner's,
Arndt's, Uhland's ? What love-ditties sweeter than the best
of Goethe's and the best of Heine's ? What songs of sentiment
tenderer than those which any one of these masters of the
German lyre upon occasion sings ? And finally, what hymns of
worship nobler than a few at least which Luther and Paul
Gerhardt have led the whole Christian Church in lifting up
on high ?

If we go now from verse to prose, we light at once upon a kind of literature in which German prose and German verse find common ground, and in which German literature easily surpasses every other national literature in the world. We refer to the literature of folk-lore: the traditionary tale, the fairy story, the popular myth, the romance of the supernatural. Goethe speaks of the "eternal womanly." So we might speak of the "eternal child-like," and predicate this as a common characteristic of the German mind. And of the German child-likeness of genius there is no better expression than that found in its "Märchen," so-called; a class of stories in which the improbable, the whimsical, the weird, the ghostly, the grotesque, runs riot without check. The brothers Grimm are universally known as masters in this kind. Goethe, who loved to try his hand at whatever man could do, wrote Märchen. So did Tieck, so did Hoffman.

In history—to make the transition now from the world of fancy to the world of fact—in history, considered as science and as philosophy, Germans have long been pioneers, discoverers, leaders, marching in the van and forefront of the world; but in history, considered as literature, they are not proportionately conspicuous. The historians Niebuhr, Neander, Ranke, Mommsen, are great names; but even Mommsen, the most brilliant writer of the four, is less brilliant as a writer than he is profound and exhaustive as an historical scholar. And it is curious, almost paradoxical, that of the brilliancy which does belong to him as a writer, a large part is the brilliancy of the advocate and the sentimentalist, rather than the brilliancy of the narrator. Respecting Schiller, it may be said that it is chiefly his fame as poet that keeps up his credit as historian.

In criticism, Germany again takes high rank—the very highest, perhaps, according to what is now accepted as the wisest current opinion. This remark applies to criticism in that wide sense of the word which includes criticism of art, as well as criticism of literature. Winckelmann, Lessing, Herder, Schlegel, Humboldt, Goethe, are held to have ad-

vanced the work of the critic from mere empiricism to the
dignity of a science and a philosophy.

In metaphysics, in psychology, in speculative theology,
and in exact scholarship as well, there have always been
found Germans to take great delight and to achieve remarkable results. There are, in the realm of pure thought, no
names, ancient or modern, mightier than Kant, Fichte,
Hegel, Schelling. German theologians we need not name,
nor German scholars. But, as has already been hinted, the
results of such intellectual activity have not often been
presented to the world by Germans in form to constitute
elegant literature.

There is one kind of literature in which Germans have
always been singularly weak, and that is the literature of
public discourse, eloquence, oratory. Whether it is due to
fault in the language, to defect in the national genius, or to
infelicity of historical circumstance, the fact remains, that
there is absolutely almost no great oratory in German literature. If Luther is not the only exception, we at least can
not name any other. With the growth of freedom in Germany, perhaps, this will change. But which is it that produces
the other? Does freedom give birth to eloquence? Or is
it eloquence that gives birth to freedom?

So much for the different recognized species or forms in
which German literature has appeared.

In the course of its appearing in these various forms,
German literature has exhibited certain exterior peculiarities
of which something has been already incidentally said in
preceding pages. We may perhaps usefully resume and
supplement the suggestions thus made.

The abundance of books in German, the comparative scar-
city of German books highly admirable at once for matter
and for form, the lateness of German literature in beginning,
the interruptedness of its subsequent history, are points
which have been sufficiently remarked.

A further point attracting attention in the present survey
is the dependent, imitative, parasitic disposition constantly

manifested by the Germans in their literature. Menzel reckons five different epidemics of literary imitation in Germany, which he names in order—a Gallomania, a Græcomania, an Anglomania, a New Anglomania, a New Gallomania.

Another noteworthy thing is the tendency, at once quarrelsome and social, prevalent among German writers, to classify and cluster themselves in mutually conflicting local schools or coteries. There were the Göttingen group, the Leipsic group, the Hamburg group, the Zurich group, the Silesian, earlier and later, the Swabian, and, greater than any other, greater than all others, the Weimar group. The associative tendency thus pointed out may be referred to the same originating cause with the national tendency spoken of to follow foreign models in literature. Both tendencies probably sprang, we will not say from weakness, but from a sense of weakness, in the German mind, an instinctive feminine leaning toward exterior support.

It is possible, however, looking to a still different peculiarity, yet to be named—a peculiarity very profoundly qualifying German literature—to find an alternative explanation, one more honorable to the national intellect, for the extraordinary tendency characteristic of German authors to attach themselves to one another in groups, and to addict themselves to foreign literary leaders. The quest, however, of this alternative explanation carries us over from a consideration of the exterior, to a consideration of the interior, characteristics of German literature. Let us then take, finally, some account of those fundamental traits which make up what we may call the national literary idiosyncrasy of Germans.

One of the most distinctive and most admirable gifts belonging to the national genius of Germany is its unrivaled catholic capacity to recognize and appreciate intellectual merit abroad as well as at home ; in fact, indifferently, wherever found, no matter in what age or what race of mankind. German literary admiration is the least jealously patriotic, the most open-heartedly hospitable, the most cosmopolitan, in the world. Beyond all other men, Germans believe in intellectual free-trade. With them there is no restriction to the commerce of ideas. Breadth, generosity, welcome, is accordingly a legend covering the whole face of German literature.

Nearly allied to this embracing catholicity of literary spirit, on the part of the Germans, is a trait, to be additionally reckoned, of their intellectual character, namely, their passion for philosophy. This passion is with Germans a universally penetrating literary influence. It makes them wish to be deep, to go to the bottom of things; it makes them wish to be broad, to work with a radius long enough to sweep their circumference around every thing knowable—and unknowable, too, for that matter. The Germans are often credited with having been the first to ground literary criticism in principles of philosophy. The "philosophy of history" is, if we mistake not, a German phrase, whether or not, also, a German idea.

Once more. Profound thinking and broad thinking imply free thinking. Freedom of thought, accordingly—paradoxical though it be to make the assertion—is as salient a thing in German literature as is imitativeness of literary form. Freedom—in fact, intrepidity—in thinking, intrepidity carried not seldom to the verge of foolhardy, eccentric caprice, is a characteristic of the German mind. We shall not exceed the truth to say that Germany, in the realm of ideas, leads the van of the world; leads, but, alas, too often misleads. It was, we suppose, in part for the purpose of expressing this leadership of his country in thought, that Richter once, with a humor which probably had for its author a tinge of patriotic pathos in it (it was the time of nadir, or near it, in the national humiliation of Germany), remarked, "Providence has assigned to France the empire of the earth, to England the empire of the ocean, and to Germany the empire of—the air!"

The present writer lately, in quoting this remark of Jean Paul's, was surprised and confounded by a straightforward hearer with the challenge, proposed in perfect good faith, to explain exactly what the remark meant. Then, for the first time, he was brought distinctly to perceive that the oft-quoted saying of Richter, which he had supposed himself to understand well enough to enjoy it keenly for its witty expressiveness, was, in truth, less clear than it seemed. This leads us naturally to name an additional trait of German literature—its lack of clearness, definiteness, solidity, point. The Germans think deeply, they think boldly, but they do not think clearly. Perhaps if they thought more clearly they would think less boldly. Perhaps, too, if they tasked themselves to think more clearly they would less seem to be thinking deeply. This vagueness, this insubstantialness, this disappointing cloudiness, in German thought, may have been a part of what was consciously meant—it is certainly a part of what we well may understand as conveyed—in Richter's remark.

Unsophisticated sentimentalism, disposition to wear the heart on the sleeve, to have no personal secrets whatever from readers—this is a further singularity observable in German literature. What we mean goes beyond that certain degree of simplicity, of unreserve, of confidingness, on the part of writers, with which, though some might be surprised, most would be pleased. German outspokenness in literature is often, to English or American taste, something excessive, something almost egregious. It resembles what in society we should call lack of requisite reticence, of decorous self-control.

The sentiment of delight in the contemplation of nature is a sufficiently striking thing in German literature to deserve separate note. This sentiment, in its later exhibition, may be a derivation from abroad—from Rousseau, from Spinoza, for example. But Luther, too, loved nature, and there are some exquisite bits of idyllic description of natural beauty interspersed through his letters. At any rate, however inspired, whether imported or indigenous, the passion has become a distinctive German literary trait.

Of near kindred with the two traits last named is, finally, a certain religiosity giving its tinge to German literature. Your German writer may be an infidel, but he will not therefore cease to have his religiosity. He may be a libertine in practice, but his religiosity will still be dear to him. Religiosity never gave up harboring in Heine's heart, cheek by jole with mockery, with ribaldry, with blasphemy. The religiosity of which we now speak, is not religion. It is rather simply the irrepressible, though half-perverted, witness borne in literature by the German temperament to its own ineradicable instinct for religion. Of religion itself, however, the authentic thing, beautiful and sweet, there is also, in German literature, no lack. We have, in saying this, to suppose a broad distinction made in thought between religion and orthodoxy, as orthodoxy is commonly conceived. A German strictly orthodox in religion may, indeed, exist; but such a one, we judge, has never yet made himself known to the world in literature.

We have said "finally," and we accordingly herewith bring our characterization of German literature abruptly to its close. A word or two only of related information, and we go without more delay to the exhibition of those select German authors who will furnish the subject and the material of the present volume.

German generosity in literary appreciation—perhaps we should say German generosity as toward English authors in particular—has enjoyed the return from English-speakers of an overflowing reward in kind. Never, on behalf of any other coeval foreign literature than the German, has there been exercised among us a championship so importunate and so influential. Coleridge and Carlyle, by eminence, in England; in America, Felton, Ripley, Brooks, Hedge, and, indeed, in one way or another, nearly all our chief literary powers, have conspired to commend to Englishmen and Americans the study of German literature, and have accumulated a popular apparatus of means for that study far beyond what exists in the case of any modern literature except the German. The deep-lying difference in mental genius between the purely Teutonic and the mixed Anglo-Saxon race interposes a barrier, which will, perhaps, never be surmounted, to perfect freedom of literary interchange flowing back and forth from the one to the other. We may, however, safely wish well to every effort made on either side to promote mutual literary acquaintance.

For the benefit of those among our own readers who may desire to prosecute their explorations of German literature farther than, with the single aid of this volume, they can do, we mention now a few accessible books in English which they will find variously serviceable to their purpose.

Among living American teachers of the German language and literature, the place of honor belongs, we suppose, by right of seniority, to the veteran Dr. F. H. Hedge, whose two books, *Prose Writers of Germany,* an ample repertory of translation issued many years ago, and *Hours with German Classics,* recently published, a collection of university lectures on German literature, have gained wide acceptance with the public. In the older and larger book, translation (limited to originals in prose) is the principal object, biographical and critical comment being secondary. In the smaller, recent volume, that relation is reversed. Even this smaller volume of the two much exceeds the present book in size.

Professor James K. Hosmer's *Short History of German Literature* is not, what its title might seem to import, a complete, though compendious, sketch of German literary history. It is rather a series of essays or lectures on selected topics in German literature, designed by the author to be so treated as virtually to cover the whole field indicated in the title to his book. The book is by no means a primer in size. It contains more than six hundred fairly large pages. It is fresh and vigorous in style, and its tone is, on the whole, pure and bracing. It breathes unwasted youthful enthusiasm and joy in its subject. There are in it frequent translations from German interspersed.

A formal history of German literature has lately been translated, under the best auspices, from German, which may be mentioned as constituting a popular manual for general purposes probably not inferior to any now existing in English on its subject. This is the work of W. Scherer, commended in its English form to the public by the name of Max Müller on its title-page as editor. Scherer is a well-informed, judicious historian and critic, having at command a more than ordinarily clear and unembarrassed style—for a German. His book is not free from errors, and his plan of treatment seems to us faulty, involving as it does, on the historian's part, repeated recurrences here and there throughout the volume to a given name, and thus obliging the student, with much confusing use of his index, to piece out as best he can for himself that whole view of each particular author which his manual will rarely be found in any one place to supply. German-like, Scherer begins remotely, and stores his first volume with a mass of uninteresting information painstakingly gathered, such as it is a great satisfaction to have within reach—for future reference.

The special difference to characterize the volume herewith offered to the public—apart from its less comparative size, a very important feature of contrast—is, first, that while, on the one hand, it will not be either merely or chiefly historical and critical, it will, on the other hand, be both historical and critical incidentally; and, second, that while, on the one hand, it will not present long translated extracts in bare unbroken bulk, it will, on the other hand, present considerable extracts, interrupted, connected, elucidated, and appreciated, by means of quasi-editorial comment in explanation and appraisal. In other words, taking translated German text, select and representative, for the basis, the backbone, of the book, we shall seek so to edit that text as to invest it with flesh, its own flesh, to inspire it with breath, its own breath, to give it a heart, its own heart; in short, to make it live, and with its own life, to our readers. If we succeed in our efforts our readers will here have under their eye, neither, on the one

hand, simply so much translated German literature, to understand, as best they may, for themselves, and to form their
own unguided judgment upon, nor, on the other hand, simply so much unexemplified critical expression to take on pure
trust from the critic, without fully apprehending, and, of
course, without verifying. The idea of this book is, therefore, not quite like that of any other book known to the
present writer. The execution is such as his best conscien-
tious endeavors could make it.

II.

LUTHER.

1483–1546.

A WORLD-HISTORICAL personage, emphatically and by eminence such, is Luther. The adjective we thus apply—a compound adjective so much more German than English in genius—seems made for our purpose, to express densely at the same time this man's personality, his influence, and his fame. For no other man perhaps ever lived who, simply by what he was, stamped himself so broadly, so deeply, and so indelibly as did Luther upon the universal imagination of the human race; no other man who, by his own single force, did so much to turn into a new channel the main current of human history ; no other who so imperiously usurped, at once and for ever, his place in the memory of all human kind.

Such was Luther, the man. We have here, however, to deal with Luther, not in these larger aspects of his genius and his achievement, but rather as a German simply; and, even more narrowly still, as a German producer of German literature. (No inconsiderable part of Luther's immensely voluminous literary production was written, not in German, but in Latin.) Luther, as we have already remarked, stands founder, at the very beginning, of proper German literary history. Fecund and manifold man that he was, he bore fruit for literature hardly less remarkable than was the fruit which he bore for religion and for politics. German literature, in the full catholic sense of that expression, may be said to date its commencement from the moment at which Luther's noble translation of the Bible into his own mother-tongue was first given to Germany. That monumental work it was which fixed for Germans the form of their literary language—in truth, which made it possible for a German literature, strictly and comprehensively so described, to be.

Before Luther, the German language seemed hopelessly distracted into dialects. As an organ of literary expression, it was despised even by the Germans themselves, and neglected.

Luther's works in authorship are as multiform as they are manifold. They consist of lectures, of sermons, of tracts, of pamphlets in controversy, of commentaries, of addresses, and, unsurpassed in importance, of letters—letters almost as numerous, and almost as various, as those of Voltaire. Above every thing else, however, that proceeded from Luther's pen towers eminent in literary value and significance his translation into German of the Old and New Testament Scriptures. Luther's own sign manual, legible on it all, renders it fair that the German Bible which, where he did not himself make it he at least effectively got made, should be called, as it invariably is called, by his name.

This, Luther's capital achievement in literature, it will, of course, be impossible for us at all to illustrate here. Luther's Bible is, and it must remain, immortally and hopelessly, as it is admirably, German. It has, for three centuries and a half, been to the German-speaking peoples all that the "King James's" translation, for two centuries, has been to the peoples that speak English.

We shall not need here to sketch Luther's life. The world knows it by heart. It will not, however, be amiss to recall to our readers an image, at once lively and just, of the man Martin Luther, by giving a few glimpses of him as self-disclosed in his letters, or again as acting the true "autocrat of the breakfast-table," at his ease and freely, among his friends. How the great reformer seems to be living again, as often as one listens to that racy and that abundant "table-talk" of his—silent now so long from the lips that uttered it, but resounding still, and forever resounding, in the books in which it is printed, for all races and all generations of his fellow-men to hear ! Luther, with shrewd self-knowledge, contrasted himself against his friend Melanchthon by saying: "Philip is straiter tied than I am; I am more a rhetorician and a talker." To talk was indeed Luther's genius and his

delight. He talked when he preached, talked even when he
wrote; but he was at his best—also, it must be owned, at
his worst — when he ungirded himself to talk freely and
flowingly, in the communications of social or of convivial
life.

Such most characteristic utterances of Luther are preserved for us, perhaps in overlarge supply. The great man
had his devoted admirers, who valued, not merely for themselves, but for the whole world of mankind, every syllable
of speech that issued from those extremely out-speaking
oracular lips. These earlier Boswells of a far mightier
Johnson waited on their master as often as they got the
chance—and they got the chance very often—and took down
his words in writing as fast as he spoke them. His least
considered utterances seem not to have differed from those
best considered, in the perilous risk they ran of being thus
"treasured up on purpose to a life beyond life." Never perhaps was mortal man more completely, more pitilessly, ex-
posed, to be known to the world for what he really was, than
was Martin Luther. And this exposure we have, in not its
least startling degree of distinctness, in the volumes of his
table-talk. No conventional, no posturing Luther is here—
no Luther deceptively draped by artful admirers for decorous appearance to history. It is an actual, not an ideal,
man, a man, too, caught as it were, at unawares—his attitude
sighted under many different angles—that lives before us, as
we listen, and speaks these breathing words.

The most conveniently accessible popular form in which,
until lately, Luther's *Table-Talk* could be read in English
was found in a much abridged translation, from the hand of
William Hazlitt, constituting one of the issues of the well-
known Bohn Library. Professor Henry Morley now edits, for
the very useful "National Library," in course of publication
by Cassell & Company, one small volume of selections,
promising a second, from the pioneer English version of
Captain Henry Bell.

We go ourselves to the original text for our extracts from

the *Table-Talk*. Luther is discussing astrology, in which pretended science he did not believe, although his friend Melanchthon did. Luther says:

> I have often talked of the subject [astrology] with Philip [Melanchthon] and recounted to him in order my whole life, how one thing after another has befallen, and how it has fared with me. I am a peasant's son; my father, my grandfather, my great-grandfather, were nothing but peasants. My father went to Mansfeld, and there became a miner. Such is my origin.
>
> Now that I should become bachelor of arts, master of arts, monk, and so forth, that was not written in the stars. Did I not get myself great shame though, by becoming monk, by laying aside my brown cap and wearing a different one? The which, truly, vexed my father sore and offended him. After that I got into the pope's hair, and he, forsooth, back into mine; I took a runaway nun to wife, and had children by her. Who saw all that in the stars? Who would have told me beforehand that so it was to happen?

With the foregoing passage cited from the *Table-Talk*, Michelet begins his lively biography of Luther. But the passage is "edited" by the Frenchman. The fact of its being in argument against astrology that Luther was sketching his own career does not at all come out, and Michelet omits altogether the particular about Luther's becoming a "monk," apparently because to include it, after "bachelor of arts, doctor of divinity," would spoil a climax—a climax, by the way, quite the Frenchman's own, and not in the least belonging to Luther's simple statement. In short, Luther is exhibited by Michelet as swaggering about himself, instead of merely telling, for argument's sake, a few incidents from his own experience. In addition, the clause, "Such is my origin," is mistranslated to read, "There I was born," Luther being thus caused to say that he was born at Mansfeld, whereas Eisleben was his birthplace. It will do to add a good pinch of salt, in allowance for rhetorical variations, whenever you read M. Michelet's citations from the *Table-Talk* of Luther. Care, in fact, is always to be exercised in using Luther's *Table-Talk*. The nature of things forbids that there should not, from one cause or another, be many

3

errors in the existing records of such hurrying reports, never, we suppose, verified by Luther, as were taken of his winged words.

When Martin's father, John Luther, died, the son wrote thus to his friend Philip Melanchthon :

> It is just and right that I, his son, should mourn such a father, through whom the Father of mercy created me, and through whose sweat he nourished me and made me what I am, such as that is. But how I rejoice that he lived in these times, that he saw the light of truth ! Blessed be God in all his works and counsels for evermore !

The filial piety of the foregoing, as well as its piety toward God, is touching and beautiful. Melanchthon's character and spirit seem to have been such as always to draw out toward him the sweetest and the best that was in Luther. If only there were now left of Luther nothing but the sweetest and the best that was in him ! What bounds then would there be to the reverence with which we should study and admire ! Alas, the dross, too, of him has come down, with sad inextricableness entangled in the gold!

The stormy soul of the battle-welcoming reformer was sensitive and tractable to music ; the lion listened, and, listening, became the lamb. Luther himself played the guitar and the flute. He never tired of sounding the praises of music as being, nigh to theology, one of the best gifts of God to men. In his *Table-Talk* many pleasing allusions to the subject occur. For instance, he says :

> It [music] drives away the devil. . . . It makes one forget anger, lust, pride, and other evil passions.

Again (speaking to a harper) :

> Friend, strike me up a song, as David struck it up. I hold that if David were now to rise from the dead, he would be very much surprised finding to what a pitch people have got in the matter of music. Music never reached a higher point than now.

Might not we, adapting, say, in our turn, of Luther what Luther said of David in reference to music, "If Luther were now to rise from the dead ?"

Once more:

> How happens it that in the worldly sphere we have so many fine poems and so many fine songs, while in the spiritual sphere we have such cold dull things?

The truculence, the coarseness, the grossness, of Luther, in his championship against Rome, and, it must be added, toward all who ventured to differ with himself, were astounding, were staggering, were incredible. But they belonged to the age as well as to the man; and we are prepared to say that if, without miracle, the Reformation was to make head against Rome, they were, under the circumstances of Luther's case, a necessity, a dire necessity, of his cause. Luther had to reassure himself, had to inspirit his followers, had to overawe his enemies, with mien and with voice as defiant as the tone and the aspect of Rome were threatening, or, humanly speaking, he and his cause would have gone instantly under. It was his bravado, hardly less than his bravery, that saved him and carried the day. But Luther had a tender conscience, and his conscience sometimes misgave him. Will not God judge gently a sinful man who expresses himself as did Luther in the following words? But first read and contrast Rousseau's effrontery, in the preface to his *Confessions :*

" Let the last trumpet sound when it will, I will come, with this book [the *Confessions*] in my hand, and present myself before the Sovereign Judge. I will boldly proclaim, ' Thus have I acted, thus have I thought, such was I,' . . . and then let a single one tell thee, if he dare, ' *I was better than that man.*' "

Now Luther (we venture, in this citation, as in one or two more next following, to depend, without verifying, on Michelet, who here gives no references):

> I have learned from the Holy Scripture that it is a thing terrible and full of danger to raise one's voice in the Church of God, to speak in the midst of those whom we shall have for judges when, in the last day of judgment, we shall find ourselves in the presence of God, and of his angels—every creature there looking, listening, bending the ear to dwell

on the Divine Word. Certes, when I think on it, I feel that I could
heartily wish to bury all in silence, and pass a sponge over what I have
written. To have to render an account to God of every heedless word—
'tis hard, 'tis horrible!

Heinrich Heine is certainly in general a poor authority
to quote in appreciation of any thing pure, any thing lovely,
any thing of good report; but the following words of his
on Luther do seem to have in them the charm of sincerity as
well as of truth:

"Renown, eternal renown to the dear man to whom we
owe the preservation of our noblest goods, and by whose
merits we live to-day. It becomes us little to complain of
the narrowness of his views. The dwarf who stands upon
the shoulders of a giant can indeed see farther than the
giant himself, especially if he puts on spectacles; but to the
higher position are lacking the lofty feeling and the giant
heart, which we cannot make our own. It becomes us still
less to pass a harsh judgment upon his failings. These failings have benefited us more than the virtues of a thousand
others. The subtlety of Erasmus, the gentleness of Melanchthon, would never have carried us so far as did often the
divine brutality of Brother Martin."

Of his own temper, and of his management of that temper,
in approaching the great crisis of his life, his appearance
before the Diet of Worms, Luther finely says:

Though, in truth, I was physically fearful and trembling, I replied to
him, [to one incredulously inquiring of Luther, "Do you still mean to go
there?"] "I will repair thither, though I should find there as many
devils as there are tiles on the house-tops."

On coming first in sight of the old bell-towers of Worms—
so Audin, a French Roman Catholic biographer of Luther,
relates—Luther, standing up in the carriage in which he
rode, broke out singing that memorable and magnificent
hymn of his, well called by Heine the "Marseillaise of the
Reformation," *Ein feste Burg ist unser Gott;* the words
and the music he had meditated and composed two days before. A better account makes the occasion of this hymn a

fight of Luther's with the devil, occurring six years later. Here is Thomas Carlyle's rendering of the original—a rendering in which not only is the sense well given, but the ruggedness of the German rhythms well preserved:

A safe stronghold our God is still,
    A trusty shield and weapon;
He'll help us clear from all the ill
    That hath us now o'ertaken.
The ancient prince of hell
Hath risen with purpose fell;
Strong mail of craft and power
He weareth in this hour—
On earth is not his fellow.

With force of arms we nothing can,
    Full soon were we down-ridden;
But for us fights the proper Man,
    Whom God himself hath bidden.
Ask ye, Who is this same?
Christ Jesus is his name,
The Lord Zebaoth's Son,
He and no other one
Shall conquer in the battle.

And were this world all devils o'er,
    And watching to devour us,
We lay it not to heart so sore,
    We know they can't o'erpower us.
And let the prince of ill
Look grim as e'er he will,
He harms us not a whit,
For why? His doom is writ—
A word shall quickly slay him.

God's word, for all their craft and force,
    One moment will not linger,
But, spite of hell, shall have its course;
    'Tis written by his finger.
And though they take our life,
Goods, houses, children, wife,
Yet is their profit small,
These things shall vanish all,
The city of God remaineth.

Dr. Hedge has a less literal, but smoother, version of this song, beginning, "A mighty fortress is our God." Dr. Hedge's version is often printed in our collections of hymns.

In a ballad of Luther's, the "Martyrs of Brussels" (two young men who suffered at the stake for Christ, in 1523), occurs the following stanza, which seems to be the original of a hymn sometimes attributed to Luther, beginning, "Flung to the heedless winds:"

> Their ashes will not rest; world-wide
>   They fly through every nation;
> No cave nor grave, no turn nor tide,
>   Can hide th' abomination.
> The voices which with cruel hands
>   They put to silence living,
> Are heard, though dead, throughout all lands
>   Their testimony giving,
>   And loud hosannas singing.

The striking thought about those restless martyr ashes finds prose expression in an extract, soon to be given, from one of Luther's fiercest controversial pamphlets.

Every one knows how Luther, on his way home from Worms, was spirited away by friends, and hidden on high in Wartburg Castle, till that first storm were overpast of threat and danger against his life. Hence he dated his letters variously, for example:

"From the region of the air;" "From the region of the birds;" "From amidst the birds which sing sweetly ou the branches of the tall trees and praise God night and day, with all their might;" "From the mountain;" "From the Isle of Patmos."

Poor caged man, how he chafed and fretted against the bars that confined, while they preserved, him! He suffered horribly from dyspepsia during those days. To Melanchthon he wrote desperately, as follows:

You greatly err in attributing to me so much, as if I were so careful for the cause of God. It shames and pains me, this idea of yours so favorable about me, while I, quite insensible and hard, sit here in idleness, and for the Church of God, alas, pray little, sigh not all, nay, through the fierce flames of my untamed flesh, feel set on fire. In short, I, who should be fervent in the spirit, am fervent in the flesh, grossness, idleness, sloth, lethargy, and do not know but God turns away from me, because you do not pray for me. . . . It is now eight days since I have written any thing, or prayed, or studied—vexed, partly, by the temptations of the flesh, partly through other trouble.

We are not to take too literally Luther's witness against himself. The pen of the man thus self-accused of sloth was in reality raining down, from his home in the clouds, all sorts of writings on Germany.

Luther's captivity at Wartburg Castle in time relaxed enough to permit him to go out hunting, for exercise and recreation. Very characteristically, and withal in a manner to win one toward the womanly soul that lay hid within that manly breast, he writes of this experience as follows:

I have been out sporting two whole days. I have long had a desire to appreciate for myself this princely pleasure, this γλυχυπίχρον [bitter-sweet]; I caught two hares and two poor little partridges. 'Tis a fine occupation for any one who has got nothing else to do. However, I did not entirely waste my time, for I theologized amid the nets and the dogs, and I found a mystery of grief and pain in the very heart of all the joyous tumult around me. Is not this hunting the very image of the devil going about seeking what poor beasts he may devour by the aid of his nets, his traps, and his trained dogs—that is to say, of his bishops and his theologians? There was an incident which made the mystery and the image still more manifest. I had saved alive a poor little hare I picked up, all trembling from its pursuers; after keeping it in my sleeve some time, I set it down, and the creature was running off to secure its liberty, when the dogs, getting scent of it, ran up and first broke its leg and then pitilessly killed it. The dogs were the pope and Satan, destroying the souls which I seek to save as I sought to save the poor little hare. I have had enough of such hunting as this; the hunting I shall keep to is that wherein I desire to pierce, with sharp darts and javelins, wolves, bears, foxes, and the whole iniquitous troop of Roman beasts that afflict the world. Ah, vile courtiers of Rome, eaters of poor hares and partridges, and eaters of us too, you will find in the other world that you yourselves have become beasts whom Christ, the great hunter of all, will cage up! While you think you are hunters, 'tis you who are hunted!

Luther's vivid sense of a personal devil always at work against God, and therefore notably against himself as signal champion for God, was an incessant exasperation to his eagerly combative spirit. He lived in one life-long, unintermittent duel with the devil. Speaking of some excesses committed during his absence by his own adherents at Wittenberg, he says:

> I can imagine Satan grinning and saying to himself, "Now I shall have depressed Luther's courage and conquered his so unbending mind. This time he will not get the better of me."

Luther took the risk of descending unpermitted from his aerie in Wartburg Castle, and going back to Wittenberg to right things there. He succeeded to his mind. Called by the Elector of Saxony to account for his temerity, he, with stimulating freedom, told that great prince:

> My conscience will permit me to make no longer delay, and rather than act against that, I would incur the anger of your electoral grace and of the whole world. The Wittenbergers are my sheep, whom God has intrusted to my care; they are my children in the Lord. For them I am ready to suffer martyrdom. I go, therefore, to accomplish, by God's grace, that which Christ demands of them who own him.

In the preceding brief citations from Luther's letters, we have thought that we ran little risk in following Michelet translated by Hazlitt without strict verification. Bluff King Henry VIII., of England, who had taken it into his royal head to stand forth as defender of the Roman Catholic faith, in a book written by him against Luther, got more than he bargained for, in reply, from the intrepid reformer. We must give a few specimens of the astounding "great plainness of speech" with which the peasant treated the prince. Luther:

> Not to me but to himself let King Henry charge it, if he shall experience somewhat hard and rough treatment at my hands. . . . If he merely erred in a human way indulgence should be accorded to him. But when with malice aforethought that rottenness and worm concocts lies against the majesty of my King in heaven, it is right for me on behalf of my King to besprinkle his Anglican majesty with his own mire and ordure, and to trample under foot the crown that blasphemes against Christ. . . . . .
> Let these swine come on and burn me if they dare. Here I am, and I

will wait for them; and my ashes alone having been after my death cast
into a thousand seas, I will persecute and harass this abominable crowd.
As long as I live, I will be the enemy of the papacy; burned, I will be
twice an enemy. Do what you can, Thomist [adjective noting a follower
of Thomas Aquinas] swine, you shall have Luther as a bear in your way,
and as a lioness in your path. He will confront you on all sides, and
will let you have no peace till he shall have destroyed your iron necks
and brazen brows either unto salvation or unto perdition.

The indescribably telling prose in which Luther writes,
with its homeliness, its idiomaticity, its nervousness, its di-
rectness, its pith, its point, its bite, suffers cruelly in any
possible English translation. The immediately foregoing
extracts were furnished to the present writer in the English
form in which they here appear, by a distinguished professor
of ecclesiastical history, whom by permission we name; the
Rev. A. H. Newman, D.D., LL.D., of Toronto Baptist College. His scholarship may be trusted to have represented
the original truly. Very coarse writing these paragraphs
undoubtedly are, and specimens still coarser might easily be
adduced. But coarseness it always is, never uncleanness, on
the part of Luther. He wavered, too, sometimes in his conduct, where to us it seems clear that he should have stood
firm. For example, he paltered once with a truculent prince
to let him practice concubinage. Shame and pity indeed;
but we should judge Luther unjustly to charge him with a
prurient mind. That notorious couplet, often attributed to
Luther as author, does not represent the spirit of the man.
And there is not, as after careful investigation we fully believe, the shadow of evidence that Luther ever either wrote
or repeated the words :

> " Who loves not wine, woman, and song,
> Abides a fool his whole life long."

There is, of course, a sense in which, without taint to his
pure name, such an expression might, as Heine says this did,
have " blossomed out " of the mouth of Luther. But, we
repeat, there is not a shadow of evidence adducible to justify
Heine's assertion, quoted, as if accepted, by Dr. Hedge.

Professor M. Günther, of Concordia College, in a note to the present writer, sets forth the facts of the case succinctly as follows: " It [the couplet] is traced back to the year 1777, when the German poet Johann Heinrich Voss published in *Musen Almanach* a poem containing the couplet as a saying of Luther. On account of this forgery, the Lutheran ministers of Hamburg protested against his being appointed professor of the gymnasium of that city. Voss never justified himself."

Our space for Luther runs rapidly away, and we go abruptly now to other illustrations, different in kind, of the genius of the man.

Luther wrote a kind of encyclical, or circular, letter to the councilmen of all the cities of Germany, urging them to found and maintain Christian schools. He says:

. . . Dear Germans! Buy while the market is at the door. Gather while the sun shines and the weather is good. Use God's grace and word while it is at hand. For you must know that God's grace and word is a traveling shower, which does not again come where it once has been. It was once with the Jews, but gone is gone; now they have nothing. Paul brought it into Greece, but gone is gone; now they have the Turk. Rome and Italy have also had it, but gone is gone; they have now the pope. And ye Germans must not think that you will have it forever; for ingratitude and contempt will not let it abide. Therefore seize and hold fast, whoever can. . . . . . .

Yea, sayest thou, schools there should and must be; but of what use is it to teach the Latin, Greek, and Hebrew tongues, and other liberal branches? Could we not teach, in German, the Bible and God's word, which are sufficient for salvation? Reply: Yes, I well know, alas! that we Germans must aye be and abide brutes and wild beasts, as the surrounding nations call us, and as also we well deserve. But I wonder we never say: Of what use are silks, wine, spices, and other foreign articles, seeing we have wine, corn, wool, flax, wood, and stones, in German lands, not only an abundance for sustenance, but also a choice and selection for elegance and ornament? The arts and languages, which do us no harm, nay, which are a greater ornament, benefit, honor, and advantage, both for understanding Holy Writ and for managing civil affairs, we are disposed to despise; and foreign wares, which are neither necessary nor useful to us, and which, moreover, peel us to the very bone, these we are not willing to forego. Are not people like that well called German fools and beasts? . . . And be this understood, that we shall not be able to keep the Gospel without the languages.' The languages are the sheath in which this sword of the Spirit is hid. They are the casket in which this jewel is borne. They are the vessel in which this drink is contained. They are the store-house in which this food is laid by. And, as the Gospel itself shows, they are the baskets in which these loaves and fishes and fragments are kept. Yea, if we should so err as to let the languages go (which God forbid!) we shall not only lose the Gospel, but it will come to pass, at length, that we shall not be able to speak or write correctly either Latin or German. . . . . . .

Yes, sayest thou; but let each one teach and train his own. Reply: Yes, we know very well what kind of teaching and training that is. . . . The education which is given at home, without such schools [as I recommend], attempts to make us wise through our own experience. Before that comes to pass we die a hundred times, and have acted inconsiderately all our life long; for experience requires much time. . . . . . .

How much time and trouble are bestowed in teaching children to play at cards, to sing, and to dance! Why will we not spend as much time in teaching them to read, and other accomplishments, while they are young and have leisure and capacity and disposition for them? I speak for myself; if I had children and were able, they should not only hear me languages and histories, but they should also sing and learn music and all mathematics. For what is all this but mere children's play, in which the Greeks anciently trained their children, whereby they afterward became wonderfully skillful people, capable of all sorts of things? Yea, what grief is it to me now that I did not read poets and histories more, and that, also, no one taught them to me! . . . . . .

I have done my part. I would gladly have counseled and helped the German lands. And albeit some may contemn me in this thing, and give to the winds my faithful advice and pretend to better knowledge, I must even endure it. I well know that others might have done better; but seeing they are silent, I have done as well as I could. It is better, besides, to have spoken, however unskillfully, than to have remained wholly silent on the matter. . . . . . .

Herewith I commend you all to the grace of God. May he soften and kindle your hearts so that they shall earnestly take the part of these poor, pitiable, forsaken youth, and, through divine aid, counsel and help them to a happy and Christian ordering of the German land as to body and soul with all fullness and overflow, to the praise and honor of God the Father, through Jesus Christ, our Saviour! Amen.

We could not find it in our heart not to let discourse so wise and so eloquent, on a subject still so living, flow on to some length.

Now let us learn, from a letter of father to son, how Luther, as a kind of Sunday-school teacher with pen, could himself practice the art of education, in the case of a boy, and that boy his own "Johnny." We quote Luther's celebrated letter, "To his son John." In its pretty parable of heaven will be found the whole idea of Miss Phelps's *Gates Ajar* anticipated:

Grace and peace in Christ, my dear little son. I am glad to see that thou learnest well and prayest diligently. Do so, my son, and continue. When I come home I will bring thee a fine fairing.

I know a fair, delightful garden wherein many children run about, wear little golden coats, and gather fine apples under the trees, and pears, cherries, prunes, and plums. They sing, spring, and are gay. They have fine little horses, too, with gold bits and silver saddles. And I asked the man to whom the garden belongs, whose the children were? And he said, "They are the children that love to pray and to learn, and are good." Then I said, "Dear man, I have a son, too, his name is Johnny Luther; may he not also come into this garden and eat such fine apples and pears, and ride such fine little horses and play with these children?" Then the man said, "If he loves to pray and to learn, and is good, he shall come into this garden, and Lippus [Melanchthon's son Philip] and Jost [Jonas's son Jodocus], too; and when they all come together they shall have fifes, drums, lutes, and all sorts of stringed instruments, and they shall dance and shoot with little cross-bows."

And he showed me a fine lawn there in the garden, made for dancing. There hung fifes of pure gold, drums, and fine silver cross-bows. But it was early, and the children had not yet eaten; so I could not wait for the dance, and I said to the man, "Ah, dear sir, I will immediately go and write all this to my dear little son Johnny, that he may pray diligently, and learn well, and be good, so that he also may come to this garden. But he has an Aunt Lene [Johnny's great-aunt, Magdalen], he must bring her with him." Then the man said, "So it shall be; go and write him so."

So, dear little son Johnny, learn and pray with good heart, and tell Lippus and Jost, too, that they must learn and pray; and then you shall come to the garden together. Herewith I commend thee to Almighty God, and greet Aunt Lene, and give her a kiss for my sake.

Thy dear father,   MARTINUS LUTHER.
Anno 1530.

We reluctantly forbear our hand from passages that tempt us, in illustration of Luther's love for teaching the doctrine of the ministration of angels. One short extract we give

from a letter of his to his wife, whom he affectionately
chides for excess of the care-taking spirit exercised on his
own behalf. The form of personal address in a letter from
Luther to his wife is generally, as it is in this case, something out of the usual :

> To my dear Housewife, Katherin Lutherin, Doctoress, Self-martyress,
> my Gracious Lady—for her hands and feet.
> Grace and Peace in the Lord! Dear Kate, do thou read John and the
> little catechism, concerning which thou once saidst, that all contained in
> that book is by me. For thou must needs care, before thy God, just as
> if he were not Almighty, and could not create ten Doctor Martins if the
> single old one were to drown in the Saale, or the Ovenhole, or Wolf's
> Vogelheerd. Leave me in peace with thy anxiety. I have a better
> guardian than thou and all the angels are. He lies in the crib, and hangs
> upon the Virgin's teats, but sitteth, nevertheless. at the right hand of
> God, the Almighty Father. Therefore be in peace. Amen!

We are most courteously permitted to make free use of
the translations by Dr. Hedge appearing in that distinguished
German scholar's *Prose Writers of Germany*. We draw
from this source the foregoing extract, and the one to follow.

With all his faults—which were mostly the faults of his
country and age—the lordliest and the loveliest of the Germans was Luther. Let him now be fitly last imprinted in
image on our minds, standing in that act and attitude of his,
the most memorable, or at least the most impressively characteristic of his life, his prayer at the Diet of Worms :

> Almighty, eternal God! What a strange thing is this world! How
> doth it open wide the mouths of the people! How small and poor is the
> confidence of men toward God! How is the flesh so tender and weak,
> and the devil so mighty and so busy through his apostles and the wise
> of this world! How soon do they withdraw the hand, and whirl away
> and run the common path and the broad way to hell, where the godless
> belong! They look only upon that which is splendid and powerful, great
> and mighty, and which hath consideration. If I turn my eyes thither
> also, it is all over with me; the bell is cast and the judgment is pro-
> nounced. Ah, God! ah, God! O, thou my God! Thou my God, stand
> thou by me against the reason and wisdom of all the world. Do thou so!
> Thou must do it, thou alone. Behold, it is not my cause, but thine.
> For my own person I have nothing to do here with these great lords of

the world.   Gladly would I too have good quiet days and be unperplexed. But thine is the cause, Lord; it is just and eternal.   Stand thou by me, thou true, eternal God!   I confide in no man.   It is to no purpose and in vain.   Every thing halteth that is fleshly, or that savoreth of flesh.   O God!   O God!   Hearest thou not, my God?   Art thou dead?   No! Thou canst not die.   Thou only hidest thyself.   Hast thou chosen me for this end?   I ask thee.   But I know for a surety that thou hast chosen me.   Ha! then may God direct it.   For never did I think, in all my life, to be opposed to such great lords; neither have I intended it.   Ha! God, then stand by me in the name of Jesus Christ, who shall be my shelter and my shield, yea, my firm tower, through the might and strengthening of thy Holy Spirit.   Lord! where stayest thou?   Thou my God! where art thou?   Come, come! I am ready, even to lay down my life for this cause, patient as a little lamb.   For just is the cause and thine.   So will I not separate myself from thee forever.   Be it determined in thy name.   The world shall not be able to force me against my conscience, though it were full of devils.   And though my body, originally the work and creature of thy hands, go to destruction in this cause—yea, though it be shattered in pieces—thy word and thy spirit, they are good to me still.   It concerneth only the body.   The soul is thine, and belongeth to thee, and shall also remain with thee, forever.   Amen.   God help me! Amen.

Who can doubt that God helped him?

III.

KLOPSTOCK.

1724–1803.

NAPOLEON once, in that witty, incisive, imperial phrase of his, said, or is reported to have said, with paradox, concerning Dante, "His fame is increasing, and it will increase; for he is no longer read."

The case with the German poet Klopstock is partly like and partly different.   There is no present, and there is not likely to be any future, increase of his fame, presenting a problem to be solved.   But if there were, Napoleon's easy solution would serve ; for Klopstock is no longer read.   The solution, however, would, in Klopstock's case, serve without paradox ; for in pure soberness, this poet's fame could not possibly increase—on the rigorous condition that his poetry continued to be read.

Such, frankly disclosed, is the strict truth as to the subject of the present chapter. And still, Klopstock is now, and he always will be, a clear and venerable name in the history of German letters. He is secure of being permanently remembered as a German poet who, in his life-time, filled, not Germany alone, but Europe, with his renown, and who wrote the first ostensibly great epic—an epic remaining yet without a fellow of its own rank—in the German language.

For the *Messiah* of Klopstock, at least in ambition—which already is much—as likewise in theme, in purpose, in scope, and in conception, is a great epic. The execution falls short, nay, painfully short; but not short so far, even at that, as in justice wholly to defeat the poem of its fame. As the idea of the *Messiah* was rather bold and lofty than felicitous, so the realization also failed rather in judgment than in power.

Thus redoubtable and thus unreadable—for absolutely unreadable, to the living generation, this German epic, in its immense entirety, is—the *Messiah* may well engage the curiosity of every liberally inquiring mind, sufficiently, at least, to make the question a perennially interesting one, What is the true character of the poem that in its time enjoyed such fame and exerted such influence? For the influence, too, of the *Messiah* was commensurate with its fame. German literary history has run a different course, because Klopstock wrote the *Messiah*.

The slight notices to be given of this poet's uneventful, but honorable, and on the whole placid and happy, life will, we think, be more likely to interest readers, if postponed for them first to form to themselves some image of the man directly from his works. Klopstock wrote in prose as well as in verse; but his writings in prose, if we except one sacred tragedy of his, the *Adam*, and an historical drama in three parts, are neither entertaining nor important. His writings in verse consisted of odes, of tragedies (mostly on Scripture themes), and of one epic, his masterpiece, the *Messiah*. Let us begin at once with surveying this chief corner-stone of his fame

The *Messiah*, then, as befitted its title, is a religious poem. Its subject is the redeeming work of Jesus the Christ. The time covered by the action of the poem is short, the action commencing a few days only before the crucifixion, and closing with the ascension and glorification, of Christ. The substance of the poem consists of matter invented by the poet. This matter, for the most part, relates to transactions imagined by Klopstock to pass in the unseen spiritual world synchronously with the events narrated by the evangelists as occurring in the earthly sphere of things, within the period of time embraced between the beginning and the ending of the poet's plot. The invention of the *Messiah*, it will thus be seen, is sufficiently profuse. In fact, the fecundity of Klopstock's imagination is prodigious. No student of the work can possibly deny to the author of the *Messiah* the possession, " in overmeasure forever," of at least one great attribute of genius—inexhaustible faculty to invent. Judgment, however, to keep invention under guidance and in check, but, above all, supreme constructive capacity, a certain original vivific creative power, to organize the teeming products of invention into one comprehensive, consistent, harmonious, living and moving whole—these gifts were wanting to Klopstock.

Of such a production as that which is thus described, obviously it would not be easy to give an abstract in brief. A very large proportion of the expansile bulk of the *Messiah* consists of speeches made by the various personages of the plot. These speeches are chiefly either soliloquies or mutual addresses exchanged in conversation, which might equally well have been more in number or less, longer or shorter, than they in fact are; since, as a general rule, they are simply expressions of thought or of emotion leading to no issue in conduct on the part of the actors. Often, indeed, the action might better have spared them altogether. As the case stands, it is much as if, in a Greek tragedy, the drama proper should give nine tenths of its time to the chorus.

The *Messiah*, in fact, is less an epic than a scarcely coherent succession of lyrics.

Our best way of enabling readers to form for themselves a right idea of a poem like this will be, simply to give them some fairly representative specimens of what it contains; since what it contains, rather than what it is, constitutes its just title to fame. Every body will like to see how the *Messiah* begins. Here are the opening lines :

> Sing, O deathless soul, of apostate man's redemption,
> Which the Messias on earth in man's own nature accomplished,
> And through which, himself (a sufferer, slain, victorious),
> To God's favor anew the race of Adam exalted.
> For thus willed the Eternal—against that heavenly Saviour
> Satan arose in vain : in vain Judea resisted
> Him, the beloved Son—he wrought his work of atonement.

> But, O work, which only the Great All-merciful knoweth—
> Darkling here, from afar, may Poesy dare to approach thee?
> Hallow her, Sacred Spirit, whom here I worship in silence!
> Lead her to me, as thine imitatress, breathing of rapture,
> Full of unperishing strength, in veil-less majesty hither!
> Arm her with thine own fire, O thou, who awfully searchest
> The deep things of God; and man, albeit of the dust formed,
> Choosest to be thy temple, thy own terrestrial dwelling!
> Pure be this heart! so dare I, though with tremulous accents
> Mortal and weak, to celebrate Him, the divine Reconciler,
> Into that dread career with pardoned frailty ent'ring.
> Fellow-men, if that ye know the height which then ye attained
> When thus a world's creator became its atoner—O, listen,
> Listen to this my strain; and chief ye few but ennobled,
> Loved, heart-cherished friends of that all-lovely Redeemer,
> Who with habitual hope await his coming to judgment,
> Listen, and sing the eternal Son through a blissful existence!

Klopstock was not fortunate in attracting qualified English translators. We have accordingly had great difficulty in se-curing suitable versions even of passages from the *Messiah.* The foregoing extract we found in an old and rare English periodical of the year 1821, the *Congregational Magazine*, now nearly inaccessible. The translator, evidently a scholar, signs himself simply with the Greek letter Delta. He prefaces his work, which is fragmentary, with the statement that he had spent some time in a German university, led thither chiefly by his desire to become acquainted with Klopstock's poetry. This circumstance may be taken to indicate in what estimation, two generations ago, our poet was held. There is something truly pathetic in the thought irresistibly suggested by the contrast, existing in the case, between what was then and what is now—the thought, namely, of the uncertainty of human fame. The translator, with much modest misgiving, ventures the innovation of hexameters in English. There was propriety in this. For, with the exception of certain formally lyric passages, in rhymeless irregular metres, occurring toward the close, the original poem is in dactylic hexameter verse—a poetic form which Klopstock, if not the first among Germans himself to adopt, was first, by truly successful example, to get adopted by his countrymen. This difficult metre remained somewhat rough and intractable in Klopstock's hands; it waited almost one generation for Goethe's master plasticity to subdue it perfectly to smoothness and grace. But the mere use of the hexameter by Klopstock was significant. It meant the beginning of emancipation for German literature from the bondage of foreign literary models. Here, at least, was a genuinely German poem. Before Klopstock raised in the *Messiah* his standard of revolt, the French canons of literary art were, for generations, supreme and almost undisputed in Germany. Klopstock was German to the core. True, he was powerfully influenced by English models. Bishop Taylor, Young, in his *Night Thoughts*, Milton, in his *Paradise Lost*, Ossian, were teachers to him. Without these foreign sources of instruction and inspiration, Klopstock would not, probably he could not, have written his *Messiah*. The *Messiah*, in fact, is a virtually self-confessed parasite of the *Paradise Lost*. The *Paradise Lost* is assumed, is taken for granted, by the *Messiah*, much as the Bible itself is assumed, is taken for granted, by the *Paradise Lost*. We are about to exemplify this in a remarkable instance. Still, in

substance, in form, and in spirit, Klopstock is thoroughly
German. If Milton, if Young, become his sources and his
standards, if toward them he holds himself docile and dependent, for all that they do not succeed in anglicizing him.
He remains stoutly, resistantly German. Nay, he germanizes
them. Coleridge's saying, often taken as a witticism and a
sneer, might wisely be taken as a merely candid and just
appreciation of Klopstock. Some one called Klopstock " a
German Milton." "Yes," said Coleridge, "and a very
German Milton." It was the strict truth happily expressed.

Early in the first canto, occurs a famous passage on which we
have felt forced to try ourselves a translating hand. It follows a conversation reported by the poet, between the Divine
Father and the Divine Son, on the subject of the atonement,
now about to be accomplished in the crucifixion of Jesus.
The pervasive effect on the universe, resulting from the cov-
enant for human redemption entered into between the two
Divine Persons, is described. Our readers will not need to be
reminded, in parallel, of those two celebrated places of Milton, describing the ominous sympathy of nature shown on
occasion of the fall of our first parents:

> Earth felt the wound, and Nature from her seat,
> Sighing through all her works, gave sign of woe
> That all was lost.

> Sky lowered, and, mutt'ring thunder, some sad drops
> Wept at completing of the mortal sin
> Original.

Here is Klopstock's modification and adaptation,—as we
have been able, hugging the original closely, to convert the
German hexameters into lines of English blank verse:

> So spake he, and ceased speaking. While they spake,
> The two Eternal Ones, there went through all
> The universe a shudder full of awe.
> Souls that but now were forming, nor to think
> Had yet begun, trembled and learned to feel.
> A mighty quaking seized the seraph, smote
> His heart in him, while round about him lay
> Waiting, as waits the earth the coming storm,

> The silence-keeping circle of his world.
> Soft transports only came into the souls
> Of Christians yet to be, and sweet-absorbing sense
> Of everlasting life. But impotent,
> And only of despairing capable
> Now, impotent to think blaspheming thoughts,
> Rushed ruining from their thrones in the abyss
> The spirits of hell. As down headlong they sank,
> On each there rolled a rock, rent under each
> The deep with dreadful rupture, while with noise
> Of thunder bellowed the profoundest hell.

An invention of Klopstock's as likely, for several reasons, as any thing in the *Messiah*, to interest our readers is that of the character and fortune of a personage named Abbadona. It is a characteristically Klopstockian invention; it associates itself with a familiar and magnificent imagination in Milton's *Paradise Lost;* and it is, in its own right, intrinsically worthy of some attention. Abbadona is an evil spirit—not wholly evil, for he is repentant. He was, according to Klopstock, originally a kind of twin to the Abdiel of Milton, having been created at the self-same moment with that noble, upright spirit, the loftiest severe conception of moral character in the *Paradise Lost*, nay, the loftiest, perhaps, in the whole realm of imaginative poetry. Abbadona, in the crisis of the great angelic apostasy, was for a moment minded to side with Abdiel in standing out against Satan. But he wavered, and finally he fell. But he did not so revolt from God as not to regret that he had revolted.

A council of the wicked angels is held, to plot the destruction of Jesus, and Satan, in a characteristic speech, has propounded his scheme. At this point Abbadona is introduced by Klopstock. We quote from the second book of the *Messiah*, using this time the prose version of Joseph Collyer:

Before the throne sat Abbadona by himself in deep dejection, ruminating with keenest anguish on the past and the future. Before his face, which was deformed by melancholy, internal anguish, and sad dismay, he beheld tortures accumulated on tortures, extending into eternity. He then looked back to those happy days when he himself was a bright seraph and the friend of the exalted Abdiel; who, on the day of the revolt, bravely vindicated the cause of God, and having zealously contended for the truth before the apostate legions, returned without him to his Creator, invincible, and crowned with immortal glory. Abbadona was near escaping with that heroic seraph; but being surrounded with the rapid chariots of Satan, and the bright bands of those who fell from their allegiance, he drew back; and though Abdiel, with looks of menacing love, chid his delay, and strove to hasten his escape from those reprobate bands, inebriated and dazzled with the delusive prospect of his future godhead he no longer attended to the once powerful eye of his friend, but suffered himself to be carried in triumph to Satan. Now lamenting in pensive silence, he revolves the history of his once spotless innocence and the fair morning of his days when he came pure and happy out of the hand of his Creator. At once the Almighty Source of Goodness formed him and Abdiel, when, filled with inborn rapture, they thus addressed each other: "Ah, beauteous form, what are we? Where, my beloved, didst thou first see me? How long hast thou—how long have I existed? Come, O come, my divine friend, embrace me—admit me into thy bosom—let me learn thy thoughts."

In the meantime came the glory of God, shining from afar with ineffable splendor, fraught with benediction. They looked around and beheld an innumerable host of new immortals. A silver cloud then gently raised them to the Eternal. They saw their Creator. They called him Father, and enraptured adored him as the source of their happiness.

Abbadona, tortured by these thoughts, shed a torrent of tears, and now resolved to oppose the blasphemous speech of Satan, which had filled him with horror. He thrice attempted to speak, but his sighs stopped his utterance. ["Thrice he assayed, and thrice, in spite of scorn, | Tears, such as angels weep, burst forth; at last | Words interwove with sighs found out their way."—*Paradise Lost*, I, 621–623.] Thus, when in a bloody battle two brothers are mortally wounded by each other's hand, at last, each to the other being mutually known, they are unable to express the strong sensations of their hearts, and sighs only proceed from their dying lips. At length Abbadona thus broke silence:

"Though I incur the everlasting displeasure of this assembly, I will not refrain from speaking. Yes, Satan; I will boldly speak, and perhaps the heavy judgments of the Eternal may more lightly fall on me than on thee. O thou seducer, how I now hate thee! This essence, this immortal essence, which thou hast snatched from its Creator, he will perpetually require of thee. . . . He will require of thee the whole assembly of immortal spirits, by thee involved in ruin. Thou execrable deceiver, with thee I renounce all connection. I will not participate in thine impotent project of putting to death the divine Messiah. Against whom, O spirit accursed! dost thou rave? It is against him who thou art forced to confess is more mighty than thyself! Has not his irresist-

ible thunder sufficiently disfigured thine audacious front? ["His face
Deep scars of thunder had intrenched." — *Paradise Lost*, I, 600.]
. . . Satan heard him with impatient rage, and instantly from the top
of his throne attempted to hurl at his devoted head an enormous rock;
["Jaculation dire," indeed, in the present case. The original in Milton
had at least some semblance of a Titanic majesty. Compare *Paradise
Lost*, VI., 635–666], but his destructive right hand dropped, shriveled
and void of strength. Then, stamping with impotent fury, three times
his disappointed malice shook his whole frame, three times he cast a look
of malignant fury at Abbadona, while his struggling passions stopped his
voice. Abbadona, with an afflicted countenance, still stood before him,
firm and intrepid.

Adramelech now intervenes with a speech in bitter scorn
of Abbadona—Adramelech, a second evil angel invented by
Klopstock. This invention, by the way, bears the stamp of
real genius. Adramelech is secretly rival and foe to Satan,
whom he plots to supplant and overthrow. His speech, in
opposition to Abbadona, elicits universal applause. Satan
and Adramelech, amid tumults of acclamation, start on their
earthward way. Klopstock again:

Abbadona, who alone had remained unmoved, followed at a distance,
either still to persuade them [Satan and Adramelech] from engaging in
the dire attempt, or to behold the consequences of the dreadful deed.
Now, with steps dilatory and slow, he advanced, and, before he was
aware, found himself before the angels who guarded the gate. But how
was he confounded when he saw there the invincible Abdiel! Sighing he
held down his head and thought of retiring; then resolved to advance;
then, trembling and filled with perturbation, determined to fly into the immense abyss of space; but instantly collecting himself he moved toward
the seraph. His beating heart spoke the terror of his mind; distressful
tears, such as fallen angels weep [*Paradise Lost*, I, 622, already quoted],
fell from his eyes; deep sighs burst from his agonizing breast, and a con-
tinual tremor, never felt by mortals, shook his whole frame. Abdiel,
with an open, tranquil eye, stood in fixed attention, gazing up the bright
stream of light, and with sweet serenity was viewing the distant worlds,
formed by the Creator, to whom he had ever remained faithful. He saw
not Abbadona. As the sun on its natal day poured his resplendent
beams on the new created earth, so shone the bright seraph; but the
afflicted Abbadona felt no genial influences from his refulgent rays.
Sighing, he cried to himself, in plaintive voice, Abdiel, my brother! wilt
thou forever shun me? Etc., etc., etc.

In our anxiety, on the one hand, not to do Klopstock injustice, and, on the other hand, not to fail of showing him as he
is to our readers, we are constantly in doubt at what point
to suspend our citations and content ourselves with simply
asserting, in place of actually proving, our worthy poet to be
tedious.   For instance, here, will it not be accepted as sufficient if we say that Klopstock makes Abbadona go on from
this point, page after page, expressing his distracted and
wretched thoughts and emotions?   There is never, with this
poem, a moment when the action, always languid, is not likely
to come to a dead standstill, for a speech from some one, in-
terjected, to express a series of reflections and emotions—reflections and emotions generally, it must be acknowledged,
appropriate enough, but also generally, it must be lamented,
conscientiously commonplace.   You may suppose, when a
speech thus introduced from some actor—or, quite as likely,
from some mere spectator—in the plot, has come to its apparent
term, and when the author himself resumes the word—you
may, we say, suppose that now, at least, the action will proceed without further delay; but that will be because you
have not yet learned your poet.   The apparent term to the
speech was not a term at all—far from it—it was just a
pause.   The pause over, the speech takes a new start refreshed, and ambles exhaustlessly on.   There was, in fact—
as in the author, so in the author's subject—no reason why
that speech should ever end.   Klopstock's speeches have
often the effect of simply so much utterance, cut off in
lengths, greater or less, as happens.   They might as easily
have been shorter; but be thankful, they might also as easily
have been longer.

It constantly seems to Klopstock that, for translating
phlegm into passion, reason into imagination—in one word,
prose into poetry—nothing at any time is necessary beyond
suddenly breaking out into a personification and apostrophe.
There is no object so inanimate, no idea so abstract, as to be
for an instant safe against a galvanic touch of this sort from
Klopstock that shall make it spring up in momentary impotent

mimicry of life.   Klopstock was a true poet, but it is strange indeed that any true poet could write as Klopstock wrote and fail to feel how purely a trick of form this use of rhetorical figure was becoming in his hands.

Abbadona re-appears as permitted beholder, deeply moved, at the spectacle of the crucifixion; then once more, and for the last time, in a vision, vouchsafed to our forefather Adam and reported by him, of the final judgment of men and angels.   During the period occupied by Klopstock in the composition of the *Messiah*, it was, with some theologians, a matter of grave concern, on behalf of the public, what destiny, whether of restitution to his original happy state, or of hopeless condemnation, should be assigned by the poet to Abbadona.   One solicitous divine wrote to Klopstock earnestly beseeching him, for the sake of religion, not to save the fallen angel.   Klopstock replied reassuringly, though vaguely; but his feelings at last were too much for his orthodoxy. He relented toward the creature of his hands, and saved Abbadona.

So much for one episode of the *Messiah.*

And so much for the *Messiah* itself, which is made up of episodes.

For the poem has now been fairly, and, for our purpose, sufficiently, represented.   The quality of it is all here.   It is the quantity only that is lacking.   Or, if there lacks any part of the quality too, it is chiefly that element of homily which in the day of its first fame made this sacred epic a quarry of material for preachers.

We almost fear that, to sympathetic readers, we shall seem to have been too little appreciative of our poet's merit.   But we have sincerely sought to be candid and just.   There is really scarce any limit to the tireless, tiresome prolixity of Klopstock.   For instance, three whole books are occupied with an inconceivably detailed and delayed account of the crucifixion.   This part of the poem, which should have been its strongest, is its weakest.   Should have been, we say; but we know well that, in the nature of things, it could not be; and that impossibility is what condemns Klopstock's choice of subject as one unfit to have been made. If this German writer had but learned how, on some occasions, to condense, as, alas, by instinct he knew only too well how on all occasions to expand—who can say?—he might have made his poem a "possession forever," instead of a possession for a day.

Of the odes of Klopstock, a single specimen, much condensed, must suffice, but that shall be one of the best. It is the ode referred to so significantly in Goethe's *Sorrows of Werther*. Werther and Charlotte, in that work of Goethe's, witness together a thunder-storm, and Charlotte interprets to Werther the sentiment of what they behold by simply exclaiming, "Klopstock!" The sudden obtrusion of this not very poetic proper name, breaking the tenor of over-strained intensity which prevails throughout the *Werther*, has an extremely odd, even whimsical, effect on the English reader—quite the reverse of a climax in the sublime. "Klopstock" was felt by the Germans themselves to be a name lacking in dignity. But what in this respect the name lacked, the owner of the name amply supplied. Goethe notes that Klopstock's air was that of a man conscious of a high moral mission in the world. To the present writer, however, "Klopstock!" as an exclamation of sublimity, remains a bit humorous. Not in the least so is the ode itself thus referred to, which we here condense from Taylor's prose translation. The German original is in irregular, unrhymed verse, Pindaric in bold abruptness and freedom of form, but Hebrew in devotional spirit. It is entitled *The Festival of Spring:*

Not into the ocean of all the worlds would I plunge. . . .

Only around the drop on the bucket, only around the earth, would I hover and adore. Hallelujah! hallelujah! the drop on the bucket flowed also out of the hand of the Almighty.

. . . And who am I? Hallelujah to the Creator! more than the earths which flowed, more than the seven stars which conglomerated out of beams.

But thou, worm of spring, which, greenly-golden, art fluttering beside me, thou livest, and art, perhaps, ah! not immortal?

I went out to adore, and I weep.   Forgive, forgive this tear also to the finite one, O thou who shalt be!

Thou wilt unveil to me all doubts, thou who shalt guide me through the dark valley of death—I shall then learn whether the golden worm had a soul.

. . . The morning sun grows sultry; clouds stream aloof; visible is he who comes—the Eternal.

Now swoop, rush, whirl the winds; bows the wood; billows the stream. . . .

The wood bows, the stream flees, and I fall not on my face? Lord, Lord, God merciful and gracious, thou approaching power! have mercy on me! . . .

See ye the new sign of his presence, the darting beam? Hear ye, high in the cloud, the thunder of the Lord?   It calls: Jehovah . . . Jehovah . . . and the struck forest smokes.

But not our hut. Our Father bade his destroyer to pass over our hut.

Ah! already rushes heaven and earth with the gracious rain; now is the earth (how it thirsted!) refreshed, and the heaven (how it was laden!) disburdened.

Behold, Jehovah comes no longer in storm; in gentle, pleasant murmurs comes Jehovah, and under him bends the bow of peace!

We here, as promised, conclude our exhibition by example of Klopstock as poet. As poetical critic, however, using himself for his subject, he deserves still to have hearing for a moment or two. Klopstock felt the necessity of instructing his public in the principles on which he sought to write poetry of the highest kind. From an essay of his, printed in preface to one of the installments in which his *Messiah* originally appeared, we separate a few expressions of opinion on the subject of *Divine Poetry*. There is abundant self-revelation, on the poet's part, in every paragraph of this prefatory essay. Klopstock:

A piece of sublime poetry is a work of genius in which strokes of wit are to be sparingly used.

There are masterpieces of wit that neither reach the heart nor flow from it; but a genius without the tender feelings of the heart is very imperfect.

The highest and utmost effect of genius is to move the whole soul.

. . . Young's *Night Thoughts* is perhaps a work that has the merit of having fewer faults than any other. If we take from him what he

says as a Christian, Socrates remains; but how does the Christian rise
above Socrates ! . . .

His [the sacred poet's] design is more extensive than awaking a single
passion. . . . By a masterpiece of skill he lays before us views at which,
by a sudden and powerful touch, he makes us cry out with joy, stand
immovably fixed in astonishment, or, filled with grief and terror, turn
pale, tremble, and weep.

The last foregoing sentence reveals what was the perfectly
conscious aim of Klopstock, in those innumerable passages
of his poem in which, with exclamation points, with superla-
tive phrases, with grammatical and rhetorical figure, in short,
with all the futile exterior artifices of intense writing, he in-
vokes the passions of the reader. He will now set forth
why he cultivated prolixity on principle :

When the poet, in some important part of his work, designs strongly to
affect the soul he will perhaps proceed unabsorbed in the following
manner. . . . He will say, In order strongly to affect the mind, I gradually rise, that every step may prepare for what is to follow. In order
to fill my readers with a sorrow mixed with silent astonishment, I must
insensibly encompass them with sorrowful images. I must first remind
them of certain truths that open the soul to the reception of the last and
most powerful impressions. . . . Were I abruptly to bring them thither,
they would be rather stunned than filled with strong sensations.

Here is a critical sentence of Klopstock's, the very last
word of which, a proper name, will, we venture to say, surprise every reader :

The Greeks, the Romans, and the French have all their short golden
age of polite literature; and I do not know why we have not given
one to the English; they have long had their masterpieces, and these
have not ceased with—Glover !

"Glover" is the name of an English poet whose now for
gotten epics, especially the *Leonidas*, enjoyed a great fame
in their day. To Coleridge and Wordsworth, paying together
a visit of youthful reverence to the venerable German poet
in his home, Klopstock expressed the opinion that Glover's
blank verse was superior to Milton's ! Such are the phases
of fame, and such may be the value of critical opinion pronounced by authority enjoying its moment of imperial sway!

What follows, finishing our citations from this essay of Klopstock, is perhaps as significant as any thing it contains. The poet seems to be reassuring at once himself and his admirers as to their spiritual state :

> Here [in sacred poetry] both the poet and his reader may certainly know whether they are Christians. For he can be nothing less who here moves our whole souls, nor he who finds himself thus moved. For how shall a poet, of the greatest genius, without feeling the strong impressions of religion, without an upright heart, glowing with all the fervor of piety, produce in our minds the most lively and devout sensations ?

It is in strict keeping with the sentiment of the last foregoing, that Klopstock should in his old age have used, as he did use, his own *Messiah* for a manual of private devotion. Klopstock's piety was probably genuine ; but it had in it a strong tincture of self-complacency, and it was highly sentimental. It by no means prevented its subject, so Scherer assures us, from smoking, from drinking, from promiscuously kissing, on first introduction, girls whom he met, and in general from deporting himself with a freedom and levity quite scandalizing to the grave Swiss Bodmer, who had made haste to invite the author of so edifying an epic as the *Messiah* to visit him at his home in Zurich. The deliberately calculating young bachelor poet had his peculiar plans of self-culture. Before accepting Bodmer's invitation, he bargained with that gentleman on the subject of being provided with the privilege of young ladies' society in Zurich:

> How near are you [so he asks his Swiss correspondent] to any young ladies of your acquaintance, into whose society you may think I would be admitted? The heart of a young woman is an extensive scene of action into whose labyrinth a poet must frequently penetrate, if he wishes to acquire profound knowledge.

Klopstock became remarkably communicative and open to his Zurich admirer. "I love," he writes—this, remember, to a man whom he has never seen, a married man, a man fifty years old, that is, more than twice as old as himself (for Klopstock published the first installment of his epic when he was twenty-four years of age)—"I love a tender holy maid, to whom my first Ode is addressed, with the most tender holy love." This "tender holy" lover was, however, disconsolate. He could not be sure that his affection was reciprocated. "By Milton's shade," Klopstock continues, "by thine ever blessed infants, by thine own great soul, I adjure thee, Bodmer, make me happy if thou canst." The exact practical thing, namely, which Klopstock wanted of Bodmer, was that the latter should interest and bestir himself to get the author of the *Messiah* a snug place of some sort, a pension would be better, to enable him to marry, and, in fruitful, placid ease of mind, finish his great poem. The mendicant poet put a very fine point upon the matter. Pregnantly suggesting that the Prince of Orange was said to be a generous fellow, "What if he should give me a pension?" he asks; but adds: "If you can do any thing to assist me in this business, excellent Bodmer, I hope you will do it, but not as asking in my name ; *for I would not beg my fortune of princes, though I would of Bodmer.*"

"Fanny" was the name of the "tender holy" maid. Fanny kept poor Klopstock in dreadful suspense, until he did at length get a pension—it was from the king of Denmark when it came; but, by the time that happened, Klopstock's own anxiety seems for some reason to have become allayed, and he in fact married another lady, one who fell in love with the poet as self-revealed in his *Messiah*. "Margaret" was this lady's name, a name immortal, in the affectionate diminutive form of "Meta," by association with Klopstock. Meta was supremely happy in her husband, and she made her husband supremely happy, four years only, and then she died. Klopstock waited long a widower ; he at length married again. His second wife was a relative of Meta. All these three rest together now, side by side, in Ottensen, near Hamburg, in Germany. Klopstock himself was buried with such honors as are usually accorded only to princes.

Few poets of any country or age have had an experience of life, on the whole, so happy as was Klopstock's. The fullness of fame was his while he lived, and he seems to have

been troubled with no misgivings as to its future continuance. That his fame at least was stainless signifies more
now, to the poet, than that it should be either great or lasting.
Carlyle, with that poetic touch of his, spoke admiringly of
the "azure purity of Klopstock."

IV.

LESSING.

1729–1781.

In all German literary history, no figure whatever stands
out more boldly in relief—square-set, sturdy, stanch, strong,
positive, combative, an individual soul "whole in himself"
—none with more challenge in his attitude, peremptory, im-
perious, commanding heed, than the figure of Lessing. Heine
calls him the continuator of Luther. And indeed, during the
two hundred years that immediately followed Luther, what
German literary name emerges so worthy as was Lessing
to stand second in that mighty succession ? Lessing was five
years later than Klopstock; but Lessing did more for German literature by criticising, than Klopstock did by creating.

Lessing was supremely a critic. His critical ideas he em-
bodied, indeed, in original work of his own—work which
maintains to this day a higher than merely respectable rank
in literature; but it is by his labors in criticism, rather than
by his labors in creation, that Lessing has been, as he still is,
and as he is likely long to be, a living literary force.

The story of this man's life is at once stimulating and depressing. It is a story of struggle against adversity, struggle
always manfully maintained, but struggle almost never tri-
umphantly victorious. Gotthold Ephraim Lessing was the son
of a Lutheran pastor. The pastor destined his son to his own
vocation; but the disposition of the youth destined him far
otherwise. Sent to the University of Leipsic for the study
of theology, the Lutheran clergyman's son found in that

Saxon Paris what interested him more than theology. He found the theatre. He devoted himself assiduously to the cultivation of acquaintanceship with actors and actresses. The issue was a permanent diversion of his mental activity. He became a dramatic writer and dramatic critic. His subsequent literary production was nearly all of it determined by his bent toward the theatre.

Intellectual independence was the distinguishing note in Lessing's character. Convention counted with him for nothing. His habitual attitude of mind was that of doubt and question as to traditional ideas. Finding German literature attached as a parasite to the French, he strove, by criticism, as Klopstock strove by production, to break the ignominious bond that held it subject, and to give it rooting and grounding of its own, in reason, in nature, and in truth. It need not be concealed that Lessing's contempt of French literary models was probably pricked on by a practical disappointment which he experienced. For, like so many of his literary compatriots, Lessing, too, was at one time fain to be the virtual pensioner of a prince. He failed of appointment to a librarianship under Frederick the Great, and from that moment his natural pure " joy of fighting " was pungent with some spice of spite transferred against those French authors whom the Prussian monarch counted for all in all. Voltaire he criticised with startling boldness. He took up one after another the tragedies of that brilliant man of letters, and mercilessly showed how they violated the essential truth of reason and of nature. Nay, he vindicated Aristotle himself against Voltaire, and against that whole school, classic so-called, of dramatic writers who, claiming to represent, in fact misrepresented, the teachings of the mighty Greek.

The effect was prodigious. Rather, we should say, the effect has been prodigious. For the influence of Lessing's fruitful criticism did not exhaust itself in producing an immense immediate effect. The effect continues to this day, and it is not German literature alone that feels it, but likewise the literature of every Western nation. Lessing, in fact, is probably at this moment exercising a literary influence, extensive and intensive, not second to that of any other name whatever in the world, since Aristotle. If Luther made a German literature possible, Lessing made a German literature actual. Of all that now is most glorious in the exploits of the German literary mind, achieved since Luther, it is not too much to say that Lessing is an inseparable element.

We have thus certainly not stinted our praise of Lessing as critic. It is only just, now, to add that Lessing's destructive critical rage against the French carried with it something of the ill grace displayed by a man who should, with an air, kick down a scaffolding that had just helped him to climb. French criticism contributed to put Lessing in the way of discovering the faults in French literature. Diderot as critic was in part master to both Lessing and Goethe. To a taunt—it should have been, perhaps it was, a German taunt—leveled once against the French, that they never invented any thing, it was wittily replied, "At least Descartes invented German philosophy." Mr. John Morley, quoting this, boldly adds: "Still more true is it that Diderot invented German criticism." The boast of absolute originality is always and every-where a very precarious boast. "He that pleadeth his cause first seemeth just; but his neighbor cometh and searcheth him out."

Lessing's native independence of mind was early asserted against his parents, who, both of them, were anxious about their son, involved amid the temptations of a city. How far from being merely querulous and idle was the solicitude they felt, may be judged from some things which Taylor (of Norwich) relates of the young man's ways. Lessing had visited home, summoned thither to see his mother, said to be dying. The dying mother revived, and every seduction of home influence was applied to reclaim the youth from his irregular life. But when he went back to Leipsic it was rather to the theatre again than to the university. The actress, however, who formerly favored him had meanwhile transferred her movable affections elsewhere. "A younger actress," Taylor says, "named Lorenzin, was the Eucharis who superseded this Calypso. Lessing took an excursion with her to Vienna under a feigned name."

To his father, Lessing writes (we draw from W. Taylor):

> I beg you will send hither the manuscripts in my drawer; and not keep back those sheets inscribed "Love and Wine." They are chiefly free imitations of Anacreon, and not such as an equitable moralist can blame.

A highly liberal view, that which the didactic son thus inculcates on his father, as to what an "equitable moralist" might blame! Concerning his poetic effusions on "Love and Wine," he further says:

> In fact, the only cause of their existence is the desire of trying my hand at all sorts of poetry.

This is exactly in the line proper to the forerunner of Goethe. In the same communication to his father, Lessing lets us into the secret of his aspiring literary ambition:

> If the title of the German Molière could justly be given· to me, I should have secured an eternal name. To speak out, I heartily covet to deserve it; but I am fully conscious of its compass, and of my impotence. Am I wrong for selecting a line of pursuit in which few of my countrymen have hitherto excelled? Am I wrong for determining not to leave off producing until some masterpiece of mine shall exist?

The cool assumption of openness, on his father's part, to mere professional motive, made by the son in the *argumentum ad hominem* which follows, is suggestive. Young Lessing says :

> What if I were to write a comedy such as you theologians would praise —you think it impossible—not if I were to turn into ridicule the despisers of their profession. Own that this would blunt a little of your sharpness.

The willful son went his own way. High-spirited as he was, and really sensitive on the point of honor, Lessing seems nevertheless to have submitted, against his conscience, to subscribing a religious creed in order to secure a university degree and so get on in the world. He never got on in the world very well, for all his degree, and his degree was always hateful to him—probably from association with the cost to his pride at which it was won.

Lessing was an habitual hard student. Though never, in the strict sense, a scholar, he became immensely learned. But he was no recluse. He almost anticipated Goethe in the latter's idea of knowing every thing, and experiencing every thing, in order to full self-culture. For instance, Lessing gambled, and, though a poor man, he played high. He affected to prize, as intellectual stimulus, the excitement, thus arising, of lively hopes and fears. He wandered much about the world, insatiably fond of change. But, wherever he went, he studied and worked. He produced multifariously, his pay scarcely ever rising above the wages of a literary hack. The productions by which he is now most remembered are, a comedy entitled *Minna von Barnhelm*, and two dramas, entitled respectively, *Emilia Galotti*, and *Nathan the Wise*, together with an essay on criticism and in criticism, entitled *Laocoön*. These works are all in prose, except the *Nathan the Wise*, which is in blank verse. Lessing was distinctively a witty man, the first in time perhaps among Germans to take away from that great people the reproach of not possessing the faculty to kindle wisdom into wit. Heine, since, far less wise surely, has contrived to be, or to seem, far more witty than was Lessing. With this doubtful exception, Lessing remains easily the prince of German wits.

The two works, verse and prose, by specimens from which our readers will best gain a true idea of Lessing, are undoubtedly the *Nathan the Wise* and the *Laocoön*. These are his masterpieces, the one in creation, the other in criticism. Lessing, however, turned his hand to many different forms of literary production. It may serve to hint the versatility of his genius, if we give a few samples of the apologues in which it was one fancy of his to convey his wisdom and his wit. Here is a fable in which Lessing makes Æsop himself, his own ideal fabulist, take characteristic part in a very short dialogue with a particular animal, whom he, Æsop, had often introduced in his narrations, and never entirely to that animal's satisfaction :

> Said the ass to Æsop: "The next time you tell a story about me, let me say something that is right rational and ingenious."
>
> "You something ingenious !" said Æsop; "what propriety would there be in that? Would not the people say you were the moralist and I the ass ?"

Lessing was sufficiently unlike his own countrymen to be able at least to see one of their weak points, as the fable of *The Blind Hen*, with its bluntly expressed application, shows :

> A hen which had become blind continued to scratch for food as she had been used. What availed it the industrious fool ? Another hen, that could see, but wished to spare her tender feet, never forsook the side of the former, and, without scratching, enjoyed the fruit of scratching. For as often as the blind hen turned up a corn, the seeing one devoured it.
>
> The laborious German gathers the literary material which the witty Frenchman uses.

Here, in a fable entitled *The Ape and the Fox*, is another hard hit at a literary folly of Germans :

> "Name to me an animal, though never so skillful, that I cannot imitate." So bragged the ape to the fox. But the fox replied : "And do thou name to me an animal so humble as to think of imitating thee."
>
> Writers of my country ! Need I explain myself more fully !

Lessing wrote an essay on the fable, which Herder praised as the best philosophic inquiry into the principles of a given literary form that had appeared since Aristotle.

Now for some exhibition of the *Nathan the Wise*. "Nathan" is the name of a Jew of the time of Saladin. This Jew is an embodiment of all the virtues. It has been esteemed part of our author's boldness that he dared make a Jew his ideal character ; so hated, so despised, and so misused were the Jews of Lessing's day, in Germany. But the fact is that Lessing's ideal Jew was an actual Jew. A citizen of Berlin—already, when Lessing wrote this play, illustrious, and deservedly illustrious, for singular elevation of character—the Hebrew, Moses Mendelssohn, was the original of Lessing's Nathan the Sage.

Moses Mendelssohn is a personage even yet interesting to us, otherwise than merely as the suggestion and inspiration of Lessing's dramatic masterpiece. He was not only a virtuous and wealthy Israelite, but himself also an eminent man of letters. He stands, moreover, in the relation of grandfather to a man of his own name, better known than himself, a man the splendor of whose fame as musical composer has had the effect to obscure his merit as an author— we mean, of course, Felix Mendelssohn. For these various reasons combined, Moses Mendelssohn is entitled to more than mere passing mention at our hands. We must let him speak here for himself in at least a few printed words of his own.

His literary masterpiece is, perhaps, the *Phædon*, an argument for the immortality of the soul. This work enjoys the distinction of having been sharply criticized by the philosopher Kant. A curious circumstance it is, by the way, that, early in life, Mendelssohn, in a philosophical competition, had borne off the prize from a rival no less formidable than this same critic himself. The writing, however, of Mendelssohn's, that will, on the whole, at once most interest our readers and best display the character of the man in that connection with Lessing and with Lessing's play which makes it fit—indeed, well-nigh imperative—to introduce him here, is an open letter of his addressed to the celebrated Lavater. Lavater's name will be universally recognized as a synonym for physiognomy claiming to be a science. Lavater was a vehemently aggressive Christian, having translated into German a French work (by M. Bonnet) on the evidences of Christianity. In dedicating his translation respectfully to Moses Mendelssohn, he incorporated a challenge to that distinguished adherent of Judaism, to do one or the other of two things, namely, confute the argument for Christianity contained in the book, or else renounce his faith as a Jew. Mendelssohn was deeply affected by the challenge. His health was exceedingly fragile, and the excitement threatened serious consequences. At length, however, he so replied to Lavater that the public generally agreed, as did Lavater himself in the end, to hold the writer completely relieved from the apparently hopeless dilemma in which the challenge had placed him. Mendelssohn's letter is a document of considerable length. We extract and condense a few specimen passages. What could be more admirable in taste and in temper than the gently insinuated reproof and appeal of the following sentences, occurring early in the letter?

> HONORED PHILANTHROPIST: . . . It seems you still recollect the confidential conversation I had the pleasure of holding with yourself and your worthy friends in my apartment. Can you then possibly have forgotten how frequently I sought to divert the discourse from religious to more neutral topics, and how much yourself and your friends had to urge me before I would venture to deliver my opinion on a subject of such vital importance? If I am not mistaken, preliminary assurances were even given that no *public use* should *ever* be made of any remarkable expression that might drop on the occasion. Be that as it may, I will rather suppose myself in error than tax you with a breach of promise. But . . . what, sir, could induce you to single me thus, against my well-known disinclination, out of the many, and force me into a public arena which I so much wished never to have occasion to enter? If even you placed my reserve to the score of mere timidity and bashfulness, these very foibles should have deserved the moderation and forbearance of a charitable heart.

Mendelssohn sets forth his own unshaken religious position; as follows:

> Of the essentials of my religion I am as firmly, as irrefragably, convinced as you, sir, or Mr. Bonnet, ever can be of those of yours. . . . We must finish certain inquiries once in our life, if we wish to proceed further. This, I may say, I had done, with regard to religion, several years ago. I read, compared, reflected, and—made up my mind.

But, immovably firm for himself in his Judaism, Mendelssohn yet had no zeal to make proselytes of others. His own lack of the propagandist spirit he justifies as follows:

> It is by virtue that I wish to shame the opprobrious opinion commonly entertained of a Jew, and not by controversial writings. . . .

Pursuant to the principles of my religion, I am not to seek to convert any one who is not born under our laws. Our rabbins unanimously teach that the written and oral laws, which form conjointly our revealed religion, are obligatory on our nation only. . . . Those who regulate their lives according to the principles of the religion of nature and of reason, are called virtuous men of other nations, and are the children of eternal salvation.

Our rabbins . . . enjoin us to dissuade, by vigorous remonstrances, every one who comes forward to be converted. We are to lead him to reflect that the moment he embraces the religion of the Israelites, he subscribes gratuitously to all the rigid rites of that faith, to which he must then strictly conform, or await the punishment which the legislator has denounced on their infraction. Finally, we are to hold up to him a faithful picture of the misery, tribulation, and obloquy, in which the nation is now living, in order to guard him from a rash act, which he might ultimately repent.

. . . Whoever is not born subject to our laws has no occasion to live according to them. We consider ourselves alone bound to acknowledge their authority; and this can give no offense to our neighbors. . . .

Suppose there were among my contemporaries a Confucius or a Solon, I could, consistently with my religious principles, love and admire the great man; but I should never hit on the extravagant idea of converting a Confucius or a Solon. . . . Do I think there is a chance of his being saved? I certainly believe that he who leads mankind on to virtue in this world, cannot be damned in the next. . . .

Mendelssohn had additional reasons for abstaining from controversy against the Christian religion. He says:

I am one of an oppressed people. Rights granted to every other human being my brethren in the faith willingly forego. . . . In some places, even a *temporary domicile is denied them.* Do the laws of Zurich allow your circumcised friend to pay you a visit there? No. What gratitude, then, do not my brethren owe to the nation [Prussia], which includes them in its general philanthropy, suffering them, without molestation, to worship the Supreme Being after the rites of their ancestors? The government under which I live leaves nothing to wish for in this respect; and the Hebrews should, therefore, be scrupulous in abstaining from reflections on the dominant religion, or, which is the same thing, from touching their protectors where men of virtue are most tender.

In what immediately follows the foregoing, but especially in the closing paragraph of his letter, Mendelssohn implies a remarkable compliment to Lavater; and at the same time, in doing so, exhibits himself in the engaging aspect of a most placable, most amiable, man:

> Private appeals from men of worth I have taken the liberty silently to decline. The importunities of pedants, who arrogated to themselves the right of worrying me publicly, on account of my religious principles, I conceived myself justified in treating with contempt. But the solemn conjuration of a Lavater demands, at any rate, this public avowal of my sentiments, lest too pertinacious a silence should be construed into disregard, or into acquiescence.
>
> . . . I have now stated to you the reasons why I so earnestly wish to have no more to do with religious controversy. . . If you should prove peremptory, I *must* lay aside my scruples and come to a resolution of publishing, in a counter-inquiry, my thoughts, both on Mr. Bonnet's work and on the cause which he vindicates. But I hope you will exonerate me from this irksome task, and rather give me leave to withdraw to that state of quietude which is more congenial to my disposition. Place yourself in my situation; take my view of circumstances, not yours, and you will no longer strive against my reluctance.
>
> I am, with most perfect respect, yours sincerely,
>
> MOSES MENDELSSOHN.

BERLIN, the 12th of *December*, 1769.

The softness, the sweetness, the blandness, the ripeness, the wideness, of wisdom attributed by Lessing to his Nathan, are all present, express or implicit, in this letter of Mendelssohn to Lavater. When, now, it is considered that Lessing and Mendelssohn were not only contemporaries but fellow-countrymen, and not only fellow-countrymen but dwellers in the same city, and not only dwellers in the same city but intimate personal friends, the inference is easy, is inevitable, that the dramatist, for the conception of the leading personage of his plot and for the sentiments which that personage is made to utter, must have owed every thing almost to the example that lived before him and to the oracle that daily spoke with him, in the gentle and saintly Hebrew sage, Moses Mendelssohn. It is touching to know that a few years after *Nathan the Wise* appeared, the memory of its author, who had meantime died, was defended against the charge of Spinozism [Pantheism] by Mendelssohn, surviving him—in a letter which was considered a triumphant vindication, but the composition of which, in its drain upon the writer's vital energies, not improbably cost him his life. There is, in every case, a limit to human perfection, and some share, it is said, of the unfavorable effect on Mendelssohn's health, was due to mortification on his part, arising from its being made to appear that his real acquaintance with Spinoza's works was disgracefully less than he had virtually claimed it to be.

The apparent by-path thus pursued, of allusion to Moses Mendelssohn with illustration of his character and genius, has led us, a little blindly, perhaps, but not indirectly, on our way to the comprehension of Lessing's *Nathan the Wise;* which great and fruitful dramatic work we may now, thus prepared, more advantageously consider.

The story of the play is as follows: Saladin, with head-quarters at Jerusalem, is in want of money. It is suggested to him that Nathan is a rich Jew of the city who might be squeezed with excellent results to the sultan's exchequer. Nathan has just returned laden with gain from a mercantile expedition to Babylon. During his absence from home, his house took fire, and his daughter, Recha, an only child (his, as will transpire, by adoption), was barely rescued from the flames. The rescuer was an unknown young Knight Templar, a Christian captive, doomed to death, but reprieved by Saladin on account of his resemblance to a beloved brother of the sultan's. Various scenes exhibit the nugatory efforts made to bring the mysterious Templar into communication with Nathan and his house.

Saladin and a sister of his, Sittah, play chess with each other. Their games are frequent, the sister always winning largely from her brother. Secretly she reimburses him. Now, however, Saladin is at the very bottom of his purse. Hafi, treasurer to the sultan, is directed to borrow on his behalf; and it is the sister, Sittah, who suggests the treasures of "Nathan the rich" as an available resource. Hafi, who is fast friend to Nathan (the two had long been in the habit, as, by the way, were Lessing and Mendelssohn, of playing

chess together), Hafi, we say, talks off, in the following
strain :

> *Hafi.* In case of need he'll lend you merchandise,
> But money, money, never.   He's a Jew,
> There are but few such ; he has understanding,
> Knows life, plays chess; but is in bad notorious
> Above his brethren, as he is in good.
> On him rely not.   To the poor, indeed,
> He vies, perhaps, with Saladin in giving :
> Tho' he distributes less, he gives as freely,
> As silently, as nobly, to Jew, Christian,
> Mahometan, or Parsee—'tis all one.

Hard pressed for reasons, Hafi is reduced to talk a little,
as it were against his old friend:

> *Hafi.*   Aye, there peeps out the Jew,
> The ordinary Jew.   Believe me, prince,
> He's jealous, really envious of your giving.
> To earn God's favor seems his very business.
> He lends not, that he may always have to give.
> The law commandeth mercy, not compliance :
> And thus for mercy's sake he's uncomplying.
> 'Tis true, I am not now on the best terms
> With Nathan, but, I must entreat you, think not
> That therefore I would do injustice to him.
> He's good in every thing; but not in that—
> Only in that.   I'll knock at other doors.

Nathan, in due course, contrives to get an interview with
the Templar, and wins on the loth confidence of that suspicious man.   The two, recognizing each in the other a soul
superior to prejudice of race or of creed, shake hands in
fellowship.

But Nathan is suddenly summoned to audience with the
sultan.   He has not yet gone, when he meets Hafi.   Hafi,
conscious to himself of the sultan's purpose with Nathan,
gives the latter warning, at first in parable, but at length
plainly.   " And is that all ? " Nathan composedly replies.

The Templar calling at Nathan's house while Nathan is
with the sultan, Recha gets her coveted chance to thank the
man who plucked her from the flames.   He gives her scant

immediate satisfaction in reply, but inwardly he is perturbed by her beauty and charm. The two, indeed, fall in love with each other.

The true climax of interest and power in this drama is not in any action represented, but in a certain dialogue reported—the dialogue, namely, occurring in that interview to which Nathan was summoned by Saladin. That something said, and not any thing done, should mark the culminating point of *Nathan the Wise,* sets off the play as belonging to the class of those fitted rather for the closet than for the stage. The author was more naturally a didactic than a dramatic poet, a teacher than an artist. Certainly *Nathan the Wise* inculcates a lesson instead of delineating life. With this character of the piece, Lessing's purpose in writing it corresponded. His directly and avowedly propagandist theologic writings had been interdicted; he would try, he said, whether he might do his teaching on the stage. *Nathan the Wise* was his experiment. His experiment succeeded; the success, however, the writer himself did not live to enjoy. The kernel of the teaching intended is contained in the scene now to be given, in which Nathan talks with Saladin. Highly anachronistic, and highly out of character for the persons conversing, but highly interesting, and highly *in* character for its German author, is the conversation, abridged out of W. Taylor's translation, as follows:

Sal. Since you are a man so wise, tell me which law,
     Which faith, appears to you the better?
Nath.   Sultan,
     I am a Jew.
Sal.   And I a Mussulman;
     The Christian stands between us. Of these three
     Religions only one can be the true.
     A man like you remains not just where birth
     Has chanced to cast him, or, if he remains there,
     Does it from insight, choice, from grounds of preference.
     Share then with me your insight—let me hear
     The grounds of preference, which I have wanted
     The leisure to examine—learn the choice
     These grounds have motived, that it may be mine.

In confidence I ask it. How you startle,
And weigh me with your eye! It may well be
I'm the first sultan, to whom this caprice
Methinks not quite unworthy of a sultan,
Has yet occurred. Am I not? Speak, then—speak.
Or do you, to collect yourself, desire
Some moments of delay—I give them you—
(Whether she's listening?—I must know of her
If I've done right.) Reflect—I'll soon return—
    [*Saladin steps into the room to which Sittah had retired.*]

The reader will not fail to note the sense of awkwardness
experienced by the dramatist himself, in making Saladin
enter on such a course of conversation; neither the awkwardness, nor the sense of it in the author, is successfully disguised. It seems, too, an odd device to have Sittah play the
needless part of eavesdropper to this interview.

Nathan seizes his opportunity to soliloquize in preparation
of himself—and of Lessing's readers—for the turn he will
give to his reply. His reply is in the form of a story, a story
not original with Lessing, but borrowed by him from Boccaccio, and now told, through Nathan, as follows:

Nathan. In days of yore, there dwelt in east a man,
    Who from a valued hand receiv'd a ring
    Of endless worth: the stone of it an opal,
    That shot an ever-changing tint; moreover,
    It had the hidden virtue him to render
    Of God and man belov'd, who in this view
    And this persuasion wore it. Was it strange
    The eastern man ne'er drew it off his finger,
    And studiously provided to secure it
    Forever to his house. Thus—He bequeath'd it:
    First, to the *most beloved* of his sons,
    Ordain'd that he again should leave the ring
    To the *most dear* among his children—and
    That without heeding birth, the *favorite* son,
    In virtue of the ring alone, should always
    Remain the lord of the house—you hear me, sultan?
Sal. I understand thee—on.
Nath.   From son to son,
    At length this ring descended to a father,

Who had three sons, alike obedient to him;
Whom therefore he could not but love alike.
       . . . . . . Death approach'd,
And the good father, sore embarrass'd, . . . sends
In secret to a jeweller, of whom,
Upon the model of the real ring,
He might bespeak two others, and commanded
To spare nor cost nor pains to make them like,
Quite like, the true one. This the artist manag'd.
The rings were brought, and e'en the father's eye
Could not distinguish which had been the model.
Quite overjoy'd he summons all his sons,
Takes leave of each apart, on each bestows
His blessing and his ring, and dies—Thou hear'st me?

Sal. I hear, I hear, come finish with thy tale;
Is it soon ended?

Nath.   It is ended, sultan;
For all that follows may be guessed, of course.
Scarce is the father dead; each with his ring
Appears, and claims to be the lord o' th' house.
Comes question, strife, complaint—all to no end;
For the true ring could no more be distinguish'd
Than now can—the true faith.

Sal.   How, how? Is that
To be the answer to my query?

Nath.   No,
But it may serve as my apology,
If I can't venture to decide between,
Rings, which the father got expressly made,
That they might not be known from one another.

Sal. The rings—don't trifle with me; I must think
That the religions which I nam'd can be
Distinguish'd, e'en to raiment, drink, and food.

Nath. And only not as to their grounds of proof.
Are not all built alike on history,
Traditional, or written? History
Must be received on trust—is it not so?
In whom now are we likeliest to put trust?
In our own people surely, in those men
Whose blood we are, in them who from our childhood
Have given us proofs of love, who ne'er deceiv'd us,
Unless 't were wholesomer to be deceiv'd.
How can I less believe in my forefathers
Than thou in thine? How can I ask of thee
To own that thy forefathers falsified

In order to yield mine the praise of truth?
The like of Christians.

Sal.   By the living God,
The man is in the right, I must be silent.

Nath. Now let us to our rings return once more.
As said, the sons complain'd. Each to the judge
Swore from his father's hand immediately
To have receiv'd the ring, as was the case;
After he had long obtain'd the father's promise,
One day to have the ring, as also was.
The father, each asserted, could to him
Not have been false, rather than so suspect
Of such a father, willing as he might be
With charity to judge his brethren, he
Of treacherous forgery was bold to accuse them.

Sal. Well, and the judge; I'm eager now to hear
What thou wilt make him say. Go on, go on.

Nath. The judge said, If ye summon not the father
Before my seat, I cannot give a sentence.
Am I to guess enigmas? Or expect ye
That the true ring should here unseal its lips?
But hold—you tell me that the real ring
Enjoys the hidden power to make the wearer
Of God and man belov'd; let that decide.
Which of you do two brothers love the best?
You're silent. Do these love-exciting rings
Act inward only, not without? Does each
Love but himself? Ye're all deceiv'd deceivers,
None of your rings is true. The real ring
Perhaps is gone. To hide or to supply
Its loss, your father order'd three for one.

Sal. O charming, charming!

Nath.   And (the judge continued)
If you will take advice in lieu of sentence,
This is my counsel to you, to take up
The matter where it stands. If each of you
Has had a ring presented by his father,
Let each believe his own the real ring.
'Tis possible the father chose no longer
To tolerate the one ring's tyranny;
And certainly, as he much lov'd you all,
And lov'd you all alike, it could not please him
By favoring one to be of two th' oppressor.
Let each feel honor'd by this free affection

Unwarp'd of prejudice; let each endeavor
To vie with both his brothers in displaying
The virtue of his ring; assist its might
With gentleness, benevolence, forbearance,
With inward resignation to the godhead,
And if the virtues of the ring continue
To show themselves among your children's children,
After a thousand thousand years, appear
Before this judgment-seat—a greater one
Than I shall sit upon it, and decide.
So spake the modest judge.

Sal.   God!

Nath.   Saladin,
Feel'st thou thyself this wiser promis'd man?

Sal. I dust, I nothing, God!

[*Precipitates himself upon Nathan and takes hold of his hand,
which he does not quit the remainder of the scene.*]

Nath.   What moves thee, sultan?

Sal. Nathan, my dearest Nathan, 't is not yet
The judge's thousand thousand years are past,
His judgment-seat's not mine. Go, go, but love me.

We do not know whether the upshot of this interview will
strike our readers as over-effusive. In general, the *Nathan
the Wise* is remarkable rather for restraint, than for indulgence, of expression. Schiller, even in his most mature and
most chastened period of culture, that enjoyed by him under
the influence of Goethe, was far more intense and extravagant than ever Lessing permitted himself to be. The difference in this respect between the two poets is, we think,
as much the difference of the genuine from the false, as it is
the difference of true passion from frigidity.

It may not be the fault of Lessing in his manner of telling
the story—the fault may inseparably inhere in the nature of
the story itself—but Nathan's parable seems to us not so in-
stantaneously and so strikingly clear as it ought to be, for
the best effectiveness of such an illustration. Does its lack of
clearness lie perhaps in its argumentative fallacy? Or does
the converse, rather, hold, and does the fallacy lurk and hide
in the lack of clearness? The story of the rings, with its
application, is, so Scherer points out, as old as the eleventh

century in Spain. The merit of the invention is accordingly no more Boccaccio's than it is Lessing's.

This play of Lessing's is not a tragedy, for the conclusion is not unhappy. On the other hand, altogether happy it cannot be called, either in the sense of joy to the personages concerned, or of felicitous contrivance on the part of the author. It turns out that the Templar and Recha are brother and sister, the Templar being, in fact, son to that brother of the sultan whom he so much resembled. No marriage, therefore, can take place between the lovers; and it tasks, if it does not overtask, the art of the dramatist to let us down from the height of expectation to which he has raised us, without at the same time exciting some sense, on our part, of ludicrous fall in the direction of pathos. Such a conclusion is the weak point of the play, considered as a piece for the stage. But notwithstanding that there are in it some passages of dialogue effectively conducted, the *Nathan the Wise* is substantially little else than a vehicle of the author's views as a religious indifferentist. Schiller, however, exercised his practical skill to adapt this greatest boast of the earlier German drama to actual representation, and it is yet occasionally exhibited. Then, as Mr. Lowell, in his brilliant essay on Lessing, wittily says, the German public "find in seeing it represented a grave satisfaction like that of subscribing to a monument."

A remarkable sequel to the *Nathan the Wise*, purporting to be Lessing's, appeared soon after that author's death. It bore the title, *The Monk of Libanon*. It seemed in effect a relinquishment, a tacit recantation, of the doctrine of the earlier poem. As long as it was supposed to be a genuine posthumous production of the author of *Nathan the Wise*, it excited a vivid public interest and, among orthodox Christian critics, commanded high admiration. With singular fair-mindedness, W. Taylor, the free-thinking English translator of *Nathan the Wise*, translated also this forged afterpiece, and translated it with spirit. It is a drama of full length, with glimpses in it of real power.

We submit, in specimen, the following extract, which forms the conclusion to the first act of *The Monk of Libanon.* Saladin lies dying. His conscience disturbing him, he has sent for Nathan. Nathan is unable to medicine his malady. The unhappy sultan passes into delirium. We begin at the point of this transition in Saladin's mental state:

Sal. . . . Then die, die, Saladin! thy lot
Be heaven or hell, or everlasting nothing;
Die, die, for here 'tis darkness all. Thy road
Is yonder, over graves—o'er slaughter-fields,
Thick-sown with skulls of men—well moistened, too,
With human gore. Who was the sower here?
Who with his sabre ploughed the reeking soil?
Who?

Nath. Saladin, what ails thee, Saladin?

Sal. I, I, 'twas I, the valorous Saladin,
'Twas I who mowed these heaps of dead—

Nath. My Sultan,
Do recollect thyself.

Sal. Ha! now I stand
In blood up to my girdle. 'Twas well fought,
My warriors nobly slaughtered—Bury them,
For fear their God should see them, and revenge
On us their blood.

Nath. Dost thou know me no longer?
God, God, have pity on him!

Sal. What of pity?
Behold in me the mighty Saladin,
The conqueror of the world. The East is his.
Down with your arms, or die!

Nath. Canst thou not know
Thy Nathan any longer?

Sal. Get thee gone.
I will not deal with thee, Jew, usurer, cheat;
Hence with thy ware, 'tis trash! sell, sell to fools—
Avaunt! Why dost thou weep? What wouldst thou have?

Nath. Oh! this is horrible.

Sal. Ay, horrible.
I did not kill them. Dost thou claim of me
Thy children?

Nath. God!

Sal. Do bury them still deeper;

Nath. Look, there peeps out a skull; in with it!
O

What a delirium this!

Sal. Up! up! we storm it—
Forward, my brothers, brisk, and down with them—
The dogs are yielding! On, on, we shall have it:
Mine is Jerusalem! Damascus mine!
Mine is all Syria!

Nath. Teach me, Lord, to think
That I must die.

Sal. What's all yon howling for?
Give quarter now; and offer up to God
A tenth of all the booty. There a mosk,
And here a school, and there an hospital
Shall be erected. We shall need them—

[*Sittah comes in.*]

Nath. Sittah!
O my dear Sittah!

Sal. Will she not? She shall.
Will Richard not? He must—

Sit. What means this, Nathan?

Nath. Alas, thou hear'st thy brother is delirious.

Sit. My Saladin delirious? God!

Sal. Keep back—
Along this narrow footpath climbs the way
Into the fortress. They are all asleep.
Hush! follow me in stillness, we shall manage
To take it by surprise—hush!

Sit. [*also gently*]. Saladin
Is for to-day too weary for new toil.
What if he should repose a little hour
Under the shade, and then with fresher strength
Assail the fortress?

Sal. Ay, I will, I will;
Keep watch upon your posts, my comrades all,
Lest they should fall upon us.

Sit. We are going.

Sal. Mind, in an hour or so I shall be walking.

The foregoing almost suggests the famous prison scene
between the seducer and his victim in Goethe's "Faust."
The author of *The Monk of Libanon* was an estimable minister, by the name of Pfranger, court-preacher in Meiningen.
Exactly what measure of responsibility was his for the moral
offense involved in a literary forgery, we have not found the

6

means of making up an opinion. Readers of ours who may happen to have access to Taylor's *Historic Survey of German Poetry* will do well to read the whole spurious play, in sequel and contrast to the *Nathan the Wise*. They will find it refreshingly positive in conviction, and vigorously, as well as loyally, Christian.

Besides Lessing's *Nathan the Wise*, two other plays of Lessing, the *Emilia Galotti*, a tragedy, and the *Minna von Barnhelm*, a comedy, still form a part of the regular stock of the German theatres. This is not true, we believe, of any dramatic production whatever of Klopstock's. Lessing's wish for himself, expressed in his celebrated epigram on Klopstock, and his bold thrust at that poet, find thus, in a manner, their fulfillment:

> A Klopstock who not warm in lauding?
>   In reading, every body? Nay.
> We, for a little less applauding,
>   And reading somewhat busier, pray.

And there had been a day when the epigrammatist himself undertook a translation into the Latin of Klopstock's *Messiah!* The foregoing epigram may be taken as a fair specimen of Lessing's skill in this kind of writing.

We found it natural and convenient to associate his friend Moses Mendelssohn with Lessing considered as dramatist. With Lessing now to be considered as critic, it will be not less opportune to associate Nicolai, a man of letters, who was friend at once of Lessing and of Mendelssohn. Except in some such incidental manner as this, we should, for want of room, be unable to notice Nicolai at all ; and he is still prominent in the literary history, if no longer in the literature, of Germany. How prominent once in German literature he was, may be guessed from the fact that Queen Catherine of Russia, in royal token of appreciation for one of his books, forwarded a gold medal to the author, and, compliment perhaps more significant still, an autograph letter bidding him send her every volume he should write. During a considerable interval, he was heard and heeded as literary dictator in Germany. His misfortune was that he kept on swaying his sceptre, after his sceptre had become a mark for laughter instead of for awe.

Christoph Friedrich Nicolai edited, from 1765 to about the close of the century, a periodical of literature and criticism, called the *Universal German Library.* When it is considered how important has been the part played by periodical literary organs in the literary history of Germany, when it is considered further that such authors as Lessing, as Wieland, as Schiller, each in his turn, tried his hand at editing a literary periodical of his own, and when, finally, it is considered that the *Universal German Library* was, on the whole, greater, more influential, than any other German publication of its kind, some just idea may be formed of the merit of Nicolai for his achievements in this line of editorship. Nicolai's collaboration with Lessing was chiefly in a periodical conducted by the latter, to which, in the event, Nicolai's serial succeeded.

This periodical of Nicolai's, the *Universal German Library*, was to Germany something like what, a few years earlier, the *Encyclopædia* was to France. It was the German organ of "enlightenment." It became the favorite vehicle for the ideas of the "philosophers," so-called, of Germany. It pleaded the cause of intellectual, of spiritual, freedom. It flouted authority in religion; it laughed at narrowness, at sensationalism, in literature. It had the merit, and it had the demerit, of refusing to see things in any other light than the light of "common sense." It accordingly saw clearly enough, but it looked between blinders, and it did not see far ahead. The *Universal German Library*, however, as compared with the French *Encyclopædia*, its forerunner, was more moderate, less hostile at heart to the interests of true religion. It was also less formidable than the *Encyclopædia*—in proportion as Nicolai, editor of the one, was a less redoubtable man than Diderot, editor of the other.

We need not give a list of Nicolai's books, which were

in number considerable; for, though not wanting in wit, they are no longer read. To this remark, his *Anecdotes of Frederick the Great* is perhaps an exception. That book of his which so pleased her celebrated majesty of Russia, was entitled, *The Life and Opinions of Master Sebaldus Nothanker.* This is still readable, though not read. It is a satire aimed against ecclesiasticism.

Nicolai, as has been said, outlived his own fame and influence. He failed to recognize what was meant by the advent on the field of German letters of such men as Herder, Goethe, Schiller, and he frittered away his own literary credit in peevish efforts to disparage theirs. The result has been to leave Nicolai fixed in the stocks for posterity to gaze at as a warning example of purblind literary bigotry. He deserved better of himself, and he perhaps still deserves better of his fellow-men.

Lessing's *Laocoön* had, as it were, a merely casual origin. It never was finished, and what was written was written very informally. But life was in it—such life that it could not die.

Winckelmann had just published his memorable work on *Ancient Art.* An incidental remark of his on the marble group of the *Laocoön,* in comparison with the famous description by Virgil, excited doubt and then dissent in the ever-vigilant and ever-active mind of Lessing. His *Laocoön,* so entitled in allusion to this its origin, was the remarkable result. We take our first extract from the opening division or chapter:

The universal and principal characteristic of the Greek masterpieces in painting and in sculpture, according to Herr Winckelmann, is a noble simplicity and a quiet grandeur, as well in the attitude as in the expression. "As the depth of the sea," he says, "remains forever quiet, however the surface may rage, so the expression, in the figures of the Greeks, discovers, in the midst of passion, a great and calm soul.

"This soul plants itself in the face of the [sculptured] Laocoön and not in the face alone, under the most vehement suffering. . . . He raises no such fearful cry as Virgil sings of his Laocoön. Laocoön [in the sculpture] suffers, but he suffers like the Philoctetes of Sophocles."

It is scarcely to be wondered at that Winckelmann's reference to Virgil, but especially his reference to Philoctetes,
should have provoked challenge from Lessing. Lessing says:

> I confess, the depreciating side-glance which he [Winckelmann] throws
> at Virgil, first caused me to doubt; and then the comparison with
> Philoctetes.
> "Laocoön suffers like the Philoctetes of Sophocles." How does this
> character suffer? It is singular that his suffering should have left such a
> different impression upon our minds. The complaints, the screams, the
> wild execrations with which his pain filled the camp, interrupting the
> sacrifices and all solemn acts, sounded not less terribly through the
> desert island. They were the cause of his being banished thither. What
> tones of impatience, of misery, of despair ! The poet made the theatre
> resound with his imitation of them.

Lessing agrees with Winckelmann that the sculptor's
Laocoön does not exhibit the violent demonstration of pain
which might have been expected. He agrees further with
Winckelmann that the artist's moderation was wise. As
to why it was wise, he differs with Winckelmann. Vehement
expression under bodily pain, he contends, is perfectly natural even for heroes. He goes to Homer for proof :

> Homer's wounded warriors fall, not seldom, with a cry to the ground.
> . . . Notwithstanding that Homer elevates his heroes so far above human
> nature in some things, they always remain true to it when it comes to
> the feeling of pain or affront, and to the expression of that feeling by
> cries or tears, or by railing. In their deeds they are beings of a higher
> order ; but in their sensations they are veritable men.

If, by this time, some of our readers are thinking that the
standard of heroic fortitude under suffering must be different for Germans (as well as for Greeks) from that which
generally holds for Englishmen and Americans, we cannot
say that they are wrong. Robert Hall, after a paroxysm of
exquisite anguish from spinal disease, says, " O, I suffered
terribly, but I did not complain while I was suffering, did I ?
Did I complain ? " Goethe, in sickness, cried out so with
violent pain that the guard at the gate of the city heard
him. And Goethe is praised for remarkable self-control.
The Greek tragedists also, Lessing makes his witnesses,

taking occasion to have, by the way, his slant at the French
teachers of false, artificial decorum in literature:

> It is worthy of note, that among the few tragedies that have come down
> to us from antiquity, there are two in which bodily pain constitutes not
> the least part of the misery with which the hero suffers; the *Philoctetes*
> and the *Dying Hercules*. The latter, also, like the former, is represented
> by Sophocles as wailing, moaning, weeping, and crying. Thanks to our
> decent neighbors [the French], those masters of propriety, a howling
> Philoctetes, a crying Hercules, would now be most ridiculous and intoler-
> able characters on the stage.

Lessing's induction done, he comes to his inference. He
says :

> And now I come to my inference. If it is true that cries, under the
> infliction of bodily pain—more especially according to the old Greek view
> of the subject—are perfectly consistent with greatness of soul; then the
> desire of representing such a soul cannot be the reason why the artist
> was nevertheless unwilling to imitate those cries in his marble. On the
> contrary, there must be some other reason why, in this particular, he de-
> parts from his rival, the poet, who expresses these cries with the most
> deliberate intention.

So much for Lessing's first chapter, condensed.

In his second chapter, Lessing proceeds to a quest of that
true reason for the sculptor's abstaining from violent expression in marble, which he thinks Winckelmann had missed.
Contrasting ancient with modern art, he says :

> " Who would wish to paint thee, since no one likes to look upon thee ? "
> said the ancient epigrammatist, of a very deformed person. Many a
> modern artist would say : " Be thou as deformed as it is possible to be, I
> will paint thee notwithstanding. Though no one loves to look upon thee,
> yet shall men look with pleasure on my painting, not because it represents
> thee, but as a proof of my art which knows how to copy such a scare-
> crow so accurately."

From certain discursive illustrations of his point he returns to say, with the most admirably suggestive criticism :

> But I wander out of my way. I only wished to establish this point,
> that, with the ancients, beauty was the highest law of the plastic arts.
> And, this point established, it follows necessarily that every thing
> else, to which the plastic arts might likewise extend, must yield alto-

gether where it was found incompatible with beauty; and where it was compatible with beauty must, at least, be subordinated to that.

Now, applying this to the Laocoön, we see clearly the reason which I am seeking. The master labored for the highest beauty possible under the given conditions of bodily pain. Bodily pain, in all its deforming vehemence, was incompatible with that beauty. It was necessary, therefore, that he should reduce it—that he should soften cries into sighs. Not because crying betrays an ignoble soul, but because it disfigures the countenance in a manner which is disgusting. Do but tear open the mouth of Laocoön, in imagination, and judge! Let him scream, and see! Before, it was a creation which inspired compassion, because it united pain with beauty. Now, it has become an unsightly, an abominable creation, from which we are fain to turn away our faces, because the sight of pain awakens displeasure, and that displeasure is not converted into the sweet sentiment of pity by the beauty of the suffering object.

With two additional extracts from this luminous and illuminating essay of Lessing's, we bring our citations to a close. The first of the two is found in the third chapter. No thoughtful reader will fail to see that in these pregnant paragraphs there speaks a consummate master of criticism—of criticism in the highest and most generous sense of that word:

Since the artist can use but one moment of ever-changing nature, and the painter, more especially, can use that moment only from a single point of view; and since their works are made, not to be seen merely, but to be contemplated, and to be contemplated repeatedly and long, it is evident that, in the selection of that single moment and that single point of view, too much care cannot be had to choose the most fruitful. But only that is fruitful which gives the imagination full play. The more we see, the more we must be able to imagine, and the more we imagine, the more we must think we see. Now, in the whole course of a passion, there is no one moment which possesses this advantage in so slight a degree as the climax of that passion. There is nothing beyond it; and to exhibit to the eye the uttermost, is to bind the wings of imagination, and to compel her, since she is unable to exceed the sensible impression, *to occupy herself with feebler images, below that impression—shunning, as limitation, the visible fullness expressed.*

In the words which we have italicized, Lessing, usually the embodiment of good sense and self-possession, seems to us to run, for a moment, into something very like mere emptiness and quiddity. Is not the harm done by climax in artistic expression rather this, that it dulls the imagination by leaving it nothing to add, than that it forces the imagination to employ itself with conceptions inferior to the climax already expressed?

We resume our interrupted extract:

> Further, since this single moment receives from art an unchangeable duration, it should express nothing that can be conceived only as transient. . . . La Metrie, who caused himself to be painted and engraved as a second Democritus, laughs but the first time he is seen. If we look at him often, the philosopher becomes a buffoon, and the laugh changes to a grin. So of cries. The violent pain which extorts the cry is either soon relieved, or else it destroys the sufferer. Although, therefore, a man of the greatest patience and fortitude may cry, he does not cry unceasingly. And it is only this appearance of perpetuity in the material imitations of art, that makes his crying seem like feminine impotence or like childish petulance. This at least, the author of the Laocoön was bound to avoid, even though the act of crying were not incompatible with beauty, or though his art would allow him to express suffering without beauty.

In the second extract, our last, taken from his fourth chapter, Lessing reaches his justification of that descriptive passage in Virgil, which Winckelmann had impliedly condemned. He does so by defining the proper province of the poet, that artist in words, as distinguished from the provinces of the painter and the sculptor, those artists in color and form. He says:

> The poet is not required to concentrate his sketch into a single moment. He can, if he pleases, take each action at its origin and carry it through to its termination. Each of those variations, which would cost the painter a separate picture, costs him but a single stroke. And though this one stroke, in itself considered, might offend the imagination of the hearer, it is so well prepared by what preceded, or so qualified and compensated by what follows, that it loses its individuality, and, taken in connection with the rest, produces the most charming effect.

> Who, then, will reproach him [Virgil]? Who will not rather confess that, if the artist did well not to represent Laocoön as crying, the great poet did equally well to let him cry?

We wish we had room for some specimen passages from Lessing's essay on *The Education of the Human Race.* This little treatise is probably to be regarded as the starting-point, indeed as the fountain-head, of German free-thinking in theology. Lessing was essentially a free-thinker, not only in the good, but also in the technical bad, sense of the expression.

There is no sentence of Lessing's more characteristic of the man, as none more universally familiar in quotation, than his really proud, though formally humble, declaration contained in the following words:

> If God should hold all truth inclosed in his right hand, and in his left only the ever-active impulse to the pursuit of truth, although with the condition that I should always and forever err, and should say to me, "Choose!" I should fall with submission upon his left hand, and say, "Father, give! Pure truth is for thee alone!"

Famous words, and words worthy of their fame! But surely they bespeak, not so much the man who loves truth supremely, as the man who supremely loves intellectual activity.

V.

WIELAND.

1733–1813.

OF all the most celebrated writers of Germany, the writer least celebrated among English-speakers is undoubtedly Wieland. Equally undoubted is another curious, a seemingly incongruous, fact. Wieland is the author of a poem, of which, despite a certain grave inextricable fault involved, it may be affirmed that it is, by eminence, of all the poetic productions of German genius—considerable in length and not dramatic—the one poem best fitted to interest and to please the English-reading public. The singularity of the case is increased by the circumstance, that of this exceptional poem of Wieland's there exists, and there has long existed in English, a version scarcely less charming than the charming original. To carry the paradox to its height, there was formerly a time when Wieland's *Oberon*—for such is the title of the poem to which we refer—was, through Sotheby's translation, almost as popular in England and America as it was in Germany.

The explanation is simple enough. Wieland belongs in a class of writers whom the world, in its progress, has left somewhat behind. He is a little antiquated now—like Klopstock, and unlike Lessing. The distinctively modern, the new, the progressive, spirit in literature, was not Wieland's. The order of things that came in with Goethe and Schiller was one in which Wieland at length appeared out of place. He had the effect of an anachronism in it. Not so with Lessing, by a few years the senior of Wieland; and not so with Herder, by a few years Wieland's junior. The difference is, that it was *through* Lessing and *through* Herder that the new era opened, while it was *with* Wieland that the old era closed.

But the old era closed splendidly with Wieland. He was a brilliant man of letters; upon the whole, the most brilliant mere man of letters that Germany has ever produced. His term of activity was long, and it was fruitful to the end. He became the patriarch of German letters—by universal acclamation recognized as such, alike for the transcendency and the seniority of his fame and for the personal charm of the man. He was, in some respects, for Germany what Voltaire was for France.

Wieland, in fact, approximated the French type by some traits of his literary character. Like the French, he studied, and he achieved, lightness, liveliness, clearness, grace, beyond any other German of his time. No German, unless it be Heine, has in this respect surpassed him since. He wrote for readers, and not for himself. He wrote for readers among people in general, and not for readers among scholars or specialists merely.

We thus describe a popular writer, and a popular writer Wieland was. But he was popular rather by the manner than by the matter of what he wrote. He was a superficial man, with no deep convictions of any sort to trouble him—

or for him to trouble the world withal. He wrote what he thought would please, and he generally succeeded. With this success he was satisfied. Setting out as a pietist of the Klopstockian pattern, he ended by being an epicurean after the model of Voltaire. He was probably as earnest at first as he was at last, and at last as he was at first.

Wieland's literary genius blossomed early. The youthful piety which seemed to consecrate it commended Wieland, as the same thing had commended Klopstock, to the notice and patronage of Bodmer. Wieland, in personal habits and general style of deportment, accommodated himself better than did Klopstock to the views and feelings of Bodmer, whose favored guest he in his turn, like Klopstock, became. Wieland drank water instead of wine, and he did not smoke. But the illusion, which probably was as much Wieland's own as it was Bodmer's, did not last long. Young Wieland, from denouncing Anacreon and Anacreontists, became himself such in practice of life that he could write Anacreontic odes from experience of his own. The "Seraphic" school—so called by the German critic Gervinus —of Klopstock, made, and no wonder, a public *auto da fé* in Göttingen of the books of their renegade fellow-disciple, Wieland.

Wieland was a literary courtier, and a good one, some time before Goethe, eclipsing his precursor, became the world's proverb and paragon of such. Wieland began making little Weimar what it became as centre and focus of literary light; though the chief glory belongs, and justly belongs, to Goethe. At Weimar, Wieland long continued to live and labor, still enjoying a sufficient, but by no means splendid, pension from the duke, after the latter's arrival at his majority had brought the relation of teacher and pupil to an end. About Wieland gathered, one after another, the stars in that resplendent constellation of literary genius and fame which has made Weimar "a name forever" and a "Mecca of the mind" to all lovers of letters.

Wieland, Goethe, Herder, Schiller, and we may add Richter —though Richter never was properly a resident of Weimar —shine, perhaps, the brightest, as they shine with nearly equal lustre; but there were brilliant inferior names besides, that we need not here stay to reckon.

The attitude assumed by Wieland toward the "new gods" who were taking Olympus by storm, under his very feet, was strikingly different from that which we have already described as the attitude of Wieland's contemporary, Nicolai. Like Nicolai, Wieland, too, to be sure, at first confronted his junior rivals with challenge; but soon he smilingly gave them his hand and helped them gain their seat on the summit.

The way in which the old order first met the new was, naturally, by encounter of Wieland with Goethe. Wieland edited a periodical, the *German Mercury.* In this he criticized Goethe. Goethe responded by a satirical farce, entitled, *Gods, Heroes, and Wieland.* Wieland good-naturedly reviewed the farce in his magazine, and praising it, over-praising it, pronounced it a piece of wit that every body should read. Goethe was fairly beaten. He acknowledged this himself. He said, "Wieland is gaining as much in the public estimation by the line he takes as I am losing." The two became, outwardly at least, good friends.

The amount and the variety of the literary work that Wieland did was prodigious. We pass his other productions, all of them, without even giving their titles, to take up at once his masterpiece, the *Oberon.*

We feel obliged to say, and to say strongly, in preface to our exhibition of this poem, that the *Oberon* is not free from the blemish of things doubtful in ethical and in æsthetic propriety. The spirit of the verse is not positively evil. There is in the story no intentional, and hardly is there practical, seduction to sin. Wieland was not, like Voltaire, a bad-hearted man. He was not, like Goethe, a good-hearted man whose good-heartedness did not stand in the way of his indulging himself freely to the ruinous cost of others. Wieland apparently became, in mature life, a man of unimpeachable correctness in personal behavior. His writings were still loose, but his looseness now was all in his writings.

The things to which we allude in the *Oberon*, and which we must pass with allusion, are touched as delicately in phrase as the nature of the case permitted. They are so nearly innocent that at least the sin is rather against taste than against morals. And they are not mere wanton recreations in the equivocal, on the part of the author. They belong inseparably to the plan of his poem, a plan dictated to the poet by his subject.

The story in *Oberon* is the story of a knight, Sir Hüon of Bordeaux, who unwittingly slays a son of Charlemagne, and is, by the implacable father, sentenced to do a series of impossible deeds in ransom of his life. These impossible deeds he happily accomplishes, with the very important assistance of Oberon and Titania, king and queen of the fairies, who have themselves a momentous interest of their own staked upon the success and virtue of the knight. For the elfin royal couple have, to their great misery, become hopelessly estranged from each other—Oberon having hastily bound himself by a mighty oath to stay away from his spouse until one human pair should be, by proof of uttermost temptation, found impregnably pure in chastity and in mutual truth. It goes without the saying that Sir Hüon, and the bride that he will win, become the blameless twain to bring Oberon and Titania happily together once more. But this does not result without much remarkable adventure and mischance befalling meantime both the knight and the fair. Of such varied experience on their part, is made up the substance of the story told in *Oberon*.

Oberon opens with Sir Hüon already far on his way to achieve the feats required by vengeful Charlemagne. The first chance encounter that he meets is a happy one. It occurs in the region of Libanon in Asia. He there falls in with

an old retainer of his father's house, who is overjoyed to recognize in the handsome stranger his own youthful lord. "Sherasmin" is the shrewd and honest fellow's name. Sherasmin,
loyal soul, offers himself as squire to Sir Hüon for complet-
ing the forlorn and distant errantry of the gallant knight.
No Don Quixote is Sir Hüon in the representation of Wieland, but Sherasmin is a kind of Sancho Panza. The homely
humor of the squire affords a welcome and a needed relief to
the tension threatened at first in the heroic character and
exploit of the knight.

True epic fashion, Wieland makes Sir Hüon relate retro-
spectively to Sherasmin the incidents that led to his setting
out on his present quest. The final fierce sentence of Charlemagne is recited as follows. Said Charlemagne (we now
give the text of Wieland in metrical translation):

" Go hence to Bagdad; in high festal day,
At his round table when the caliph, placed
In stately pomp with splendid emirs graced,
Enjoys the banquet, ranged in proud array,
Slay him who lies the monarch's left beside.
Dash from his headless trunk the purple tide;
Then to the right draw near, with courtly grace
The beauteous heiress of his throne embrace,
And thrice with public kiss salute her as thy bride.

" And while the caliph, at the monstrous scene,
Such as before ne'er shocked a caliph's eyes,
Stares at thy confidence in mute surprise,
Then, as the Easterns wont, with lowly mien
Fall on the earth before his golden throne,
And gain (a trifle, proof of love alone)
That it may please him, gift of friend to friend,
Four of his grinders at my bidding send,
And of his beard a lock with silver hair o'ergrown."

So much for the occasion and the motive of Hüon's
expedition.

After the first night of bivouac together, Sir Hüon, who
has been " on this occasion " guest of Sherasmin, fares forth
with his squire in a light-hearted temper of welcome for

fate, which Wieland, through Sotheby, thus buoyantly describes :

> The day awakes ; and straight from sound repose,
> Fresh as the morn, our warrior gaily rose:
> Buckles his armor on ; while seen to stand
> With knapsack on his shoulder, club in hand,
> Cheerily smiles his host, and forth toward Bagdad goes.

Therewith ends book, or canto, first. There are twelve cantos in all.

The fresh, bright, breezy verse of Wieland is well represented by his English translator, William Sotheby. Our readers lose surprisingly little by becoming acquainted with *Oberon* in this secondary, instead of the original, form. We consider Sotheby's rendering of Wieland's *Oberon* one of the most successful feats of translation in verse that the English language contains. The transfusion of spirit from Wieland to Sotheby is wonderful. The chief abatement of praise to be made is, that Wieland's free, idiomatic, often homely, expression, and the caprice of his verse, get transposed by Sotheby into a key of somewhat greater form and stateliness.

The stanza in which Wieland composed his *Oberon* is a free variation of that of Ariosto in the *Orlando Furioso*. The German original has eight lines only, where the English translation has nine. Wieland rhymes irregularly, and he makes his lines irregular in length, as the fit takes him. Sotheby, it will be observed, submits to rule, and has one mold for all his stanzas.

The tone of the *Oberon* is most felicitously chosen, and it is maintained throughout with excellent art. It is, of course, not the high epic. Homeric, Wieland is here, rather than Miltonic; but he is Homeric in fluent ease and flexile grace rather than in loftiness of occasional flight. Still, Wieland can rise when he chooses ; only he never chooses to wing an ether quite so high and thin as that which Homer, when sublimest, reaches. What a pretty, downward swoop, skimming the ground, of Wieland's swallow-muse, is in the last line of the following stanza, the opening one of canto second :

> Thus go the noble pair—and blithe and gay
> Journey by sunshine and the starry light,
> Three days down Libanon's romantic height.
> And when the fervor of meridian day
> Strikes on their heads, they seek some shadowy lair
> Where groves of ancient cedars cool the air;
> While sweet around from silver throats are heard
> Melodious songs from many a beauteous bird,
> That pecks with wanton bill the travelers' scattered fare.

Various "moving accidents" which befall the errant knight, we may pass in silence. The momentous encounter is imminent now of Sir Hüon with Oberon.

The apparition of the fairy king, drawn in a silver car by leopards, is too much for the nerves of Sherasmin. Sir Hüon gazes delighted, but Sherasmin shudders with horror. The well-nigh burlesque consequence (Sherasmin shrieking in terror to his master, and therewith seizing the knight's horse by the bridle to pull him after in headlong flight), is thus described by Wieland :

> "O, fly, sir! or your life's not worth a song!"
> Sir Hüon strives, indeed, but strives in vain;
> The old man speeds in fullest flight amain,
> And after him drags Hüon's horse along;
> O'er stock and stone, through bush and brake they race,
> Nor hedge nor ditch impedes their desperate pace;
> Nor ceased the wight to scamper, fear-pursued,
> Till, clear from out the compass of the wood,
> They find themselves at last amid an open space.

Oberon is not so to be thwarted. He raises a tempest, which drives the knight, ignobly dragged by his flying squire, to seek shelter in a convent met in their course. Nuns and monks from neighboring closes, out that day together on a short pious pilgrimage, are, at the same moment, driven to the same refuge. Sherasmin, without ceremony of leave-asking, rushes incontinently in, and while the knight tarries without, in better form to beg admittance, up comes Oberon, in appearance like a boy, and works a change which, with its surprising sequel, is thus described by Wieland. A certain magic pipe or horn, on which much depends in the development of the plot, is brought into use:

> At once the storm is fled, serenely mild
> Heav'n smiles around, bright rays the sky adorn,
> While beauteous as an angel newly born
> Beams in the roseate dayspring, glow'd the child.
> A lily stalk his graceful limbs sustain'd,
> Round his smooth neck an ivory horn was chain'd.
> Yet lovely as he look'd, on all around
> Strange horror stole, for stern the fairy frown'd,
> And o'er each sadden'd charm a sullen anger reign'd.
>
> He to his rosy lip the horn applies,
> And breathes enchanting tones of fairy sound:
> At once old Sherasmin in giddy round
> Reels without stop—away the spinner flies,
> Seizes a hoary nun without a tooth,
> Who dies to dance, as if the blood of youth
> Boil'd in her veins; the old man deftly springs,
> Bounds like a buck, while every caper flings
> Her veil and gown in air, that all laugh loud forsooth.
>
> Cloister and convent burn with equal rage,
> Nor hoary hairs, nor rank the dance withstand;
> Each sinner takes a sister by the hand,
> And in the gay contention all engage.
>
> .   .   .   .   .   .

Meantime Oberon talks graciously with the knight. Sherasmin, too, he first relieves from the necessity of dancing, and then comforts with a most reviving draught from an empty-looking bowl, from which, lifted to his lips, flowed delicious wine. Finally, the fairy monarch presents both bowl and horn to Hüon, with explanation and with solemn adjuration, as follows :

> "Does but its snail-like spiral hollow sing
> A lovely note soft swell'd with gentle breath,
> Though thousand warriors threaten instant death,
> And with advancing weapons round enring;
> Then, as thou late hast seen, in restless dance
> All, all must spin, and every sword and lance

7

Fall with the exhausted warriors to the ground.
But if thou peal it with impatient sound,
I at thy call appear, more swift than lightning glance.

"If, at that time, my path from thine recede
Far as the world, if boundless space between,
I at thy side am in a moment seen;
Yet, oh! reserve thy call for utmost need;
And take this bowl, whose golden round contains
Pure wine, self-springing from a thousand veins,
If touch'd by guileless mouth; but if base lip
Dare with rash taste the conscious nectar sip,
'Tis void, and burns the wretch with guilt-avenging pains!"

The knight with grateful hand each wonder takes,
Pledge of the favor of his fairy friend;
And when he sees the rays of morn ascend,
And paint the purple clouds with golden flakes,
He asks the way to Bagdad's destin'd wall—
"Hence!" cries the dwarf, "where fame and honor call:
And, oh! may never Oberon behold
That dreadful hour, when Hüon, good and bold,
May yield to deeds of shame, that need his soul appal!

"Not that thy heart and spirit I mistrust;
But, ah! thou art a child of Adam's kind,
Form'd of soft clay, and to the future blind!
Woes without end oft spring from transient lust:
My warning words thy happiness intend;
Forget not, youth, the counsel of a friend."
Then with his lily wand he touch'd the knight,
And Hüon views, O unexpected sight!
Roll'd from his azure eyes two liquid pearls descend.

The raillery of Wieland, playful, and not acrid like the
mockery of Voltaire, throws out, it will have been noted, a
lambent tongue of bright unburning flame that fastens, this
time, on the brethren and sisters of those religious houses.
These all dance, perforce, while, always, the knight, "because
his heart is pure," is able to stay his feet against the enchantment of that fairy horn. Readers must be mindful
throughout the story that every thing good for Hüon hinges
on his maintaining his firmness against the temptation, of
which Oberon, with tears, warns him in his farewell words,

The magic equipment of the knight, wonderful as it already is, is not yet complete. One other delightfully potent weapon of might, Sir Hüon will win for himself with his own knightly emprise. There is, of course, a lady sore beset, in the case. The impossible sort of thing that our young knight, in sheer valor, would cheerfully undertake, and, what is more, accomplish felicitously, without receiving so much as a scratch on his person or a dint on his mail, is well illustrated here. The distressed lady is shut up in a castle— how guarded, and despite such guard how entered, let the poet in the following stanzas show :

> Th' enormous fabric form'd of iron ore,
> Close barr'd around, all avenue denied,
> Save where a little gate, scarce two feet wide,
> Stood open, and the little gate before,
> Metallic monsters of colossal height,
> Through sorcery alive, so swiftly smite
> The ground, rebellowing to their iron flail,
> That stroke and stroke between, more thick than hail,
> No beam of day can pass with undivided light.

> .   .   .   .

> Yet bound by knighthood, Hüon firm remain'd
> Not to recede, though death his course oppose!
> Yet since no counsel can these dangers close,
> Since all must be by force, not prudence, gain'd,
> Forward he dashes through the iron flails,
> Sword rais'd, eyes clos'd—such confidence prevails!
> Heaven deigns to second his heroic trust;
> Each fierce colossus at his foremost thrust,
> Stands motionless as death, nor other foe assails.

Such valor and such prowess fail not of their reward, The maid's deliverer wins from the heathen giant, who meant her harm, a certain magic ring stolen by him. This ring will by and by stand Sir Hüon in good stead.

Oberon soon after sends to Hüon, sleeping, a lovely dream, lovely and terrible. The knight sees the fairest of women, and at once loves her with all his heart. But, almost immediately, he sees her involved in peril from which, as will happen in dreams, he cannot move hand or foot to save her,

The high-wrought sentiment of the dreaming knight is rudely disturbed. Squire Sherasmin speaks, and he and the knight talk matters over. Readers will relish the humorous Sancho Panza quality in what Sherasmin says:

> "That was a heavy dream," the old man cries;
> "Too long, perchance, upon your back you lay."—
>
> . . . .
>
> 'Now tell me,' says the knight, with earnest air,
> 'Think'st thou not, friend, that dreams, at times, declare
> The will of Heaven to man, and future scenes disclose?'
>
> "Such instances are known," returns the squire,
> " And since I've followed your adventurous way,
> Wonders are things of course, seen every day;
> Yet, as your words the truth, plain truth, require,
> Freely to speak, your dreams mere dreams I hold!"

Sir Hüon, at his squire's request, relates his dream, doing so with much effusion of feeling. Sherasmin at last advises him to cheer up and look on the bright side. He says:

> "Were I, sir, in your place,
> I should erase what grieves me from the case,
> And stick to what the spirit promis'd fair.
> Courage, sir knight! my bodings good declare!
> Go forth! the living maid in Babylon embrace!"

Onward they fare, and now they are nearing Bagdad ("Bagdad" and "Babylon," indifferently, Wieland, for convenience, reads the "Babilone" of the original romance), when a pregnant adventure befalls. Sir Hüon rescues from the jaws of a lion a Paynim knight, who rewards his Christian deliverer by stealing the champion's horse, riding therewith safely away. The reader's feeling is, by this act of baseness on the Saracen's part, well prepared to regard with less displacency what will happen to the fellow from his cheated rescuer's hand on the occasion of a second fateful encounter impending.

At Bagdad, all by happy chance, the knight learns that the caliph's daughter, she, too, had had her dream—a marvelous match to his own. Her maid's mother confided the matter to Sir Hüon, who had become the old woman's guest. So far, so good; but the reluctant princess was, the very next day, to be married to a man she abhorred!

But Oberon is on the right side, and that is a great matter—as the story, trippingly told by Wieland, abundantly shows:

As fays not sparingly their favorites aid,
A stately courser at the cottage door
Champs, with gay trappings richly cover'd o'er.
Two beauteous youths in silver cloth array'd
Wait at the stirrups, bright with burnish'd gold—
Up vaults the knight; the boys before him hold
Their nimble course, through secret pathways guide,
Rich meads fair blooming by Euphrates' side,
Till his impatient eyes the imperial tow'r behold.

.   .   .   .   .   .

Now to the table he advances nigh,
And with uplifted brow in wild amaze
Th' admiring guests upon the stranger gaze;
Fair Rezia, tranc'd with fascinated eyes,
Still views her dream, and ever downward bends;
The sultan, busy with the bowl, suspends
All other thoughts, prince Babekan alone,
Warn'd by no vision, tow'rds the guest unknown,
All fearless of his fate his length of neck extends.

Soon as Sir Hüon's scornful eyes retrace
The man of yesterday, that he, the same
Who lately dar'd the Christian God defame,
Sits at the left, high-plum'd in bridal grace,
And bows the neck as conscious of his guilt;
Swift as the light he grasps the saber's hilt;
Off at the instant flies the heathen's head!
And o'er the caliph and the banquet shed,
Up spirts his boiling blood, by dreadful vengeance spilt!

The rest of the commission, enjoined by Charlemagne on the knight, proceeds to accomplishment in manner following:

Low on his knee Sir Hüon humbly bends;
With cool, heroic look, and gentle tone
Begins—"Imperial Charles, before whose throne
"I bow, his faithful vassal hither sends,

" To hail thee, Asia's lord! with greeting fair,
" And beg—forgive, what duty bids declare—
" (For, as my arm, my tongue obeys his laws—)
" And beg—great sir!—four grinders from your jaws,
" And from your reverend beard a lock of silver hair!"

The caliph naturally declines the complimentary loss of his grinders, and rejects also certain alternative proposals made him by the knight.   The scene at length becomes highly uproarious in that festal hall, when suddenly Oberon presents himself.   Wieland :

Loud rings the castle with rebellowing shocks;
Night, tenfold midnight, swallows up the day;
Ghosts, to and fro, like gleams of lightning play,
The stony basis of the turret rocks !

.   .   .   .

With miracle on miracle oppress,
The caliph struggles with the pangs of death ;
His arm hangs loose, deep drawn his heavy breath,
Scarce beats his pulse, it flutters, sinks to rest.
At once the storm is hush'd that roar'd so loud;
While sweetly breathing o'er the prostrate crowd,
A lily vapour sheds around perfume,
And, like an angel image on a tomb,
The fairy spright appears, array'd in silver cloud !

Every thing is easy to Oberon.   One of his elfin retinue featly plucks, without pain to the owner, four teeth from the jaws of the caliph, and packs them, with a tuft of his beard to boot, as if they were jewels, for Sir Hüon to carry home with him.   As for Hüon and his bride, Rezia by name, they, with their respective attendants, Sherasmin and Fatme, go sailing far away, borne softly through the air in a fairy chariot drawn by swans.   Sherasmin may think his thoughts, but—now Wieland :

Far other thoughts inspire the youthful pair,
Whom love with Cytherea's swans conveys—
Whether they speed along unwonted ways,
Winged through the pathless regions of the air;
Whether they roll on earth, or swim the main;
Whether with flying course, or flagging rein;

How borne, thro' rough or smooth, by swan or steed;
What perils threaten, or what scenes succeed;
Of these no transient thought e'er flits across the brain.

The lovers have a lovely time of it together—too lovely, alas! and not Sherasmin, with long instructive tale of Oberon and Titania's estrangement, avails to impress them sufficiently with the need of self-control. (Sherasmin's didactic tale, by the way, is a borrowing of Wieland's from Chaucer, in that poet's piece entitled, *January and May.* Probably, however, Wieland got it, not directly from Chaucer, but indirectly through Pope, who paraphrased Chaucer's story. This interlude of the *Oberon*, Sotheby judiciously omits. It is a salacious affair.) The over-tempted travelers fail of fulfilling the condition on which Oberon's favor depends, and the fairy king, immeasurably vexed that he has so lost his hoped-for chance of honorable return to his forsworn Titania, plunges the hapless pair in manifold miseries. But Titania, tired, as is her husband, of long conjugal separation, intervenes, and a fresh hope dawns on their future. If now, against resistless temptation, they both resist, and keep true to each other in perfect faith, Oberon and Titania may yet come together. The trial of their steadfastness is described by Wieland in long detail, with wonderful delicacy for realism so daring. The two are torn asunder, and each without the knowledge of the other undergoes the terrible test. Both stand firm, and for their firmness are condemned to death by fire. The pyre is built, and, by way of well-plotted coincidence, the two, bound face to face, are laid on it together. But their enemies have reckoned without Oberon. At the exact critical moment, Hüon finds the miraculous horn miraculously about his neck. He of course winds it, and sets his enemies dancing. The prosperous ending of all speeds on apace.

The aerial ride which Oberon gives to Sir Hüon and his Amanda (so his wife, the sultan's daughter, Rezia, was christened) is, with its paradisaical conclusion, thus described by Wieland. The meeting and reconciliation of Oberon

with Titania are, it will be seen, introduced. The translator's verse, like his original's, seems to experience an access
of ease and swiftness in sympathy with a voyage so luxurious
and an arrival so delightfully welcomed:

> They mount the car—the Moors may ceaseless prance
> Long as such fancies please the fairy king;
> Though Sherasmin, who views the giddy ring,
> Thinks that to delve the dike, not weave the dance,
> Were better pastime for that roguish crew.
> Th' aerial steeds their noiseless course pursue;
> Nimble as thought itself, and soft as sleep,
> O'er land and sea their pinions smoothly sweep,
> While zephyrs fan the clouds that round the chariot flew.
>
> Already they behold where twilight sweeps
> Her veil of shapeless mist o'er mount and hill;
> And see the moon admire her image still
> In many a lake that calm beneath her sleeps.
> Night far and wide her silent shadow flings,
> As earthward gradual with descending wings
> The self-reined swans their course celestial leave;
> When, as if woven from the rosy eve,
> Radiant before their sight a floating palace springs!
>
> Girt with a pleasant grove, sweet shades between,
> Where arching rose-trees meet in wavy play,
> Appeared the palace whose alluring ray
> Bright through the wood's o'ershadowing foliage seen,
> Diffused around its wide resplendent light.
> "This, was not this the place?" soft breathed the knight;
> Yet, ere he forms the sound, a golden gate
> At once expands, and lo! in graceful state,
> Twice ten fair virgins float before their ravished sight.
>
> With ever-blooming cheeks the virgins move,
> Beauteous as May, and decked in robes of snow;
> And hail, triumphant from the world of woe,
> The pair whom Oberon greets with boundless love.
> To graceful measures glide the choral throng,
> And truth's immortal guerdon swells the song—
> "Come, faithful pair!" (while golden cymbals ring,
> Light as they weave the dance, and sweetly sing)
> "Blest pair! receive this wreath! to you these flowers belong."

The lovers, scarce themselves, in blissful trance
Rapt in another world, float hand in hand,
Where ranged on either side the virgins stand;
There, as a sun, before their dazzled glance,
And like a bridegroom robed in radiant sheen,
The fairy monarch stood with graceful mien.
No more in sweet disguise, a lovely child;
On youth's full bloom eternal beauty smiled,
And sparkling on his hand th' enchanted ring is seen.

Titania, by his side, with roses wreathed,
Gleams like a bride in moonlight's modest ray;
Their wedded hands a myrtle crown display;
" Take," with sweet tone their souls harmonious breathed,
" Thou faithful pair ! for you alone decreed,
This well-earned chaplet, victory's heavenly meed !
Receive from friendly hands the gift divine !
And long as ye retain this favored sign,
So never from your hearts shall happiness recede ! "

The final incidents form a fit and felicitous issue to so
much remarkable vicissitude of fortune. The return of the
pair to Charlemagne's court happens upon the occasion of a
tournament, of which the prize proposed to the victorious
knight is—what, to be sure, but Sir Hüon's own ancestral
castle and domain, confiscated to this purpose in view of the
supposed certainty of his never returning! Sir Hüon is not
left in the lurch by his fairy friend Oberon. How he is sumpt-
uously provided, to make good his claim to his own; and how,
with fortune equal to his virtue, he accomplishes this—it
may be safely left to the imagination of the reader to guess.
Here is the very last stanza of the poem; in it, the emperor
handsomely recovers himself to something like imperial mag-
nanimity:

Charles from his throne descends, with noble grace
Bids welcome to the court the beauteous bride:
The peers that press around on every side
The youthful hero in their arms embrace—
The youthful hero, from such perils freed,
Who, home returned, achieved the adventurous deed—

The emperor clasps him with paternal hand—
"And ne'er," he cries, "be wanting to our land,
A prince like thee, to win high virtue's heavenly meed."

Oberon is unique in German literature for happy wholeness and oneness. The plot is a masterpiece of felicity and skill in invention and joinery. Wieland was indebted for his idea to an anonymous French *chanson de geste*, so-called, that is, "song of exploit," belonging to the Middle Ages, entitled *Huon of Bordeaux*. This work, in Wieland's time, existed only in manuscript. A year or two, however, before *Oberon* was begun, a bare abstract of the old romance was printed. This became in Wieland's mind the quick seed which sprang up and bloomed in the brilliant flower of the *Oberon*.

Wieland used great freedom with his original romance. Generally, his changes were for the better. We have seen the French critic, Saint-Marc Girardin, quoted as expressing a preference for *Huon of Bordeaux* over Wieland's *Oberon*. He seemed to find the mediæval poem more delicate in describing the passion of love than is its modern version. This criticism is to us incomprehensible. The present writer has had the curiosity to look with some care over the pages of *Huon de Bordeaux*, now accessible in print to the public, and he has lighted upon nothing there deserving the praise of delicacy, in contrast with Wieland's *Oberon*. The caliph's (admiral's) daughter, for example, in the *chanson de geste*, is so unscrupulously eager for her foreign and unknown Christian lover that, to get out of the way all obstacles to the union she desires, she is even fain to put her father to death with her own hands.

And yet we do not rate very high the delicacy of *Oberon*. Delicacy the poem has, but it is delicacy of touch rather than delicacy of tone. The tone is not high. There is little to uplift in the *Oberon*. The poem runs along on a somewhat lowly moral level. It is of the earth, earthy. The intellectual level of the poem is not much higher than the moral. There is some imagination, some fancy, much felicity of phrase, of metre, of rhythm, sufficient wealth of invention, but there is no thought save what is perfectly commonplace thought. This commonplaceness in thought may be praised as a virtue of the *Oberon*, and we will not gainsay ; but as at least a characteristic of the *Oberon*, it cannot be denied. It is truly surprising how simple, how ordinary, how obvious, how matter-of-course, how commonplace, every thing in the *Oberon* is—the plot and the machinery being supposed given. This perhaps is as it should be. It probably constitutes the absolute triumph of the poet and the artist. But it is a triumph achieved in a comparatively humble order of things. In short, the *Oberon* is the finest poem that exists of its class ; but its class is modest indeed compared with that of such a modern handling of an ancient theme as Tennyson gave us when he wrote his *Guinevere*. Some readers, with those verses of Milton in mind appealing every thing to the "perfect witness of all-judging Jove," and awarding fame strictly,

> As he pronounces lastly on each deed,

may like to see the Olympian sentence of Goethe: "So long as poetry remains poetry, gold gold, and crystal crystal, Oberon will be loved and admired as a masterpiece of poetic art."

Wieland's prose works have none of them resisted the antiquating influence of time. In one of his "dialogues of the gods" there is a rather interesting anonymous introduction, as "The Unknown," of Jesus Christ in the character of an interlocutor. This unknown personage converses with Jupiter and Numa. He sketches to those pagan divinities, quite as a Voltairean deist might be expected to make him do, his own enthusiastic scheme of beneficence to the human race. Jupiter, somewhat satirically, treats him with the condescension of seniority. The time chosen for the dialogue to occur seems to be that of Constantine the Great (A. D. 300). When, in due time, the mysterious stranger vanishes, the dialogue concludes with the following exchange of question and reply between Numa and Jupiter, left alone together :

> *Numa* (to *Jupiter*). What sayst thou to this apparition, Jupiter?
> *Jupiter*. Ask me fifteen hundred years hence.

Heinrich Heine has somewhere a very striking sentence, representing the assembly of the Olympian gods disturbed by the entrance of the crucified Galilæan, who flings his bloody cross on their banqueting-table, and puts a stop to their carousal. One is reminded of this, by the foregoing far paler, far less imaginative, and far less powerful conception of Wieland's. Bayard Taylor's *Masque of the Gods* might almost seem to have found in Wieland's dialogue its seed of suggestion.

Wieland died repeating, in his own translation, the soliloquy of Hamlet. "To die—to sleep," were his last words—so spoken, and by such a man, words of mournful skepticism, rather than of Christian trust and rest.

We cannot forbear adding still a note of Wieland's own, respecting a personal interview that it was his fortune once to have with the invading and conquering Napoleon at Weimar. It will afford an interesting contrast with a like experience of Goethe's, to be noted hereafter. Wieland writes :

> The Duchess presented me to him in form, and he addressed me affably with some words of compliment, looking me steadily in the face. Few persons have appeared to me so rapidly to see through a man at a glance. He instantly perceived that, notwithstanding my celebrity, I was a plain, unassuming old man ; and, as he seemed desirous of making, forever, a good impression on me, he at once assumed the form best adapted to attain his end. I never saw a man in appearance calmer, plainer, milder, or more unpretending. No trace was visible about him of the consciousness that he was a great monarch. He talked to me like an old acquaintance with his equal, and, which was very rare with him, chatted with me exclusively an entire hour and a half, to the great surprise of all who were present. At length, about midnight, I began to feel inconvenience from standing so long, and took the liberty of requesting his majesty's permission to withdraw. "*Allez donc,*" said he in a friendly tone; "*bon soir.*" [Go, then; good night.]

The more remarkable traits of our interview were these: The previous play having made Cæsar the subject of our conversation, Napoleon observed that he was one of the greatest characters in all history; and that, indeed, he would have been, without exception, the greatest, but for one blunder. I was about to inquire to what anecdote he alluded, when he seemed to read the question in my eye, and continued: "Cæsar knew the men who wanted to get rid of him, and he ought to have been rid of them first." If Napoleon could have read all that passed in my mind, he would have perceived me saying, Such a blunder will never be laid to your charge. . . .

He preferred Ossian to Homer. . . . Notwithstanding the flattering friendliness of his apparent manner, he repeatedly gave me the idea of his being cast from bronze.

At length, however, he had put me so much at my ease, that I asked him how it happened that the public worship, which he had in some degree reformed in France, had not been rendered more philosophic, and more on a par with the spirit of the times. "My dear Wieland," he replied, "worship is not made for philosophers; they believe neither in me nor in my priesthood. As for those who do believe, you cannot give them, or leave them, wonders enough. If I had to make a religion for philosophers, it should be just the reverse." In this tone the conversation went on for some time, and Bonaparte professed so much skepticism as to question whether Jesus Christ had ever existed.

There is, in Wieland's character both as author and as man, so much to engage the kind feeling of the reader, such cheerfulness, such brightness, such versatility, such pliancy, such good-nature, such amiable desire to please, that, notwithstanding his faults, of levity, of fickleness, of lasciviousness, of skepticism, one does not part from him without a certain regret. His company, at least to your slacker moods of mind, is not—though perhaps it ought to be—the less delightful, that it never threatens to "disturb" you "with the joy of elevated thoughts."

VI.

HERDER.

1744–1803.

AMONG the greater divinities of the German literary Olympus, Goethe is generally the one selected to stand for Jove, the monarch of them all. This, if regard be had chiefly to supremacy of fame and of influence, is, of course, an arrangement of the hierarchy not to be quarreled with. We, however, imagine that Goethe's noble personal presence, " the front of Jove himself," has, by natural, if illogical, associative effect, had something to do with the instinctive and almost universal acclamation which has crowned this elect favorite of fortune the German literary Zeus.

Herder was a less impressive-looking physical man than was Goethe; but, if physical qualities were to be carefully denied any influence, and if moral qualities were to weigh, and to weigh equally with intellectual, in making their possessor a candidate for pre-eminent place; if a certain inborn kingliness of soul, a certain proud consciousness imprinted on the brow, of inalienable native right to reign, were to be accepted in evidence of title—in one word, if ethical height as well as mental breadth were to be measured, in finding out the true Jove among German literary men, then Herder, and not Goethe, would undoubtedly be that monarch. In our own opinion, at least, the erectest, the stateliest, in short, seen by the eye of the morally-judging mind, the kingliest, of all his peers is he.

But this majestic man was not, like Goethe, born to ease and leisure. The mien of courtliness and command, the grace of elegance in manner, which in Herder so well comported with his fame, were not the fruit to him of early habit and example. Herder was of poor, almost squalid, extraction. Burke proudly told the Duke of Bedford: " *Nitor in adversum* [' I struggle against adverse circumstance '] is the motto for a man like me." With much more force of truth, Herder might have said the same concerning himself.

Herder's life was still bound in shallows and in miseries, when, from the great tide in affairs created by Frederick the Great, a sudden flush flowed into his native village, which bore the eager youth unexpectedly out into sea-room. A regiment returning from the Seven Years' War was quartered at Mohrungen. The regimental surgeon got his eye on Herder, and proposed making him a student of surgery. The beneficiary was in return to translate a professional treatise of his patron's into Latin. This was done ; but the first surgical operation witnessed by the student settled the business for him. He fainted away at the sight, and renounced the profession forever. He was destined, as will presently appear, to be, later, a subject, instead of a practitioner, of surgery. Then, suffering such as he could not see in another, he endured himself with stoic fortitude. His imagination, more sensitive than his nerves, made sympathy to him more painful than pain.

Herder was fairly out in the world now ; alas, however,— the business of surgery abandoned—with nothing to do, but starve—or return to Mohrungen. He chose starving; and remained at Königsberg, whither he had gone with his friend the surgeon. His acquaintances in Königsberg helping him a little, and his kindred helping him a little from home, he entered the University of Königsberg, to study theology. "Plain living and high thinking " sustained him—sometimes it would seem to have been more the " high thinking " than the "plain living"; the living was so very plain, and therewithal so scant—mere bread, and short rations of that. This lofty spirit, when, toward the end of life, he felt himself sinking, sighed and said, " O, if some grand new thought would come and pierce my soul through and through, I should be well in a moment." Who knows? That may have been a wind of reminiscence out of his own past. Perhaps he unconsciously remembered "nourishing a youth sublime" on that nobler than Olympian fare, the diet of "high thinking," when he was a penniless student at the University of Königsberg.

At Königsberg, he fell upon the time of the great philosopher Kant.

Not Kant, however, but a man far less known than Kant, a man in fact scarcely known at all except to the specialist in German literature, exerted in Königsberg the leading influence on Herder's intellectual development and history. Hamann was nothing less than an indispensable factor in the making of Herder into what he became. Herder became one of the acknowledged chief ruling powers in the world of German thought and German letters; and this without writing any single work that can justly be called a masterpiece of literature. His fame was greater than any literary achievement to which it could appeal, and his influence was still greater than his fame. Herder taught his countrymen to study the literatures of the East, Herder taught his countrymen to explore the treasures of popular poetry among different peoples; and the teacher was really Hamann through Herder. Unconsciously, Hamann had moved a mind that was to move the world—the world, that is, of German literature. The character, in especial, of breadth, of catholicity, of open hospitality to ideas, which we have already attributed to German letters, was an impression and impulse received more from Herder than from any other hand. Herder was, early, by personal contact, as well as through the influence of his books, one of the chief teachers of Goethe. Later, the growing moral separation between them left Goethe less capable of receiving the elevating influence which Herder was not less, but more and more, capable of imparting. A letter of Herder's on the subject of Goethe's *Wilhelm Meister* makes dignified but melancholy note of this. It is a letter addressed to a lady, the Countess Bandissin, who seems to have applied to Herder for his opinion of that production of Goethe's. Herder writes:

I owe you an answer respecting Goethe's novel (*Wilhelm Meister*). Do not reproach me as though I were myself the author, for I have only read it the other day, later than most people. Many years ago, indeed, he read us some passages that pleased us, although we even then regretted the bad company that his hero keeps so long. But then the story was quite a different thing. We made the young man's acquaintance in his childhood, and conceived an interest in him that gradually increased, even when he went astray. Now it has quite another cast; we see the hero from the first where we had rather not see him at all, and are left to find out for ourselves how he got there, while at the same time he is no longer sufficiently interesting in himself to merit our sympathy. I have expostulated without effect, and none of the scenes where Philina appears were shown to me in manuscript. My own opinion of all that part is the same as yours, and, I should imagine, as that of all right-thinking people. Goethe thinks otherwise; truthfulness of scene is to him all in all, and he troubles himself extremely little about elevation of sentiment or moral gracefulness. In fact, this is the fault of many of his writings, and the difference of our sentiments has caused him to desist from taking my opinion on any of them. I hate the whole generation of his Marianas and Philinas; and neither in life nor the representation of it can I endure any sacrifice of actual morality to mere talent, or what people call by that name.

Herder, widely and brilliantly famous as a preacher, had been drawn to Weimar by the invitation of the Grand Duke—to become in the end " superintendent " of the clergy of his realm. He there of course knew Goethe well, had in fact known him before going there, and he in due time became acquainted with Schiller, when Schiller also came, first to Jena, near by, and afterward to Weimar; but his relation to them was never quite easy. That Herder was felt by those two great reigning powers of Weimar to be, in example and in sentiment, a rebuke to such license as Goethe practiced and as Schiller allowed, was reason enough why that pure and strenuous spirit should be, as he was, under some cloud of disfavor with them. Schiller, for example, writing to Körner, condescended again and again to peddle out, to the disadvantage of Herder, the spiteful gossip of the frivolous, current in that corrupt little capital, Weimar. Here is one of his stories, amusing undoubtedly, and, however self-evidently unverifiable, having a certain likeness to life. It seems at least to illustrate the unwillingly reverent

8

popular conception, prevailing in the time and the place, with regard to the character of Herder ; as well as the relation which could not but subsist between a man so chaste and so serious, and the producer, or the encourager, of a literature libidinous like the *Roman Elegies* of Goethe published by Schiller in his magazine *The Hours.* ("Some of the coarsest of Goethe's Elegies were purposely omitted, not to shock decency too much," Schiller writes to Körner.) Schiller's story :

Herder and his wife live in selfish retirement, from which they exclude every other son of earth. But as both are proud and violent, these self-elected deities often dispute with each other. When this is the case they retire to their respective apartments, and letters go up-stairs and down stairs between the two, until the lady enters her husband's room and recites some portion of his writings, adding the words, "He who wrote that must be a god, and anger cannot touch him." Whereupon the appeased Herder throws his arms round her neck and the quarrel is made up. Praise the Almighty that ye are immortal!

The story reminds us that Herder has previously found a wife, without our having taken note of the fact. His marriage was a nearly ideal one. The wife he found will be spoken of in a passage presently to be shown from the auto-biography of Goethe. Meantime, one or two more bits of allusion to Herder out of the letters of Schiller to Körner. These will help still further to set out in distinctness, by contrast, that noble severity in Herder, the firm outline of which not even the enervating softness of Weimar could prevail to subdue. Schiller says:

Herder was cut out for a distinguished dignitary of the Roman Catholic Church, genially insipid and oratorically pliant when he wishes to please.

Schiller says again :

What disgusts me most with him [Herder] is an indolent carelessness, accompanied by sarcastic impudence. He shows a venomous envy toward all that is good and energetic, and affects to protect what is middling. He made the most offensive remarks to Goethe about his *Meister*. His heart is overloaded with bile against Kant and the philosophers of the new school.

The querulous, not to say termagant, tone of Schiller in the foregoing quoted expressions of his is, we regret to say, not uncharacteristic of this famous man, as he appears, often in most disadvantageous contrast with his friend, in his correspondence with Körner. Herder, it seems, was "impudent"! Of what sort his impudence was it is easy to guess, from Schiller's allusion to Herder's "offensive" remarks to Goethe about that author's *Wilhelm Meister*. Now let Goethe himself speak of Herder in the promised passage from the former's autobiography. Goethe here exhibits himself, as well as Herder, to fine advantage. Goethe is recounting the experiences that befell him when he was a student in the University of Strasburg. He says:

> The most important event, one that was to have the weightiest consequences for me, was my acquaintance with Herder, and the nearer connection with him which sprang from it. [The first meeting of the two was a casual one at Strasburg.] At parting I begged permission to wait on him at his own residence, which he granted me kindly enough. I did not neglect to avail myself repeatedly of this favor, and was more and more attracted by him. He had a certain gentleness in his manner which was very suitable and becoming without being exactly easy. . . . By various questions he tried to make himself acquainted with me and my situation, and his power of attraction operated on me with growing strength. I was, generally speaking, of a very confiding disposition; and with him especially I had no secrets. It was not long, however, before the repelling pulse of his nature began to appear and placed me in no small uneasiness.

It seems that young Goethe had a mania for collecting, not autographs, and not postage-stamps, but the "seals" of titled personages. Goethe says:

> I related to him many things of my youthful occupations and tastes, and, among others, of a collection of seals, which I had principally gotten together through the assistance of our family friend, who had an extensive correspondence. I had arranged them according to the *State Calendar*, and by this means had become well acquainted with all the potentates, the greater and lesser mightinesses and powers, even down to the nobility under them. These heraldic insignia had often, and in particular at the ceremonies of the coronation, been of use to my memory. I spoke of these things with some complacency; but he was of another

opinion, and not only stripped the subject of all interest, but also contrived to make it ridiculous and nearly disgusting. From this his spirit of contradiction I had much to endure.

At the time of which Goethe, throughout this passage, is speaking, Herder was on a visit to Strasburg to receive surgical treatment for a disorder in his eyes. Goethe says:

> I found every reason to admire his great firmness and endurance; for neither during the numerous surgical operations, nor at the oft-repeated painful dressings, did he show himself in any degree irritable; and of all of us he seemed to be the one that suffered least. . . . Herder could be charmingly prepossessing and brilliant, but he could just as easily turn an ill-humored side foremost.
>
> During the whole time of this cure I visited Herder morning and evening; I even remained whole days with him, and in a short time accustomed myself so much the more to his chiding and fault-finding, as I daily learned to appreciate his beautiful and great qualities, his extensive knowledge, and his profound views. The influence of this good-natured blusterer was great and important. He was five years older than myself, which in younger days makes a great difference to begin with; and as I acknowledged him for what he was, and tried to value that which he had already produced, he necessarily gained a great superiority over me. But the situation was not comfortable; for older persons, with whom I had associated hitherto, had sought to form me with indulgence, perhaps had even spoiled me by their lenity; but from Herder, behave as one might, one could never expect approval. As now, on the one side, my great affection and reverence for him, and, on the other, the discontent which he excited in me, were continually at strife with each other, there arose within me an inward struggle, the first of its kind which I had experienced in my life. Since his conversations were at all times important, whether he asked, answered, or communicated his opinions in any other manner, he could not but advance me daily, nay, hourly, to new views.

We have been the more willing to prolong our condensations from this part of Goethe's autobiography, because they not only exhibit in striking testimonial from the highest authority the commanding intellectual and moral worth of Herder, but also, in doing this, let Goethe, by anticipation, make an interesting and, on the whole, highly favorable impression of himself. Goethe's is a great name in German literature, which, in its own place, will demand large room for its due proportionate display. The whole of German literary history may be regarded as a vista leading up to Goethe. Let us do what we properly can to show him by occasional glimpses on the way.

If, in accordance with Richter's suggestion, Herder was rather a poem than a poet, yet he did write poetry as well as prose. His most considerable production in verse was a treatment of the theme of the Cid. We have no space to show any thing more than a very short flight of Herder's muse. This, however, shall be in a piece that admirably illustrates the elevation and seriousness of his character. And yet it is a skating song. Klopstock seems to have set the fashion that made skating so popular a recreation among cultivated people in Germany. Goethe, after him, was an enthusiastic skater. The assertion may with confidence be hazarded that there was never a lyric on sport of any kind pitched in a key loftier than that of the following skating song by Herder. It will be observed that a strong homiletic bias seems to embarrass somewhat the free lyric swing of our poet. He moralizes his song, drawing, with not, it must be admitted, the most brilliant success, an analogy between skating and living. We use Mr. C. T. Brooks's version, but shorten by omitting two of the stanzas:

Away and away o'er the deep-sounding tide
On crystals of silver we sweep and we glide:
The steel is our pinion, our roof the broad blue,
And heav'n's pure breezes our pathway pursue.
So, joyfully, brothers, we glide and we sweep
Away and away over life's brazen deep.

. . . . .

Look up, now! How sparkles that blue sea on high;
And below us, in frost, gleams a star-lighted sky.
For He who with suns studded heaven o'erhead,
Beneath us a frost-flowered meadow hath spread.
So, joyfully, brothers, we float and we glide
Through life's starry meadows away far and wide.

He made us this palace so airy and wide
And gave us steel feet amid dangers to glide;

In the frosts of mid-winter he kindles our blood;
We hover, we sweep, o'er the treacherous flood.
So, fearlessly, brothers, steel-hearted, we sweep
O'er the sounding abysses of life's stormy deep.

Let us go at once to Herder's prose. This is in quantity sufficiently ample. Sixty volumes, in one edition, his printed productions fill. But in all those sixty volumes—full of thought, quick and quickening thought, as they are—there is, we repeat, no single production generally reckoned a true literary masterpiece. Herder's mind was too eager, too versatile, too enterprising, too fond of forward movement, of pioneering, of adventure, to have the long patience necessary for the elaboration of a completely rounded and finished literary work. He loved best of all to be a life-giving force to other minds. He was by eminence, as by eminence he chose to be, a teacher.

Herder's best book Goethe pronounced to be his *Ideas toward a Philosophy of History ;* and this judgment the common opinion of critics has confirmed. Of Herder's *Philosophy of History,* accordingly, we shall do most wisely to give here some account—necessarily a very meagre account it must be.

The aim of this work is nothing less than to reduce the whole of human history to the unity and the orderly progress of a development. The human race is, by an effort of philosophic and imaginative historic generalization, conceived as a complex individual, having its infancy, its youth, its maturity. The idea is almost an anticipation, in the historic realm, of the idea of evolution—that master-thought of current speculation in science and philosophy with which we are now all so familiar. Like the true German, Herder begins, widely and remotely, with the earth itself, man's abode, as a member of the system of the universe. He wishes to be thorough, comprehensive, exhaustive. If the truth must be told, all the earlier part of his work is as dry, and much of it is as barren, as it is ambitious and profound. Of the breadth and scope of the treatment, some stimulating idea may be formed from the titles to a few of the chapters.

Astronomy, Geology, Physical Geography, appear successively in those of the first "Book," as the following citations
will show:

1. Our Earth is a Star among Stars. 2. Our Earth is one of the middle
Planets. 3. Our Earth has undergone many Revolutions ere it became
what it now is. 4. Our Earth is an Orb, which revolves round its own
Axis, and in oblique direction toward the Sun. 5. Our Earth is enveloped
with an Atmosphere, and is in conflict with several of the celestial Bodies.
6. The Planet we inhabit is an Earth of Mountains rising above the
Surface of the Waters. 7. The Direction of the Mountains renders our
two Hemispheres a Theatre of the most singular Variety and Change.

Subsequent books treat of the animal and the vegetable
creation in relation to the organization of man, of the supe-
riority of man to every other animate creature, and so forth
and so forth. No thoughtful person can barely glance over
the table of contents without feeling that here wrought a mind
of aspiring ambition, if not of masterly power, to grasp and
to wield material to its purpose. Except, however, to the
very thoughtful, and withal very studious, person, the promise held out is not of highly entertaining discussion. It is
not till Herder advances to treat, in his wide comparative
way, particular races of men and particular periods of history, that he becomes at all interesting to the general reader.
He then reminds you of Montesquieu, to whom indeed
Herder, as he himself acknowledges, is not a little indebted
for suggestion and lead in the path which he follows.

Of the really religious, while quasi-deistic, spirit in which
Herder conducted his philosophic inquiries, the work itself as
a whole is a monumental witness. The following sentences
from the preface exhibit this spirit in distinct expression:

Thus, Great Being, Invisible, Supreme Disposer of our race, I lay at
thy feet the most imperfect work that mortal ever wrote, in which he
has ventured to trace and follow thy steps. Its leaves may decay and its
characters vanish; forms after forms, too, in which I have discerned
traces of thee, and endeavored to exhibit them to my brethren, may mold-
er into dust; but thy purposes will remain, and thou wilt gradually un-
fold them to thy creatures, and exhibit them in nobler forms. Happy if

then these leaves shall be swallowed up in the stream of oblivion, and in their stead clearer ideas rise in the mind of man.

The enormous breadth and inclusion of Herder's plan is impressively shown in the mere list of the nations whose history he treats in separate chapters. You may count these literally by scores.

Opening his volumes at hazard, in that portion of their contents in which Herder luminously discusses the history of the Romans, we light on the following remarkable expression, rhapsodic almost to the point of grammatical incoherence. This, as will naturally occur to the student of Mommsen, substantially anticipates that hero-worshiping historian's enthusiastic appreciation of Julius Cæsar:

> When in the throng of battle or in the tumult of the forum the countenance of Cæsar retains its constant serenity, and his heart beats with magnanimous clemency even toward his enemies; great man, even with all the vices into which levity led thee, if thou didst not deserve to be monarch of Rome, no man ever did! But Cæsar was more than this; he was Cæsar. The highest throne on earth decorated itself with his name. O that it could have adorned itself with his spirit also! that for ages it could have been animated with the benevolent, vigilant, comprehensive mind of Cæsar!

The latter part of the work is largely occupied with the history of the propagation of Christianity. This subject is treated in the calm, dispassionate, rational spirit of the deistical philosopher calling himself and, whether truly or not, supposing himself, Christian. Herder was certainly a devout man, but as certainly he was not a Christian, in the sense of being an evangelical Christian, so-called. He was a rationalist, and the fountain-head of theological rationalism in Germany. This, in the view of those who, bearing whatever sectarian name, inherit from him the spirit of rationalism in religion, is Herder's praise. Herder's character it is, at any rate, in the view of all who judge him according to the truth.

To exhibit the attitude—rather, it will be observed, that of dignified, self-centred reverence, as toward a man, than that of supreme devotion and worship, as toward a divine being—assumed by Herder in presence of Jesus Christ, we quote the following personal apostrophe to him, occurring at the close of a sort of preface or proëm to that section of his work in which the author begins to treat of the history of Christianity:

> With reverence I bend before thy noble form, thou head and founder of a kingdom so great in its object, so durable in its extent, so simple and animated in its principles, so efficacious in its motives, that the sphere of this terrestrial life appears too narrow for it. Nowhere in history find I a revolution so quietly effected in so short a time, planted in such a singular manner by feeble instruments, propagated over all the earth with yet indeterminable effect, and cultivated so as to produce good or bad fruit, as that, which has spread among nations under the name, not properly of *thy religion*, that is to say, of thy vital scheme for the welfare of mankind, but mostly of *thy worship*, that is, an unreflecting adoration of thy cross and person. Thy penetrating mind foresaw this; and it is dishonoring thy name to affix it to every turbid stream from thy pure fountain. We will avoid it as much as possible; thy placid form shall stand alone before the whole history, that takes its rise from thee.

The whole treatment of this important topic of Herder's discussion is very much in the tone and manner of Professor Seeley's *Ecce Homo*.

Finally, we may display at once the entire scheme of Herder's *Philosophy of History* by condensing here his chapter of general reflections on the history of Greece. The instance of Greece, he says himself, presents a kind of microcosm of the history of humanity at large. The process of historic evolution, complete, may thus, according to Herder, be studied here in an example existing on a scale conveniently reduced. Let us begin with Herder's statement of what he calls his " first grand principle: "

> *Whatever can take place among mankind, within the sphere of given circumstances of time, place, and nation, actually does take place.*
>
> Of this Greece affords the amplest and most beautiful proofs. . . . The whole history of mankind is a pure natural history of human powers, actions, and propensities, modified by time and place. . . .
>
> This philosophy will first and most eminently guard us from attributing the facts that appear in history to the particular hidden purposes of a

scheme of things unknown to us, or the magical influence of invisible powers which we would not venture to name in connection with natural phenomena. . . .

Why did enlightened Greeks appear in the world? It was because Greeks existed, and existed under such circumstances that they could not be otherwise than enlightened. Why did Alexander invade India? Because he was Alexander, the son of Philip; and from the dispositions his father had made, the deeds of his nation, his age and character, his reading of Homer, etc., knew nothing better that he could undertake. But if we attribute his bold resolution to the secret purpose of some superior power, and his heroic achievements to his peculiar fortune, we run the hazard, on the one hand, of exalting his most senseless and atrocious actions into designs of the Deity, and, on the other, of detracting from his personal courage and military skill, while we deprive the whole occurrence of its natural form. . . . History is the science of what is, not of what possibly may be according to the hidden designs of fate.

Secondly. *What is true of one people holds equally true with regard to the connection of several together—they are joined as time and place unite them; they act upon one another as the combination of active powers directs.*

We are incorporating the present condensation of Herder's general reflections on the history of Greece, not because these reflections constitute the most vividly interesting thing that we could produce out of the work—this is far from being the case—but because they are in the highest degree *representative* of his attempted philosophy of history. If we should speak out our own individual mind on the point, we should have to say that Herder's great principles sometimes—for example, in the case of the one last given—seem to us chiefly futile and barren truisms. We omit Herder's expansion and exemplification of his second great principle, and go on to the third. He says:

Thirdly. *The cultivation of a people is the flower of its existence; its display is pleasing indeed, but transitory.*

. . . The cultivation of Greece grew with time, place, and circumstances, and declined with them. Poetry and certain arts preceded philosophy; where oratory or the fine arts flourished, neither the patriotic virtues nor the martial spirit could shine with their highest splendor; the orators of Athens displayed the greatest enthusiasm when the state drew near its end and its integrity was no more.

But all kinds of human knowledge have this in common, that each aims

at a point of perfection which, when attained by a concatenation of fortunate circumstances, it can neither preserve to eternity, nor can it instantly return, but a decreasing series commences.

. . . When Homer had sung, no second Homer in the same path could
be conceived; he plucked the flower of the epic garland, and all who followed must content themselves with a few leaves. Thus the Greek
tragedians chose another track; they ate, as Æschylus says, at Homer's
table, but prepared for their guests a different feast. They too had their
day; the subjects of tragedy were exhausted, and their successors could
do no more than remold the greatest poets, that is, give them in an
inferior form; for the best, the supremely beautiful, form of the Grecian
drama, had already been exhibited in those models. In spite of all his
morality, Euripides could not rival Sophocles, to say nothing of his being
able to excel him in the essence of his art; and therefore the prudent
Aristophanes pursued a different course. Thus it was with every species
of Grecian art, and thus it will be in all nations—the very circumstance
that the Greeks in their most flourishing periods perceived this law of
nature, and sought not to go beyond the highest in something still higher,
rendered their taste so sure, and its development so various. When
Phidias had created his omnipotent Jove, a superior Jupiter was not
within the reach of possibility; but the conception was capable of being
applied to other gods, and to every god was given his peculiar character;
thus this province of art was peopled.

. . . Our youth returns not again; neither returns the action of our
mental faculties as they then were. The very appearance of the flower is
a sign that it must fade; it has drawn to itself the powers of the plant
from the very root; and when it dies, the death of the plant must follow.
Unfortunate would it have been could the age that produced a Pericles
and a Socrates have been prolonged a moment beyond the time which
the chain of events prescribed for its duration; for Athens it would have
been a perilous, an insupportable period. Equally confined would be the
wish that the mythology of Homer should have held eternal possession
of the human mind, the gods of the Greeks have reigned to infinity,
and their Demosthenes have thundered forever. Every plant in nature
must fade; but the fading plant scatters abroad its seeds, and thus reno-
vates the living creation.

Shakespeare was no Sophocles, Milton no Homer, Bolingbroke no Pericles, yet they were in their kind, and in their situation, what those were
in theirs. Let every one, therefore, strive in his place to be what he can
be in the course of things; this he will be, and to be any thing else is
impossible.

Why "every one" should "strive" to be that which he inevitably "will be," is not so clear to the present writer's mind

as, let us hope, it was to the mind of Herder. Herder's doctrine of historic necessity, or fate, is adapted to be more satisfactory to the anti-Christian, than to the Christian, evolutionist. We have seen pantheism, as a derivation from Spinoza, attributed to Herder. Atheism, rather, his reader might suspect to have been the dominating spirit of Herder's philosophy of history; such curious anxiety he manifests to exclude the Great Being, for whom, in words—sincere words, doubtless—he professes unspeakable adoration, from any active share in the concerns of his universe or in the on-goings of history. But, as we said, Herder's religious point of view is that of the devout deist.

Our next citation, and our last, from this work shall be Herder's *fourth* great "principle"—which, without comment, we leave to the leisurely digestion of our readers:

> Fourthly. *The health and duration of a state rest not on that point of its highest cultivation, but on a wise or fortunate equilibrium of its active living powers. The deeper in this living exertion its centre of gravity lies, the more firm and durable it is.*

We have called Herder's spirit in the present work dispassionate and calm. This characterization, however, is true, rather of the matter, than of the manner, of what he says. He is not seldom oratoric in his style; he even tends to swell into the grandiose and turgid. The merit of the whole work is in fairness to be estimated with constant regard to the fact that the author was, to a considerable extent, finding his own path in a new, untrodden field of philosophic inquiry. That Herder was not strictly original in his idea of history, as subject to a law of development, as enfolding within itself a principle of philosophy, we have already pointed out. Montesquieu was before Herder in this, as Bossuet in it was perhaps before Montesquieu. But the first man to attempt actually forcing this expansile and resistant idea into the forms and terms of a system, was Herder. And Herder's *Philosophy of History*, never quite completed according to the plan of the author, is still a standard treatise on its subject.

We feel that we ought not to dismiss Herder without adding yet a citation or two that may serve to suggest something of the versatility of his genius. Herder was a critic. Of his critical quality, let the following parallel of his between Klopstock and Milton stand for illustration. We might find an example better adapted to exhibit his boldness and his suggestiveness; hardly perhaps any more likely to interest our readers. We use the translation of W. Taylor:

> We are accustomed to call Klopstock the German Milton; I wish they were never named together, and that Klopstock had never known Milton. Both have written sacred poesy, but they were not inspired by the same Urania. They bear to each other the relation that Moses bears to Christ, or the old to the new covenant. The edifice of Milton is a steadfast and well-planned building, resting on ancient columns. Klopstock's is an enchanted dome, echoing with the softest and purest tones of human feeling, hovering between heaven and earth, borne on angels' shoulders. Milton's muse is masculine, and harsh as his iambics. Klopstock's is a tender woman, dissolving in pious ecstasies, warbling elegies and hymns. Klopstock had studied deeply the language of his country, and won for it more powers than the Briton ever suspected his to possess. A single ode of Klopstock outweighs the whole lyric literature of Britain. The *Herman* of this writer awaked a spirit of simple nervous song, far loftier than that which animates the chorus-dramas of antiquity. The *Samson* or Milton attains not these models. When music shall acquire among us the highest powers of her art, whose words will she select to utter but those of Klopstock?

Herder was a writer of parables; allegories or fables they were, conceived by him in the Oriental rather than in the ancient Greek or Roman spirit. Of these serious recreative pieces of Herder, we regret to say that we can spare no room for even a single specimen.

Already it is time that we bow ourselves respectfully out of this most unbendingly august of the presences to be found in the halls of German letters. We cannot do so more appropriately than by quoting, condensed, the words of hail and farewell nobly pronounced by Richter in one of his books on occasion of Herder's death. These two kindred though differing spirits loved each the other as his own soul.

Richter came to Weimar that he might be near Herder; and
Herder leaned on Richter as Paul did on Timothy. A loftier
strain, more pathetic, of funereal triumph, has seldom been
chanted by the voice of friendship and genius, than that
which Richter here lifts up, in clear and steady tenor, over
the just-closed grave of Herder.

Having said this, we need to prepare our readers against
a first disappointment. This mingled wail and eulogy from
Richter will seem to them written in a strange, almost an
outlandish, style. It will puzzle and confound at first. Read
it thoughtfully, read it studiously, read it repeatedly. It will
need, and it will repay, the pains. Return to it after having
gone through the chapter to follow, that devoted to the study
of Richter, and see if then this strain, which to us seems of a
mournful and triumphing beauty so rare, does not take possession also of your sentiment and imagination:

> That noble spirit was misunderstood by opposite times and parties, yet
> not entirely without fault of his own. For he had the fault that he was no
> star of first, or of any other, magnitude, but a clump of stars out of which
> each one spells a constellation to please himself. . . .
>
> If he was no poet, as he often, indeed, thought of himself—and also
> of other very celebrated people—standing as he did close by the Homeric
> and Shakespearean standard, then he was merely something better,
> namely, a *poem*, an Indian-Greek *epos* made by some purest god. . . .
>
> In his beautiful soul, precisely as in a poem, every thing coalesced, and
> the good, the true, the beautiful, constituted an inseparable trinity. . . .
> He wished to see the sacrifices of poesy as fair and undefiled as the thun-
> der of heaven permits to scathed humanity. . . .
>
> Few minds are learned after the same grand fashion as he. . . . Many
> are clasped by their learning as by a withering ivy, but he as by a grape-
> vine. . . .
>
> He exhibited the Greek humanity, to which he restored the name, in
> the most tender regard for all purely human relations, and in his Lutheran
> indignation against all whereby they were poisoned, however sanctioned
> by Church and State. He was a fort overgrown with flowers, a northern
> oak whose branches were sensitive plants. How gloriously irreconcilable
> he burned against every creeping soul, against all looseness and self-contra-
> diction, dishonesty, and poetical slime-softness; as also against German
> critical rudeness and all sceptres in paws; and how he exorcised the ser-
> pents of his time! But would you hear the softest of voices, it was his

in love—whether for a child, or for a poem, or for music—or in mercy for the weak. He resembled his friend Hamann, who was at once a hero and a child, who, like an electrized person in the dark, stood harmless, with a glory encircling his head, until a touch drew the lightning from him. . . .

Altogether, he was little weighed and little estimated; and only in particulars, not in the whole. That task remains for the diamond-scales of posterity. . . . His life was a shining exception to the ofttimes tainted endowment of genius; he sacrificed, like the ancient priests, even at the altar of the muses, only with white garments.

He seems to me now—much as death usually lifts men up into a holy transfiguration—in his present distance and elevation, no more shining than formerly, by my side, here below. I imagine him yonder, behind the stars, precisely in his right place, and but little changed, his griefs excepted. Well, then, celebrate right festively yonder thy harvest-feast, thou pure, thou spirit-friend! May thy coronal of heavy wheat-ears blossom on thy head into a light flower-chaplet! thou sunflower, transplanted to thy sun at last!

In his song to the night, he says to his sleeping body:

> Slumber well meanwhile, thou sluggish burden
> Of my earthly walk. Her mantle
> Over thee spreads the Night, and her lamps
> Burn above thee in the holy pavilion.

Otherwise, now, and colder, stands the star-night above his mold. Alas! he who only read him has scarcely lost him, but he who knew and loved him is not to be consoled any more by *his* immortality, but only by the immortality of the human soul. If there were no such immortality; if our whole life here is only an evening twilight preceding the night, not a morning twilight; if the lofty mind is also let down after the body by coffin-ropes into the pit—O, then I know not why we should not, at the graves of great men, do, from despair, what the ancient savage nations did from hope; that is, throw ourselves after them into the pit, as those did into the tombs of their princes, so that the foolish, violent heart, that will obstinately beat for something divine and eternal, may be choked at once. . . . O, I well know that he tolerated such griefs least of all. He would point now to the glittering stars of spring, above which he now dwells; he would beckon to us to listen to the nightingales which now sing to us and not to him; and he would be more moved than he seemed to be. . . .

We will now love that great soul together, and if, at times, we are moved too painfully by his memory, we will read over again all whereby he made known to us the immortal and divine, and himself.

There has been of late a revival of interest in Herder, and
the prospect is fair that he will eventually be rehabilitated
to something like his contemporary fame. Any change of
dominant taste tending to make more of morals in literature,
and of mere culture, apart from morals, less, might work
against Goethe ; but it would, to the same degree, work in
Herder's favor.

VII.

RICHTER.

1763–1825.

The largest, softest, most loving heart in literature—heart
pure, too, of the purest—was Richter, Richter the unique,
the only. So the German themselves call Richter, and so,
much more, may we, not Germans, call him, since with a
far stronger feeling than can be theirs of his unexampled
peculiarity. Not quite, however, "Richter the Only," is the
favorite form of the name. For well-nigh universally still,
as was the case during his life-time, he is, among those who,
knowing him best, love him most, affectionately designated
(after his double first name, Gallicized by himself), "Jean
Paul," rather than Richter.

To the heart, great and tender, of this man, was married
a brain only less remarkable for both quantity and quality.
Still, less remarkable the brain was than the heart, in Richter ; and what Goethe, in German phrase—phrase to be
transferred rather than translated—spoke of as the "eternal
womanly" predominated in his character. But it was a
most manly womanliness. Richter was a sentimentalist, but
he was a sentimentalist of a robust and virile type. You
are not unbraced in reading him. On the contrary, you feel
him to be tonic. Richter is full of ozone, moral, but especially intellectual. He possesses the stimulating value of
difficulty. It is impossible to read him in a lax and languid

mental mood. You have to gird up the loins of your mind to understand him. His conceptions are unexpected and extraordinary. They still take you by surprise. You cannot get used enough to Richter to calculate him beforehand. Beyond all men he has the gift to "startle and waylay." If Richter ever had a commonplace thought, or a commonplace association of thought, he had it as an awful secret to himself—he never breathed it to mortal.

Conceptions thus remote and unusual, to the very verge of unbalanced eccentricity, Richter had a vocabulary and a syntax of his own, to express. It is literally true that there was a special Richter lexicon published to explain to his fellow-countrymen the strange words—his own coining, his own compounding, or his own polarizing—employed by Richter in delivering his message to the world.

We shall of course seem to describe a not wholly pleasing writer. And a wholly pleasing writer certainly Richter is not. There is out-of-the-way beauty, but there is out-of-the-way deformity too. Grotesqueness masquerades hand-in-hand with grace everywhere through Richter's pages. You wonder that a soul capable of beauty in thought so ravishing, should be at the same time capable of ugliness so undisguised. But it is æsthetic, not ethical, ugliness of which we speak. Taste, not conscience, was wanting to Richter. He had little sense of proportion, fitness, form. He had so much material that his material mastered him. He could not reduce it to order. He produced not a cosmos, but a chaos—a chaos, however, full of every beauty save the beauty which would have transferred all into a cosmos. Richter's reason was all imagination, and his imagination was all fancy. His thoughts were images, images with winged feet. His images went, or flew, in pairs. There was first the original idea, and then its similitude. For every thing in heaven or earth had its similitude with Richter. There was never another human eye that could invariably see double like his. "Thick-coming fancies" is a phrase that seems made to describe the perpetual state of this man's brain. His couriers

9

arrived so fast that he could hardly find time to give them separate audience. They trod on one another's heels, and mixed and confused their messages in his ears. The consequence is that if—which you are half-tempted to think doubtful—Richter succeeds himself in preserving his mental balance as he writes, you at least go near to losing your mental balance as you read. You find it sheerly impossible to co-ordinate into any mutual relation of unity the discordant emotions awakened. You are enraptured with a form of beauty almost divine, developing itself unexpectedly out of the most wanton grotesque ; when, lo, while you are still wondering with delight, already that evanescent evolution has dived and disappeared in the grotesque again. You are irresistibly moved to laughter at humor incalculably droll, but your laughter has not half satisfied itself before the wizard has reversed his wand and capriciously summoned you, beyond your power of gainsaying, to weep.

But we must not linger, seeking vainly to describe what nevertheless we fear we shall as vainly seek to exemplify.

Richter's production was chiefly, perhaps exclusively, prose in form. But no prose was ever more instinct than Richter's with the spirit of poetry. His works are valuable, not for what they are, but for what they contain. Not one of them all has the merit of being an organized and beautiful whole—not one produces on the mind of the reader the effect of unity. The reason in the writer seems to have been that, as we have intimated, with all his unbounded exuberance of fancy, he lacked imagination. He saw things separately, or rather in pairs, never together as composing a "universal frame."

It did not much signify in what ostensible species of literature such a writer might choose to wreak himself upon expression. The result in any case would inevitably be the same. We should have an impetuous torrent of thoughts, sentiments, images, fancies, rolling out confusedly as from an inexhaustible fountain—or at times almost as if from a volcano in eruption. The actual fact is, that Richter's best works are "novels," of a peculiar sort. Of these *Hesperus* was the one that first made its author decisively and widely famous. *The Invisible Lodge* was an earlier success. *Titan,* however, a later book, is generally, among Germans, held to be Richter's masterpiece. From the *Titan,* accordingly, as admirably translated by Mr. C. T. Brooks, we present some specimen passages—selected with a view to exhibiting fairly both the beautiful and the ugly, of this extraordinary writer. We do not exaggerate when we say that, as for the plot, or the course of the story, in Richter's "novels," that is literally almost undiscoverable, beneath the luxuriant overgrowth of incidental thought and fancy which constantly "high overarched imbowers." The interest of story as story is nothing. It is only what is other than story that counts. For this reason, our citations, comparatively brief as they must be, need not leave Richter in any important respect, except that of quantity, unexemplified. We shall quite disregard the narrative of the *Titan ;* but that is exactly what Richter himself does, and what, moreover, every one who reads Richter in full is virtually compelled to do.

Take, for a first specimen, this sweet, benignant sigh of pensive reflection, suggested by a scene of reconciliation that has just been described:

> Verily, I have often formed the wish—and afterward made a picture out of it—that I could be present at all reconciliations in the world, because no love moves us so deeply as returning love. It must touch immortals, when they see men, the heavy laden, and often held so widely asunder by fate or by fault, how, like the Valisneria, they will tear themselves away from the marshy bottom, and ascend into a fairer element; and then, in the freer upper air, how they will conquer the distance between their hearts and come together.

Having read now a note which Richter subjoins, turn back and read again the foregoing extract. Here is the subjoined note:

> The female Valisneria lies rolled up under the water, out of which it lifts its bud, to bloom in the open air; the male then loosens itself from the too short stalk and swims to her with its dry blossom-dust.

Richter made wide forays into all literature and all science, and he never came back without "mountains of prey" on his shoulders. The allusion to the "Valisneria" is characteristic, alike of his learning, of his fancy, and of his taste. His method was to make vast scrap-book anthologies from his reading, and he thus had always at hand resource of the most varied illustration. We may as well advise our readers that fondness for Richter is with nearly all persons an appetite to be acquired, if it is ever to be possessed at all. In our own individual opinion, it is an appetite good to possess, notwithstanding that to acquire the appetite will cost some patience, and afterward, too, cost some leisure—more leisure, in fact, than most people can command—to indulge it and to profit properly from indulging it.

Albano, alternatively called Zesara (Cæsara), is the young hero of the *Titan*. He strides into the story, radiant with youth and health and beauty. Albano, indeed, was overcharged with energy, and to such a degree that he was " weary " with it ! For such is the extravagant representation of Richter. Let us introduce the passage in which this representation is made. It will sufficiently exemplify that excess which is one of the traits of this author:

Zesara had tasted only three glasses of wine; but the must of his thick, hot blood fermented under it mightily. The day grew more and more into a Daphnian and Delphic grove, in whose whispering and steamy thicket he lost himself deeper and deeper; the sun hung in the blue like a white glistening snow-ball; the glaciers [the scene is near the Alps] cast their silvery glances down into the green; from distant clouds it thundered occasionally, as if spring were rolling along in his triumphal chariot far away toward us at the north; the living glow of the climate and the hour, and the holy fire of two raptures, the remembered and the expected, warmed to life all his powers. And now that fever of young health seized upon him in which it always seemed to him as if a particular heart beat in every limb; the lungs and the heart are heavy and full of blood; the breath is hot as a Harmattan wind [a wind of Africa, hot and dry, named in Italy *sirocco*], and the eye dark in its own blaze, and the limbs are weary with energy. In this overcharge of the electrical cloud, he had a peculiar passion for destroying. When younger, he often relieved himself by rolling fragments of rock to a summit and letting them roll down, or by running on the full gallop till his breath grew *longer*, or most surely by hurting himself with a penknife (as he had heard of Cardan's doing), and even bleeding himself a little occasionally. [Cardan was an eccentric Italian physician of the sixteenth century.]

Richter thus prepares his reader for an actual resort in practice to blood-letting, about to be attributed on the present occasion to his hero. We may justly extenuate the whimsical extravagance of such a conception on Richter's part, by remembering that he lived in a time when phlebotomy, as a remedial measure, was habitually employed by physicians. Poor Schiller had his blood therapeutically thinned to the point of exhaustion in this way. From the *Titan* once more— but we need to explain that young Albano was now alone in a place that reminded him tenderly of his mother long dead :

He scratched himself, but accidentally too deep, and with a cool and pleasant exaltation of his more lightly-breathing nature, he watched the red fountain of his arm in the setting sun, and became, as if a burden had fallen off from him, calm, sober, still, and tender. He thought of his departed mother, whose love remained now forever unrequited. Ah, gladly would he have poured out this blood for her.

Let us see the Alps with the passionate Italian eyes of Albano. The youth has made his approach to those mountains from the other side, from Italy. The fancy strikes him that he will take in the great panoroma all at once, and not part by part ; in Richter's phrase, it shall be " one single draining draught from Nature's horn of plenty." They reach, climbing—Albano and his companions—the proper terrace for commanding the view, and then one says to Albano, " Now ! now ! " but, " No," says Albano, still luxurious in his desire for the brim, the rounding, goblet, ere he drink at all; " wait till the sun strikes it." Albano had bandaged his eyes to secure himself from seeing too soon. Now Richter:

At that moment the morning wind flung up the sunlight gleaming through the dark twigs, and it flamed free on the summits, and Dian snatched off the bandage, and said, " Look round ! " " O God ! " cried he with a shriek of ecstasy, as all the gates of the new heaven flew open, and the Olympus of nature, with its thousand reposing gods, stood around him. What a world ! There stood the Alps, like brother giants of the Old World, linked together, far away in the past, holding high up over against the sun the shining shields of the glaciers. The giants wore blue girdles of forest, and at their feet lay hills and vineyards, and through the aisles and arches of grape-clusters the morning winds played with cascades as with watered-silk ribbons, and the liquid brimming mir. ror of the lake [Lago Maggiore] hung down by the ribbons from the mountains, and they fluttered down into the mirror, and a carved work of chestnut woods formed its frame. . . . Albano turned slowly round and round, looked into the heights, into the depths, into the sun, into the blos- soms; and on all summits burned the alarm-fires of mighty Nature, and in all depths their reflections—a creative earthquake beat like a heart under the earth and sent forth mountains and seas. . . . He took . . . the hands of his friends and pressed them to their breasts, that he might not be obliged to speak. The magnificent universe had painfully expanded, and then bliss- fully overflowed his great breast; and now, when he opened his eyes, like an eagle, wide and full, upon the sun, and when the blinding brightness hid the earth, and he began to be lonely, and the earth became smoke and the sun a soft, white world, which gleamed only around the margin—then did his whole, full soul, like a thunder-cloud, burst asunder and burn and weep, and from the pure, white sun his mother looked upon him, and in the fire and smoke of the earth his father and his life stood veiled.

Silently he went down the terraces, often passing his hand across his moist eyes to wipe away the dazzling shadow which danced on all the summits and all the steps.

If you do not like the foregoing passage at first, try reading it again, and yet again—perhaps even once more, after that. Do you still not like it ? Then you do not like Richter—at least, not in his descriptive dithyrambics; for, place him in the presence of a noble aspect of nature to be described, and such as the foregoing displays him is Richter. The sentiment of nature, which was almost nothing to the ancient Greek and Roman world, finds here an expression ardent beyond the ardor of Rousseau; and Rousseau's flame it probably was that kindled Richter's. Truth requires us now to add that the Alps thus described by him Richter had never seen, except through the eyes of others.

Contagiously inspiring is the vehement moral indignation of which Richter on occasion is capable. Read the passage

we next offer, considering the while whose portrait it prob
ably is that, under an alias, is therein drawn, and you will
not wonder that Goethe—of whom Mr. Lowell well said that
his "poetic sense was a Minotaur" (the Minotaur was a fabu-
lous monster that yearly devoured seven maidens)—you will
not wonder, we say, that Goethe did not like Richter.
"Painted egotism and unpainted skepticism," Richter declared that he found in Weimar ; and what was Weimar?
Goethe might fitly have used Louis Fourteenth's formula,
and claimed, "It is I." Patriot, too, enough, as well as Puritan enough, was Richter, to say, to the deep displeasure of
Goethe—who, of course, could not but take to himself what
was so manifestly his own—that the times needed in Germany,
"not a Propertius, but a Tyrtæus—" that is, not a pander
poet of luxury and licentiousness, but a poet with trumpet
and with bugle voice summoning to freedom and to virtue.
Richter, in the following powerful description, portrays a
character of his novel:

. . . He plunged into good and bad dissipations and amours, and afterward represented on paper or on the stage every thing that he repented
or blessed; and every representation made him grow more and more hollow,
as abysses have been left in the sun by ejected worlds. His heart could
not do without the holy sensibilities; but they were simply a new luxury,
a tonic, at best; and precisely in proportion to their height did the road
run down the more abruptly into the slough of the unholiest ones. As, in
the dramatic poet, angelically pure and filthy scenes stand in conjunction
and close succession, so in his life; he foddered, as in Surinam [alter-
native name for Dutch Guiana in South America], his hogs with pine-
apples ; like the elder giants, he had soaring wings and creeping snakes'-
feet.

Unfortunate is the female soul which loses its way, and is caught in
one of these great webs stretched out in mid-heaven ; and happy is she,
when she tears through them, unpoisoned, and merely soils her bees'-
wings. But this all-powerful fancy, this streaming love, this softness and
strength, this all-mastering coolness and collectedness, will overspread
every female Psyche with webs, if she neglects to brush away the first
threads. O that I could warn you, poor maidens, against such condors,
which fly up with you in their claws ! The heaven of our days hangs
full of these eagles. They love you not, though they think so ; because,
like the blest in Mohammed's paradise, instead of their lost arms of love,

they have only wings of fancy. They are like great streams, warm only along the shore, and in the middle cold.

Now enthusiast, now libertine in love, he ran through the alternation between ether and slime more and more rapidly, till he mixed them both. His blossoms shot up on the varnished flower-staff of the ideal, which, however, rotted, colorless, in the ground. Start with horror, but believe it—he sometimes plunged on purpose into sins and torments, in order, down there, by the pangs of remorse and humiliation, to cut into himself more deeply the oath of reformation.

That we have not misrepresented Richter's *Titan*, as being mainly a miscellany of thoughts and fancies which the story only supplies excuse for introducing, let an intercalated "Cycle" (chapter), so-called, commencing the sixth "Jubilee" (book), so-called, bear witness. From this we extract its opening paragraphs, and show them as incidental exemplification of Jean Paul's humor. Overtly humorous passages, it is very difficult to separate from the text of Richter. The truly appreciative reader learns at length to make humor the qualifying master-light of nearly all his seeing, in the pages of this writer. The title stands, in usual form, "Sixth Jubilee;" under this, as one of several sub-titles, "The Ten Persecutions of the Reader." With these "ten persecutions" only (and with these condensed) here we have need to do. There is tacit Richterian allusion to the traditional "ten persecutions," long reckoned by ecclesiastical historians, of the early Christian Church. Richter begins, after his own pregnant allusive manner, with opulent reduplication of alternative phrase—appropriate enough in the present case, since the writer's object is to represent how prolific, beyond its power to disburden itself, his mind is, in ideas of all sorts:

Postulates, apothegms, philosophems, Erasmian adages, observations of Rochefoucauld, La Bruyère, Lavater, do I in one week invent in countless numbers, more than I can in six months get rid of by bringing them into my biographical *petits soupes* as episode-dishes. Thus does the lottery-mintage of my *unprinted* manuscripts swell higher and higher every day, the more extracts and winnings I deal out to my reader therefrom in print. In this way I creep out of the world without having, while in it, said any thing. . . .

But why shall I not . . . let at least one or two lymphatic veins of my water-treasure leap up and run out? I limit myself to ten persecutions of the reader, calling my ten aphorisms thus, merely because I imagine the readers to be martyrs of their opinions, and myself the regent who converts them by force. The following aphorism, if one reckons the foregoing as the first persecution, is, I hope, the

SECOND. Nothing ... winnows our preferences and partialities better than an imitation of the same by others. For a genius there are no sharper polishing-machines and grinding-disks at hand than his apes. If, further, every one of us could see running along beside him a duplicate of himself, a complete Archimimus ["The title of a man, among the Romans, who walked behind the corpse and acted out the looks and character which the deceased had when living.—*Pers., Sat.* 3." (Richter's own note)] and re-peater in complimenting, taking off the hat, dancing, speaking, scolding, bragging, etc.; by heaven! such an exact repeating-work of our discords would make quite other people out of me and other people than we are at present. . . .

THIRD. It is easier and handier for men to flatter than to praise.

FIFTH. What makes old age so sad is, not that our joys, but that our hopes, then cease.

SEVENTH. Have compassion on poverty, but a hundred times more on impoverishment! Only the former, not the latter, makes nations and in-dividuals better.

EIGHTH. Love lessens woman's delicacy and increases man's.

LAST PERSECUTION OF THE READER. Deluded and darkened man . . . thinks there is no further evil beyond that which he has immediately to overcome; and forgets that after the victory the new situation brings a new struggle.

Thus does the reader vainly hope now, after having stood out ten per-secutions, to ride into the haven of the story, and there to lead a peaceable life, free from the troubled one of my characters; but can any spiritual or worldly arm, then, protect him against scattered similes? etc., etc. . . .

Richter's pathos is the pathos of reflection and of sentiment, rather than of situation or of action. It is hardly ever quite pure; almost always there is some intermingling of the hu-morous, or, it may well chance, even of the grotesque. The following passage—wherewith we take leave of the *Titan*—may be accepted as a fairly representative specimen. Rich-ter—with sincere sympathy, but with sympathy ever ready to relieve itself by kindly humor—is dwelling, in connection with his hero Albano, on the glorious heyday of youth, that morning-time of life in which all things seem possible, to the sense of untried omnipotence within the soul. He says :

> Blissful, blissful time! thou hast long since gone by! O, the years in which man reads, and makes, his first poems and systems, when the spirit creates and blesses its first worlds, and when, full of fresh morning-thoughts, it sees the first constellations of truth come up bringing an eternal splendor, and stand ever before the longing heart which has enjoyed them, and to which time, by and by, offers only astronomical newspapers and refraction-tables on the morning stars, only antiquated truths and rejuvenated lies! O, then was man, like a fresh, thirsty child, suckled and reared with the milk of wisdom; at a later period he is only cured with it, as a withered, skeptical, hectic patient! But thou canst, indeed, never come back again, glorious season of *first love* for the truth! . . .
>
> Into this golden age of his [Albano's] heart fell also his acquaintance with Rousseau and Shakespeare, of whom the former exalted him above his century, and the latter above this life.

Jean Paul wrote a book on education, under the title of *Levana.* This has been translated, and the translation is now published as a volume in their useful series of " educational classics " by D. C. Heath & Co. The gold of the book is not without its alloy. There is plenty of whimsey and paradox in Richter's educational advice.

Prefixed to the treatise on education in the English volume, appropriately appears Richter's " autobiography." This fragment is not, as a whole, a specially fine felicity of the author's hand. Writing " lectures," as " professor," on the " history of himself " (such is his humorous form of conception for his autobiography), he did his work under urgency from others, and under protest of reluctance on his own part. Passages, however, are exquisitely beautiful. The most exquisitely beautiful of all is perhaps the one with which the fragment closes. In it, Jean Paul, drawn into fond reminiscence, describes tenderly the season of his own first communion. Their first communion, among Lutherans, as among Roman Catholics, is a great occasion for children. Jean Paul's father was a minister, and the boy at home was steeped in an atmosphere of religion. Very touchingly he adverts to the custom requiring the young candidate to make, the day before his first approach to the altar, the round of kindred and neighbors, in suit of forgiveness for all faults committed in the past. Richter :

How often did I go to the garret before the Confession Saturday, and kneel down to repent and atone! And how sweet it was on the Confession day itself to ask forgiveness with stammering lips and overflowing heart for one's faults from all the dear ones, parents and teachers, and thus to atone for them and absolve one's self!

On this evening there came, too, a mild, light, clear heaven of peace over my soul, an unutterable, never-returning blessedness, in feeling myself quite clean, purified, and freed from sin; in having made with God and man a joyful, far-reaching peace; and still, from these evening hours of mild and warm soul-rest, I looked onward to the heavenly enthusiasm and rapture at the altar next morning.

O blessed time! when one has stripped off the unclean past, and stands pure and white, free and fresh, in the present, and thus steps forth courageously into the future. But to whom but children can this time return ? . . .

On Sunday morning the boys and girls, adorned for the sacrificial altar, met at the parsonage for the solemn entrance into the church amid singing and bell-ringing. All this, together with the festive attire and the nosegays, and the darkened fragrant birch-trees, both at home and in the church, became for the young soul a powerful breeze in its outspread wings, which were already raised and in motion. Even during the long sermon the heart expanded with its fire, and inward struggles were carried on against all thoughts which were worldly or not sufficiently holy.

At length I received the bread from my father and the cup from my purely loved teacher, . . . and my rapture rose to a physical lightning-feeling of miraculous union.

I thus left the altar with a clear blue infinite heaven in my heart; this heaven revealed itself to me by an unlimited, stainless, tender love which I now felt for all, all mankind. To this day I have preserved within my heart, with loving and youthful freshness, the remembrance of the happiness when I looked on the church-members with love, and took them all to my innermost heart. The maiden companions at the holy altar with their bridal wreaths became not only dearer, but also more holy, to me as the brides of Christ, and I included them all in such a wide, pure love that even my beloved Katharina, as far as I can remember, was not otherwise loved than the rest.

The whole earth remained for me throughout the day an unlimited love-repast, and the whole tissue and web of life appeared to me to be an Æolian or ethereal harp played by the breath of love.

Jean Paul, in a subsequent paragraph, supplies the means of making an important discrimination. The ardent feelings which he has so vividly described were by no means the feelings of a strictly orthodox evangelical Christian. On the contrary, they were sentiments which pagan great men were as capable of stirring in his soul as was Jesus of Nazareth. Richter says :

> This spring festivity of the heart returned later in the years of youth, but only as a quiet, serene Sabbath—when for the first time the great old stoical spirits of Plutarch, Epictetus, and Antoninus arose and appeared before me, and freed me from all the pains of this earth, and all anger; but from this one Sabbath I hope I have gathered together a whole year of Sabbaths, or am able to make up that which may still be wanting.

The most intensely loved of German authors, to his own countrymen, is Richter. The most intensely loved, we say ; for Schiller is the one loved most widely. The reason, in Richter's case at least, is clear ; for he himself loved much. He was like gentle Saint Francis of Assisi, in loving, not his fellow-men only, but his fellow-creatures all, of earth, of air, of sea. Coleridge's lines, if to any, would apply to Richter,

> He prayeth well who loveth well
> Both man and bird and beast.

The great manly heart in him was as soft as a woman's—and as sweet and as chaste as a virgin's.

It was a long, long struggle for poor Jean Paul, before he " won his way upward and prevailed " as author. After a painfully impoverished experience at the university, he lived with his mother—become a widow now—and shared her abject poverty. In that one room which was her abode— seated there amid the din of unavoidable household occupation surrounding him—the pertinacious youth wrote painful reams of manuscript that had no market value. But he felt called to authorship, and he would starve at that rather than thrive at other work. Finally he wrote *The Invisible Lodge*. Probably he never experienced a purer joy than when he poured into his mother's lap the golden ducats paid him, in first installment, by the publisher of that production. The struggle was mainly over, and now the triumph began. With *Hesperus* published, Jean Paul became a rage. Never, perhaps, in the annals of letters was there a personal victory greater. For the man, too, was suddenly as popular as the author. He walked through the fatherland as in a royal progress, as in an endless Roman triumph. The houses of nobles, the palaces of kings, were thrown open to him. Women, women of rank and of fame, went wild over Jean Paul. Every thing feminine in Germany seemed to cast itself in offer and in worship at the conqueror's feet. One brilliant woman seriously, and even urgently, proposed, by means of a divorce, to get herself free of her husband, that she might marry the author of *Hesperus*. Her importunity proved vain. A later case is that of a pure and noble young girl who, never having seen Richter, loved him so from his books that she pined in a vain desire toward him, which finally turned back on her own poor heart and drove her to suicide. Richter was then already a married man of fifty. He had answered the child's letters to him with a mild, sweet wisdom of fatherly counsel, which sets his character in the fairest and most engaging light. It was truly astonishing how this masculine intellectual Aphrodite, this resistless Apollo, seemed unconsciously to "conquer all with love." The most singular thing about it, however—and the one thing admirable—was that Jean Paul, according to the universal testimony, remained throughout as impeccably chaste in conduct as an angel of light. Such a man was, evidently, no natural fellow-citizen of Goethe. After Goethe, during his own life-time, had published his autobiography, entitling it, *Poetry and Truth out of My Life* (so to release himself from the obligation of faithful adherence to fact), Richter, with perhaps a needless slant at this book, styled his own account of himself, *Truth out of My Life;* whereupon Goethe, with what was meant to be the extreme of severity, remarked, " Jean Paul has written *Truth out of My Life*—as if truth from the life of such a man could be any other than that the author was a Philistine." (" Philistine" was a term of opprobrium implying " vulgar, sordid fellow.") It was a disguised confession from Goethe of the hostility which he could not but feel toward a man so profoundly different in character and in life from himself.

This relation of instinctive mutual repulsion between Goethe and Richter did not at once establish itself. It was but the final inevitable result jointly of deep intellectual and of deep moral antipathy. Herder and Richter were two by themselves ; another two, also by themselves, were Goethe and Schiller. These two pairs of men were two fundamentally, though not openly, hostile alliances, offensive and defensive.

Richter himself may now tell us how it seemed to him to be at length, by way of change, successful, famous, and happy. He writes to his life-long, dearest of friends, Otto. He dates from that Weimar which Wieland had caused to be called the " Athens of Germany," and which now Goethe, as resident, made yet more widely illustrious. The natural openness of Richter's heart is set boundlessly wide and free, both by his new sensations of joy and by his sense of perfect confidence in his friend :

> God saw yesterday upon his earth a happy mortal, and that was I. Ah, I was so happy that I thought of Nemesis, and Herder consoled me with the *Deus Averruncus*. [Nemesis was the goddess of revenge, anciently supposed to follow great good fortune with a visitation of evil. The *Deus Averruncus* was a divinity supposed able, on the contrary, to avert impending calamity.] I cannot put off writing till I can send a letter. I must say something.

Knebel, chamberlain to the Duchess of Weimar, showed Richter polite attentions. The two men were walking together when (Richter's letter now again):

> Knebel said, " How gloriously it all happens ; here comes Herder, his wife, and the two children." We went to meet him, and under the free heaven I threw myself into his arms. I could scarcely speak for joy, and he could not embrace me enough. As I looked around Knebel's eyes were almost moist. With Herder I am now as familiar as with you. . . . I wish it were possible to tell you all without blushing. He praises all

my works, even the *Greenland Lawsuits.* . . . He says, "Whenever he reads the *Hesperus* he is for two days unfit for business." . . .

In the evening we supped with the Kalb. [It was Madame von Kalb who afterward wished to be divorced that she might marry Richter.] . . . I made as many satires as at Hof [his mother's home, and Otto's]—in short, I was as unrestrained and as lively as I am with you. By heaven! I have become courageous, and could trust myself to talk with twenty gentlemen, and yet more, with the burgomaster and all his kindred.

How much is here pathetico-humorously implied of Jean Paul's former humble estate ! But there was a disturbing disillusion. Weimar had previously won in Richter's eyes " a glory from its being far." He says:

I have not told you one third part ; but the bitterest drop, Otto, swims in my Heidelberg cup of joy. What Jean Paul wins, humanity loses in his eyes. Ah! my ideal of great men !

The expression " Heidelberg cup of joy" alludes to the celebrated tun for wine, in its day the largest ever built, still to be seen in Heidelberg Castle.

Five days later, June 17, 1796, Richter writes again:

I have lived twenty years in Weimar in a few days. . . . I am happy, Otto, wholly happy, not merely beyond all expectation, but beyond all description, and I lack nothing in the whole world but you, only you!

What now follows will show the peculiar awe, to which not even the free spirit of Richter could at first rise superior, inspired by the presence and influence of Goethe:

On the second day I threw away my foolish prejudices in favor of great authors. They are like other people. Here, every one knows that they are like the earth, which looks from a distance, from heaven, like a shining moon, but when the foot is upon it it is found to be made of *boue de Paris* [Paris mud]. An opinion concerning Herder, Wieland, or Goethe is as much contested as any other. Who would believe that the three watch-towers of our literature avoid and dislike each other? I will never again bend myself anxiously before any *great* man, only before the virtuous. Under this impression, I went timidly to meet Goethe. Every one had described him as cold to every thing upon the earth. Madame von Kalb said, he no longer admires any thing, not even himself. Every word is ice ! Curiosities merely warm the fibres of his heart. Therefore I asked Knebel to petrify or encrust me by some mineral spring, that I might present myself to him like a statue or a fossil. Madame von Kalb advised me above all things to be cold and self-possessed, and I went without warmth, merely from curiosity. His house, palace rather, pleased me; it is the only one in Weimar in the Italian style—with such steps! A Pantheon full of pictures and statues. Fresh anxiety oppressed my breast! At last the god entered, cold, one-syllabled, without accent. "The French are drawing toward Paris," said Knebel. "Hm!" said the god. His face is massive and animated, his eye a ball of light. But, at last, the conversation led from the campaign to art, publications, etc., and Goethe was himself. His conversation is not so rich and flowing as Herder's, but sharp-toned, penetrating, and calm. At last he read, that is, played for us, an unpublished poem, in which his heart impelled the flame through the outer crust of ice, so that he pressed the hand of the enthusiastic Jean Paul. (It was my face, not my voice, for I said not a word.) He did it again when we took leave, and pressed me to call again. By heaven! we will love each other! He considers his poetic course as closed. His reading is like deep-toned thunder, blended with soft, whispering rain-drops. There is nothing like it.

The same letter, that of June 17, tells of an interview with Schiller. The adjective used by Richter to characterize this great and popular poet, will probably surprise most readers. Richter's language implies that Schiller's personal presence was generally felt on first approach to be repellent:

I went yesterday to see the stony Schiller, from whom, as from a precipice, all strangers spring back. His form is worn, severely powerful, but angular. He is full of sharp, cutting power, but without love. His conversation is nearly as excellent as his writings. As I brought a letter from Goethe he was unusually pleasant; he would make me a fellow-contributor to the *Hören* a [periodical], and would give me a naturalization act in Jena.

For a moment, then, Jean Paul was with the circle of Goethe and Schiller; but he was never, for a moment, of that circle. It was soon after his return to Hof that he wrote to Knebel those words which cut so to the quick through the usually impenetrable mail of Goethe: "In such stormy times we need a Tyrtæus rather than a Propertius." Their difference in patriotic feeling worked as strongly as did their difference in intellectual and moral sentiment, among the things that held Richter and Goethe asunder. Richter was a patriot and Goethe was a lover of culture.

Richter, still unmarried, though thirty-five years old, was in due course attracted to Berlin. Here he was received with measureless welcome. The queen was his friend. The whole court, therefore, was of course at his service. "So much hair has been begged of me," he writes, "that if I were to make it a traffic I could live as well from the outside of my cranium as from what is inside it." At Berlin he met his fate, a welcome one and a fortunate, in becoming acquainted with the lovely and accomplished woman who was to be his wife. The union was, on both sides, very happy. Whoever wishes to read a fairly full sketch of the life of this most individual and most interesting man, should endeavor to find a biography written or compiled from various sources by Mrs. E. Buckminster Lee. Mrs. Lee writes in a spirit of contagious sympathy with her subject, delightful to the reader.

Jean Paul was a son of Anak in strength of health. But there came an end of this—to him, as there comes to all. He had loved to study and work out of doors. When the time arrived—and it arrived early for so stalwart a man—that he had to shut himself up and guard himself against the weather, the change was a marked one, and it boded the end as nigh. The loss of a son, cut off in young manhood, broke the father's heart. He still worked, but the spring of hope and joy in work had failed. When he wrote, he wrote with his eyes streaming tears over the memory of his son. From this cause, or from some cause, his sight was impaired. Gradually he became quite blind. Amid affectionate ministrations from wife and kindred and friends, he passed thus a lingering night of darkness, helpless, but pathetically gentle and lovely in his helplessness, till he died. They buried him by torchlight, the manuscript of his last work, still unfinished— a tractate on the immortality of the soul—borne, a symbol, on his coffin. But the tears of a nation that loved the man as well as the author made an amber to embalm him for immortality. There had ceased a German such as never was before, such as never would be after. It was Jean Paul the Only!

10

VIII.

INTERLUDE OF POETS.

RICHTER, with whom we have just done dealing, is customarily, by his countrymen, reckoned a "poet"—this, although the form of his production was prose, not verse. But Richter's writing, even if you consider it poetry, is not easy reading; and the same is true of Herder's—"poem," though, with Richter, you consider that great author to be.

In the last two chapters, accordingly, our readers may have found their task a trifle serious. A change, perhaps, will be grateful—a change, if not exactly "from grave to gay," at least from grave to less grave. Let us interrupt the regular succession of name to name, in our list of the greater classic German authors, and, "so to interpose a little ease," listen now, for a while, to the mingling voices of some German writers whom we may set down as poets, without putting the word within marks of quotation. What we hear will be, "not from the grand old masters, not from the bards sublime," but from a select few of those lesser brethren of the tuneful choir—and of such in German literature there are many—who have sung, it may be, barely a single song or two that has caught and held the ear of the generations. We shall thus find opportunity to catch a few sweet tones, at least, descending from the Christian hymnody of the Germans—a rich and varied music, when heard in full choir, constituting one of the best glories of the German Parnassus.

We begin with Hans Sachs (1494–1576). Hans Sachs was a shoemaker, but he disregarded the proverb and went beyond his last. He became what is called a master-singer (*meistersinger*). By this is meant that he attached himself to a regularly organized society, or guild, of men who made it a business to manufacture verses. Such manufacture, in those old days, went on at a redoubtable rate among Germans. The product was good or bad, of course, much according to the original gift, or lack of gift, that belonged to the particular singer. Hans Sachs was a natural poet, and he made a successful craftsman in verse accordingly. He was voluminous in production, having, to full measure, that seldom-wanting attribute of true genius, fecundity. His quantity, indeed, was so great that his quality could hardly fail to be comparatively less. When he had written poetry fifty-two years, he had turned out more than six thousand two hundred separate pieces, classified as follows: master-songs, four thousand and upward; two hundred and eight comedies and tragedies; near two thousand "merry tales," dialogues, proverbs, fables, together with seventy-three songs, devotional and other. All this in verse; and he had written prose besides.

Hans Sachs was a Protestant, with Luther. He praised the great reformer in an allegorical tale, which he entitled *The Nightingale of Wittenberg.* The nightingale, of course, is Luther, who lures the listening sheep, fallen among ravening beasts of prey, to a lovely flowery meadow where grass is green and waters are still. The pope appears in the poem, under the figure of a devouring lion.

Hans Sachs's "merry tales" are his best and most characteristic productions. These have a quality of homely humor which is very flavorous. Hans Sachs deals with things sacred in a spirit of freedom which, to the modern sense, might well seem little short of sheer irreverence. Take the following for a sufficient example. It is the story of *Saint Peter and the Goat.* Saint Peter has hinted to the Almighty that things go rather awry down in the world, and offered, with the divine permission, to set them to rights. At that very moment there presents herself a peasant girl, complaining that she has her hands more than full with a hard day's work to do, and in the bargain a troublesome goat to mind. The Lord at once turns over this affair to Peter, and Peter experimentally undertakes the care of the goat—with result described as follows in Hans Sachs's verse, translated by Gostwick and Harrison—we trust to Professor Hosmer's citation:

> The young goat had a playful mind,
> And never liked to be confined;
> The apostle, at a killing pace,
> Followed the goat in desperate chase;
> Over the hills and among the briars
> The goat runs on and never tires,
> While Peter, behind, on the grassy plain,
> Runs on, panting and sighing in vain.
> All day, beneath the scorching sun,
> The good apostle had to run,
> Till evening came; the goat was caught,
> And safely to the Master brought.
> Then, with a smile, to Peter said
> The Lord: "Well, friend, how have you sped?
> If such a task your powers has tried,
> How could you keep the world so wide?"
> Then Peter, with his toil distressed,
> His folly with a sigh confessed.
> "No, Master, 'tis for me no play
> To rule one goat for one short day;
> It must be infinitely worse
> To regulate the universe."

It would hardly seem possible that, from the same genius which produced the foregoing, there could proceed so perfectly decorous, and withal so genuinely simple and hearty, a devotional inspiration as the following, presented in the way of Hans Sachs's farewell to our readers. We give four only out of the nine stanzas contained in the hymn:

> Why art thou thus cast down, my heart?
> Why troubled, why dost mourn apart,
> O'er naught but earthly wealth?
> Trust in thy God, be not afraid,
> He is thy Friend who all things made.
>
> Dost think thy prayers he doth not heed?
> He knows full well what thou dost need,
> And heaven and earth are his;
> My father and my God, who still
> Is with my soul in every ill.

Since thou my God and Father art,
I know thy faithful, loving heart
Will ne'er forget thy child.
See, I am poor, I am but dust,
On earth is none whom I can trust.

The rich man in his wealth confides,
But in my God my trust abides;
Laugh as ye will, I hold
This one thing fast that he hath taught:
Who trusts in God shall want for naught.

The foremost hymn-writer in the German language is, by common consent, Paul Gerhardt (1606—1676). A large part of his life was passed amid the storm and distress of the Thirty Years' War. He was a man of steady adherence to principle, and in his case the hymns of the poet may, with more confidence than generally is wise in such assumptions, be taken to reflect the character of the Christian. Gerhardt's hymns are often almost more religious poems, than hymns. Lyrical they are indeed, but they run on to length beyond what, according to our own ordinary standards, is proper for pieces that are to be sung continuously through. For example, the full text of the original piece of Gerhardt from which, translated by Wesley, a section is cut out to make the familiar hymn, beginning, "Give to the winds thy fears," extends to the measure of sixty-four lines. The stanzas in one of Gerhardt's hymns will generally all of them be good; but often it seems as if there were too many of them. One stanza goes on echoing another, without apparent progress of thought. Such, in fact, tends to be the prevailing character of German hymns in general. They possess the merit of unity, but, with that, the demerit of unity too much insisted on, in rounds of repetition. We confine ourselves to a single hymn of Gerhardt's, ninety-six lines long. The hymn is throughout so very good, that in this instance the length is hardly excessive. We retrench, however, one half —with sincere regret. Our translator, for all these German hymns, is Miss Catherine Winkworth, who has two volumes of translation from German psalmody. This English lady translates consummately well:

If God be on my side,
　Then let who will oppose,
For oft ere now to him I cried,
　And he hath quelled my foes.
If Jesus be my Friend,
　If God doth love me well,
What matters all my foes intend,
　Though strong they be and fell?

.　　.　　.　　.

His Spirit in me dwells,
　O'er all my mind he reigns;
All care and sadness he dispels,
　And soothes away all pains.
He prospers day by day
　His work within my heart,
Till I have strength and faith to say,
　Thou God my Father art!

.　　.　　.　　.

He whispers in my breast
　Sweet words of holy cheer,
How he who seeks in God his rest
　Shall ever find him near;
How God hath built above
　A city fair and new,
Where eye and heart shall see and prove
　What faith has counted true.

.　　.　　.　　.

The world may fail and flee,
　Thou standest fast forever;
Not fire, or sword, or plague, from thee
　My trusting soul shall sever.
No hunger, and no thirst,
　No poverty or pain,
Let mighty princes do their worst,
　Shall fright me back again.

No joys that angels know,
　No throne or wide-spread fame,
No love or loss, no fear or woe,
　No grief of heart or shame—

Man cannot aught conceive,
　Of pleasure or of harm,
That e'er could tempt my soul to leave
　Her refuge in thine arm.

My heart for gladness springs,
　It cannot more be sad,
For very joy it laughs and sings,
　Sees naught but sunshine glad.
The sun that glads mine eyes
　Is Christ the Lord I love,
I sing for joy of that which lies
　Stored up for us above.

We next present a hymn bearing date 1631, one which goes by the name of "Gustavus Adolphus's Battle-song:"

Fear not, O little flock, the foe
Who madly seeks your overthrow;
　Dread not his rage and power;
What though your courage sometimes faints?
His seeming triumph o'er God's saints
　Lasts but a little hour.

Be of good cheer; your cause belongs
To him who can avenge your wrongs;
　Leave it to him our Lord.
Though hidden yet from all our eyes,
He sees the Gideon who shall rise
　To save us, and his word.

As true as God's own word is true,
Not earth nor hell with all their crew
　Against us shall prevail;
A jest and byword are they grown;
God is with us, we are his own,
　Our victory cannot fail.

Amen, Lord Jesus, grant our prayer!
Great Captain, now thine arm make bare;
　Fight for us once again!
So shall the saints and martyrs raise
A mighty chorus to thy praise,
　World without end. Amen.

Gustavus Adolphus often sang this hymn with his army. He sang it for the last time before that battle of Lutzen in which he fell. It is proper to say that there is a Swedish form of this hymn, which the Swedish monarch himself is said to have inspired to his chaplain. Which is prior in time, the German or the Swedish form of the hymn, seems uncertain.

It is pleasing to know that, in 1653, a royal lady, the Electress of Brandenburg, had the heart and the brain to contribute to the cheer of her time by such a lyric as the following; we omit four stanzas:

> Jesus my Redeemer lives,
>   Christ my trust is dead no more;
> In the strength this knowledge gives
>   Shall not all my fears be o'er;
> Calm, though death's long night be fraught
> Still with many an anxious thought?

> I shall see him with these eyes,
>   Him whom I shall surely know;
> Not another shall I rise,
>   With his love this heart shall glow;
> Only there shall disappear
> Weakness in and round me here.

> Body, be thou of good cheer,
>   In thy Saviour's care rejoice;
> Give not place to gloom and fear;
>   Dead, thou yet shalt know his voice,
> When the final trump is heard,
> And the deaf, cold grave is stirred,

> Laugh to scorn then death and hell,
>   Laugh to scorn the gloomy grave;
> Caught into the air to dwell
>   With the Lord who comes to save,
> We shall trample on our foes,
> Mortal weakness, fear, and woes.

A sacred singer of a somewhat different type, was Johann Scheffler (1624–1677), best known as Angelus. Angelus became in the end a Roman Catholic; but in such a hymn as the following, which is his, we Christians, all of us, Protestant and Catholic alike, may joyfully join. We take the first five stanzas only, composing just one half of the hymn. It comes near being a case in which the half is more than the whole:

Nothing fair on earth I see
But I straightway think on thee;
Thou art fairest in my eyes,
Source in whom all beauty lies!

When I see the reddening dawn,
And the golden sun of morn,
Quickly turns this heart of mine
To thy glorious form divine.

Oft I think upon thy light
When the gray morn breaks the night;
Think what glories lie in thee,
Light of all eternity!

When I see the moon arise
'Mid heaven's thousand golden eyes,
Then I think, more glorious far
Is the Maker of yon star.

Or I think in spring's sweet hours,
When the fields are gay with flowers,
As their varied hues I see,
What must their Creator be!

. . . . . .

Of the same school in hymnody with Roman Catholic Angelus, is Protestant Gerhardt Tersteegen (1697–1769), a layman, and a business man. The following hymn, bearing date 1731, well expresses Tersteegen's sweet spirit and his favorite filial aspiration; we leave out four stanzas:

Dear soul, couldst thou become a child,
While yet on earth, meek, undefiled,
Then God himself were ever near,
And paradise around thee here.

A child cares naught for gold or treasure,
Nor fame nor glory yield him pleasure;
In perfect truth, he asketh not
If rich or poor shall be his lot.

Little he recks of dignity,
Nor prince nor monarch feareth he;
Strange that a child so weak and small
Is oft the boldest of us all!

He hath not skill to utter lies,
His very soul is in his eyes;
Single his aim in all, and true,
And apt to praise what others do.

No questions dark his spirits vex,
No faithless doubts his soul perplex;
Simply from day to day he lives,
Content with what the present gives.

   .   o   .   .   .   .   o

For strange concerns he careth naught;
What others do, although were wrought
Before his eyes the worst offense,
Stains not his tranquil innocence.

   .   .   .   .   .   .

Spirit of childhood! loved of God,
By Jesus' Spirit now bestowed;
How often have I longed for thee;
O, Jesus, form thyself in me!

And help me to become a child
While yet on earth, meek, undefiled,
That I may find God always near,
And Paradise around me here.

Tersteegen is reckoned the best German hymn-writer of the pietistic school to which he belongs.

We show one hymn of Gellert's, a name which our readers will remember from mention in previous pages as that of a man possessing considerable importance in German literary history. Gellert (Christian Fürchtegott, 1715–1769) had the gift, not common among his countrymen, of brevity. The following rather dry, didactic, and formal, but sound and sensible, piece is a fair specimen of Gellert's religious hymns:

Who keepeth not God's word, yet saith,
  "I know the Lord is wrong,"
In him is not that blessed faith
  Through which the truth is strong;

But he who hears and keeps the word,
Is not of this world, but of God.

The faith his word hath caused to shine
    Will kindle love in thee;
More wouldst thou KNOW of things divine?
    Deeper thy LOVE must be;
True faith not only gives thee light,
But strength to love and do the right.

Jesus hath washed away our sin,
    And we are children now;
Who feels such hope as this within,
    To evil cannot bow;
Rather with Christ all scorn endure,
So we be like our Father, pure!

For he doth please the Father well
    Who simply can obey;
In him the love of God doth dwell
    Who steadfast keeps his way;
A daily active life of love,
Such fruits a living faith must prove.

He is in God, and God in him,
    Who still abides in love;
'Tis love that makes the cherubim
    Obey and praise above;
For God is love, the loveless heart
Hath in his life and joy no part.

Lower in time than Gellert we need not come, in exhibiting the religious lyrics of Germany. We had already, before reaching him, passed the great age of German hymn-writing.

From sacred song to secular, we may very naturally make the transition in Gellert. Gellert was a fabulist in verse— the German Lafontaine, we might, approximating the fact, pronounce him—though the poet himself, to Frederick the Great, disclaimed being an imitator of any model. The following version of one of Gellert's fables in metre, we take from W. Taylor's *Survey of German Poetry:*

Her vernal song a nightingale began,
Hoping to please the pride of creatures, man.

Boys, who were playing in a meadow near,
Pursued their bustling sport with heedless ear.
Meanwhile a cuckoo, from a neighboring tree,
Exclaims "Cuckoo;" the boys repeat with glee.
They laugh, they point at him, they join his song,
And ten times over his short tune prolong.
The cuckoo turns to Philomela's rest,
"You must allow they like my singing best."

Soon came Damætas, with his lovely bride.
The cuckoo calls.   They pass with sulky pride.
Not long the nightingale felt envy's pang;
So sweet, so shrill, so variously, she sang,
That Phillis took a seat upon the bank,
And looked aloof, with glistening eye, her thank.
"Now, prater (said the nightingale), perceive
How pure the recompense my lays receive;
The still approval of one silent tear
Is more than vulgar shouts that rend the ear."

Ramler (Karl Wilhelm, 1725–1798) was the German Horace. He both translated his Roman master and imitated him. Here is one of Ramler's imitations of Horace, translated into English by W. Taylor. "My Kleist," a personal allusion quite in the Horatian manner, means a brother poet of the lyrist, the author of a poem, celebrated in its day, on *Spring*. Kleist was the German Thomson. Ramler's ode following is inscribed *Winter:*

Storms ride the air, and veil the sky in clouds,
And chase the thundering streams athwart the land;
Bare stand the woods; the social linden's leaves
          Far o'er the valleys whirl.

The vine—a withered stalk; but why bewail
The godlike vine?   Friends, come and quaff its blood.
Let Autumn with his emptied horn retire;
          Bid fir-crowned Winter hail!

He decks the flood with adamantine shield,
Which laughs to scorn the shafts of day. Amazed
The tenants of the wood new blossoms view:
          Strange lilies strew the ground.

No more in tottering gondolas the brides
Tremble ; on gliding cars they boldly scud;
Hid in her fir-clad neck the favorite's hand
    Asks an unneeded warmth.

No more like fishes plunge the bathing boys;
On steel-wing'd shoes they skim the hardened wave;
The spouse of Venus in the glittering blade
    The lightning's swiftness hid.

O, Winter, call thy coldest east-wind; drive
The lingering warriors from Bohemia back,
With them my Kleist; for him Lycoris stays,
    And his friend's tawny wine.

Bürger (Gottfried August, 1748–1794) was a poet who singularly united with a fiery lyrical genius, willingness to expend on his work an endless labor of art. His life was dissolute, and wretched, accordingly, to an exemplary degree.

Herder turned Bürger's attention to the store of stuff for poetry to be found in the rude traditional songs of the people, and Percy's *Reliques* further helped fix the bent of his genius in the direction of ballad-writing. Bürger's ballad of *Lenore* became immensely popular, both at home and abroad. An English translation, exhibiting the German text in parallel pages, was issued in a sumptuous quarto volume, with elaborate illustrations. Walter Scott paraphrased the *Lenore*, under title, *William and Helen*, and his paraphrase is on the whole the form in which our readers will best enjoy seeing a condensation of the poem. The legend of the ballad is that a soldier, leaving his sweetheart, went away to the wars, and neither returned nor made report. The poor maiden, driven half mad with love, longing, suspense, despair, shocked her pious mother with expressions of rebellion against God. The mother prays, on her daughter's behalf, a deprecatory prayer, but the daughter in the deep of night hears a summons at her door. It is the voice of her lover returned. She eagerly lets him in, but he refuses to abide. She must forthwith up and away with him on horseback, to find a bridal bed afar. She hesitates, but—and now Bürger,

in Scott's paraphrase, which must make up to the English
reader in spirit what it loses in fidelity:

> Strong love prevailed: she busks, she bounes,
>   She mounts the barb behind,
> And round her darling William's waist
>   Her lily arms she twined.
>
> And hurry! hurry! off they rode,
>   As fast as fast might be;
> Spurned from the courser's thundering heels,
>   The flashing pebbles flee.
>
> And on the right and on the left,
>   Ere they could snatch a view,
> Fast, fast each mountain, mead, and plain,
>   And cot, and castle, flew.
>
> "Sit fast—dost fear? The moon shines clear,
>   Fleet goes my barb—keep hold!
> Fear'st thou?" "O no!" she faintly said;
>   "But why so stern and cold?
>
> .   .   .   .
>
> "O William, why this savage haste?
>   And where thy bridal bed?"
> "'Tis distant far, low, damp, and chill,
>   And narrow, trustless maid."
>
> "No room for me?" "Enough for both;
>   Speed, speed, my barb, thy course!"
> O'er thundering bridge, through boiling surge,
>   He drove the furious horse.
>
> Tramp! tramp! along the land they rode,
>   Splash! splash! along the sea;
> The scourge is wight, the spur is bright,
>   The flashing pebbles flee.
>
> Fled past on right and left how fast
>   Each forest, grove, and bower!
> On right and left fled past how fast
>   Each city, town, and tower!
>
> .   .   .   .
>
> "Dost fear? dost fear? The moon shines clear,
>   And well the dead can ride;
> Does faithful Helen fear for them?"
>   "O leave in peace the dead!"

"Barb! barb! methinks I hear the cock;
    The sand will soon be run;
Barb! barb! I smell the morning air;
    The race is well-nigh done."

Tramp! tramp! along the land they rode,
    Splash! splash! along the sea;
The scourge is red, the spur drops blood,
    The flashing pebbles flee.

"Hurrah! hurrah! well ride the dead;
    The bride, the bride is come!
And soon we reach the bridal bed,
    For, Helen, here's my home."

Reluctant on its rusty hinge
    Revolved an iron door,
And by the pale moon's setting beam
    Were seen a church and tower.

With many a shriek and cry whiz round
    The birds of midnight, scared;
And rustling like autumnal leaves,
    Unhallowed ghosts were heard.

O'er many a tomb and tomb-stone pale
    He spurred the fiery horse,
Till sudden at an open grave
    He checked the wondrous course.

The falling gauntlet quits the rein,
    Down drops the casque of steel,
The cuirass leaves his shrinking side,
    The spur his gory heel.

The eyes desert the naked skull,
    The moldering flesh the bone,
Till Helen's lily arms entwine
    A ghastly skeleton.

The furious barb snorts fire and foam,
    And, with a fearful bound,
Dissolves at once in empty air,
    And leaves her on the ground.

Half seen by fits, by fits half heard,
    Pale spectres flit along,
Wheel round the maid in dismal dance,
    And howl the funeral song.

> E'en when the heart's with anguish cleft,
>   Revere the doom of Heaven.
> Her soul is from her body reft;
>   Her spirit be forgiven!

Goethe's *Bride of Corinth* recalls this poem of Bürger's. Neither one of the two poems can be called an agreeable production, but, of the two, Bürger's is the less disagreeable. To us it seems also the more genuine. Bürger's is written as in hot blood; Goethe's is perfectly cold-blooded, like the bride that it celebrates.

Because Longfellow has translated it so charmingly, as well as because it is in itself so short and so sweet, we give from Tiedge (Christoph August, 1752–1841), a gentle and delicate genius, the following trifle, entitled *The Wave of Life:*

> "Whither, thou turbid wave?
> Whither, with so much haste,
> As if a thief wert thou?"
>
> "I am the Wave of Life,
> Stained with my margin's dust;
> From the struggle and the strife
> Of the narrow stream I fly
> To the sea's immensity,
> To wash from me the slime
> Of the muddy banks of time."

A truly remarkable poet was Frederike Sophie Christiane Brun (1765–1835)—at least to English-speakers remarkable and memorable; if only for that one poem of hers which was the original of Coleridge's celebrated *Hymn in the Vale of Chamouni*. Readers must compare this English poem, if they wish to feel the full significance of the following piece by Frederica Brunn (so the name is customarily given in English), entitled *Chamouny at Sunrise:*

> From the deep shadow of the silent fir-grove
> I lift my eyes, and trembling look on thee,
> Brow of eternity, thou dazzling peak,
> From whose calm height my dreaming spirit mounts
> And soars away into the infinite!

Who sank the pillar in the lap of earth,
Down deep, the pillar of eternal rock,
On which thy mass stands firm, and firm hath stood,
While centuries on centuries rolled along?
Who reared, up-towering through the vaulted blue,
Mighty and bold, thy radiant countenance?

Who poured you from on high with thunder-sound,
Down from old winter's everlasting realm,
O jagged streams, over rock and through ravine?
And whose almighty voice commanded loud,
" Here shall the stiffening billows rest awhile ! "

Whose finger points yon morning star his course?
Who fringed with blossom-wreaths the eternal frost?
Whose name, O wild Arveiron, does thy din
Of waves sound out in dreadful harmonies?

" Jehovah ! " crashes in the bursting ice;
Down through the gorge the rolling avalanche
Carries the word in thunder to the vales.
" Jehovah ! " murmurs in the morning breeze,
Along the trembling tree-tops ; down below
It whispers in the purling, silvery brooks.

Arndt (Ernst Moritz, 1769–1860) lacked only the conse-
cration of a death, like Körner's, in self-sacrifice on the altar
of his country, to be as dear to world-wide fame as is that
young patriot-martyr of Germany.   In real merit, and in influence as popular lyrist of freedom and nationality for
Germans, Arndt exceeded Körner hardly less than he did in
length of life-time and career.   Here is Arndt's best-known
lyric, *What is the German's Fatherland?* It may be doubted
whether either Bismarck, with his statecraft, or Von Moltke,
with his sword, has done more to secure German unity than
did Arndt with this brave tune of his on his lyre :

Which is the German's fatherland?
Is 't Prussia's or Swabia's land?
Is 't where the Rhine's rich vintage streams?
Or where the Northern sea-gull screams?
    Ah, no, no, no !
His fatherland's not bounded so !

11

> Which is the German's fatherland?
> Come, tell me now the famous land!
> Doubtless, it is the Austrian state,
> In honors and in triumphs great.
>   Ah, no, no, no!
> His fatherland's not bounded so!
>
> .   .   .   .   .   .
>
> Which is the German's fatherland?
> So tell me now at last the land!
> As far's the German accent rings
> And hymns to God in heaven sings,
>   That is the land—
> There, brother, is thy fatherland!
>
> .   .   .   .   .
>
> That is the German's fatherland,
> Where wrath pursues the foreign band,
> Where every Frank is held a foe,
> And Germans all as brothers glow;
>   That is the land—
> All Germany's thy fatherland!

Our readers lose five of Arndt's stanzas, but they miss nothing of the spirit of the song. In the stanzas retrenched, there was simply an accumulation of other territorial German names; the poet would play on every chord within his reach of national feeling.

The *Sword Song* of Karl Theodor Körner (1791–1813) was written almost literally in letters of blood. The heroic young author composed it at twenty-two years of age, only an hour before he fell on the field of battle bravely fighting, a soldier in the War of Liberation. The piece forms a dialogue carried on between the soldier and his sword, conceived as already betrothed to each other, but still awaiting battle for actual marriage. "Bridegroom" and "bride" bear this sense in German usage. With the "Hurrah!" closing each stanza, is to be imagined a chorus of swords clanging. Körner's *Sword Song* will bear abridgement without serious loss of effect. We part with eight stanzas:

> "Sword at my left side gleaming!
> Why is thy keen glance, beaming,

So fondly bent on mine?
I love that smile of thine!

          Hurrah! "

" Borne by a trooper daring,
My looks his fire-glance wearing,
I arm a freeman's hand:
This well delights thy brand!

          Hurrah! "

" Ay, good sword! Free I wear thee;
And, true heart's love, I bear thee,
Betrothed one, at my side,
As my dear, chosen bride!

          Hurrah! "

" To thee till death united,
Thy steel's bright life is plighted;
Ah, were my love but tried!
When wilt thou wed thy bride?

          Hurrah! "

" The trumpet's festal warning
Shall hail our bridal morning;
When loud the cannon chide,
Then clasp I my loved bride!

          Hurrah! "

" Well may thy scabbard rattle,
Trooper, I pant for battle;
Right eager for the fight,
I clang with wild delight.

          Hurrah! "

" Come from thy sheath, then, treasure!
Thou trooper's true eye-pleasure!
Come forth, my good sword, come!
Enter thy father-home!

          Hurrah!

" Come on, ye German horsemen!
Come on, ye valiant Norsemen!
Swells not your hearts' warm tide?
Clasp each in hand his bride!

          Hurrah! "

Let Rückert (Friedrich, 1789–1866) close the cycle of German patriot lyrists. Rückert was a learned Orientalist as well as a versatile master of metres. He was one of that numerous band of spirited German youths through whom, during the War of Liberation, the fatherland uttered musically its long-suppressed cry of desire for life from the dead. Professor C. C. Felton is our translator for the following caustic lyrical satire of Rückert's, entitled, *The Patriot's Lament*:

"What forgest, smith?" "We're forging chains; ay, chains!"
  "Alas! to chains yourselves degraded are!"
  "Why plowest, farmer?" "Fields their fruit must bear."
"Yes, seed for foes; the burr for thee remains!"

"What aim'st at, sportsman?" "Yonder stag, so fat."
  "To hunt you down, like stag and roe, they'll try."
  "What snarest, fisher?" "Yonder fish, so shy."
"Who's there to save you from your fatal net?"

"What art thou rocking, sleepless mother?" "Boys."
  "Yes; let them grow, and wound their country's fame,
  Slaves to her foes, with parricidal arm!"
"What art thou writing, poet?" "Words of flame;
  I mark my own, record my country's harm,
Whom thought of freedom never more employs."

I blame them not who with the foreign steel
  Tear out our vitals, pierce our inmost heart;
  For they are foes created for our smart,
And when they slay us, why they do it, feel.

But, in these paths, ye seek what recompense?
  For you what brilliant toys of fame are here,
  Ye mongrel foes, who lift the sword and spear
Against your country, not for her defense?

Ye Franks, Bavarians, and ye Swabians, say,
  Ye aliens, sold to bear the slavish name,
What wages for your servitude they pay.
  Your eagle may perchance redeem your fame;
More sure his robber-train, ye birds of prey,
  To coming ages shall prolong your shame!

Kerner (Justinus Andreas, 1786–1862) had a delicate lyrical vein of pathos, almost quaint enough sometimes to be humorous in effect. The following piece, translated by the sure hand of our American Bryant, is a fair specimen:

> In yonder mill I rested,
>   And sat me down to look
> Upon the wheel's quick glimmer,
>   And on the flowing brook.
>
> As in a dream before me,
>   The saw, with restless play,
> Was cleaving through a fir-tree
>   Its long and steady way.
>
> The tree through all its fibres
>   With living motion stirred,
> And, in a dirge-like murmur,
>   These solemn words I heard:
>
> " O thou who wanderest hither,
>   A timely guest thou art!
> For thee this cruel engine
>   Is passing through my heart.
>
> When soon, in earth's still bosom,
>   Thy hours of rest begin,
> This wood shall form the chamber
>   Whose walls shall close thee in."
>
> Four planks—I saw and shuddered—
>   Dropped in that busy mill;
> Then, as I tried to answer,
>   At once the wheel was still.

The same translating touch, that of Bryant, attracts us to one other lyrical piece, with which we bring our " Interlude of Poets " to its close. This is from Niclas Müller (1809–1875). It is entitled, *The Paradise of Tears:*

> Beside the River of Tears, with branches low,
> And bitter leaves, the weeping willows grow;
> The branches stream like the disheveled hair
> Of woman in the sadness of despair.

On rolls the stream with a perpetual sigh;
The rocks moan wildly as it passes by;
Hyssop and wormwood border all the strand,
And not a flower adorns the dreary land.

Then comes a child, whose face is like the sun,
And dips the gloomy waters as they run,
And waters all the region, and behold
The ground is bright with blossoms manifold.

Where fall the tears of love, the rose appears,
And where the ground is bright with friendship's tears,
Forget-me-not, and violets, heavenly blue,
Spring, glittering with the cheerful drops like dew.

The souls of mourners, all whose tears are dried,
Like swans, come gently floating down the tide,
Walk up the golden sands by which it flows,
And in that Paradise of Tears repose.

There every heart rejoins its kindred heart;
There in a long embrace that none may part,
Fulfillment meets desire, and that fair shore
Beholds its dwellers happy evermore.

Our "Interlude of Poets" is done. It was a concord of voices commingling to usher and herald the great singer Goethe.

IX.

GOETHE.

1749–1832.

IF Luther was the morning, Goethe was the meridian, sun of German literature. Schiller, it might almost be said, rising later and setting earlier, rode rival by Goethe's side through the dazzling zenith arcs of the sky. But these two orbs, both so large and so splendid, were not mutually equal, either in largeness or in splendor. Schiller was the less luminary; and of him it is praise enough to say that, shining so near to Goethe, he did not lose, did not pale, his lustre in the blaze of the superior ray.

Johann Wolfgang von Goethe was born, in Frankfort-on-the-Main, almost exactly in the middle of the eighteenth century. His parentage was excellent on both sides. His father was a tailor's son who had raised himself to some civic distinction, and his mother was daughter to the chief magistrate of Frankfort. The father was more than twice as old as the mother when they married; she indeed was a blooming young creature of only seventeen years of age. Wolfgang was the first-born of the pair. The mother was but eighteen years older than the son. There thus came to be a time when the two could share between them a fellowship approaching in kind that natural between those nearly equal in age. This, the temperament of the mother—happy, equable, serene, perennially young—made additionally easy. Such a mother was an immeasurable blessing to Goethe.

The father was a very different being. Stern, stiff, opinionated, a precisian, a pedant, he was well fitted to balance the equipment of the mother with qualities needful for the training of the boy to become the symmetrical, all-accomplished Goethe whom we know. Remarkable among the traits of the elder Goethe's character as disciplinarian to his son was his way of insisting that whatever Wolfgang began he should go on with till he carried it to completion.

> From my father I derive my frame and the steady guidance of my life, and from my dear little mother my happy disposition and my love of story-telling.

So Goethe says and sings in one of his poems.

The early years of Goethe did not pass without yielding to the precocious boy much premature experience of life. This, in such form and degree as he thought it comportable with his dignity to indulge, he has himself shadowed forth to the public, directly in his autobiography, and indirectly in his autobiographical "novel," the *Wilhelm Meister*. He contracted soil to the innocence of youth—soil which, alas, the practice of manhood and of old age rather inveterated than removed. But the father, meantime, did not remit his intellectual demands on his boy; and his boy was still able to respond, for he was magnificently endowed from nature to bear, without obvious loss, heavy overdrafts on the precious reserves of health and strength and youth. Goethe entered upon man's estate ideally well furnished to run the long career that lay before him of successful and lauded achievement. It is even, by contrast with the general lot of the race, almost depressing to contemplate the worldly prosperity that arched, like one day-long cloudless heaven, over the whole life of this man. But, stay!—when is it well to be envious? When can you be sure that you are envious wisely? Goethe, the well-attempered, the prosperous, the fortunate, of whom, when he spoke, listeners said, as those said of King Herod, "It is the voice of a god and not of a man," he, Goethe, who smiled and smiled, as if inaccessible to pain, like the easy Olympian divinities of Epicurus—this Goethe, what did he say? He said to Eckermann:

> I have ever been esteemed one of Fortune's chiefest favorites; nor can I complain of the course my life has taken. Yet, truly, there has been nothing but toil and care; and, in my seventy-fifth year, I may say that I have never had four weeks of genuine pleasure.

Let us deal gently, while we deal justly, with a happy man of this world, who, at seventy-five years of age, has to bear of himself a testimony like that.

Young Goethe went at sixteen years of age to Leipsic, to continue an education nobly commenced at home. At Leipsic, he devoted himself perhaps more to the seeing and the enjoying of life than to the prosecution of study. He had thus early formed his life-long habit of turning to literary account his own experiences, and his observations of himself and of the world; and his three years at Leipsic gave him both the matter and the leisure for writing, besides a score or so of erotic effusions, two plays—one of which, *The Fellow-Culprits,* the great man himself retained to old age a sentiment of respectful fondness for, which the critics and the general public have hardly shared with the illustrious author. Recalled from Leipsic, young Goethe, after an eighteen months' interval of unwilling sojourn at home, was entered, at twenty-one years of age, a student in the University of Strasburg. This change in situation was of the greatest importance to Goethe. At Strasburg, as has already in a preceding chapter appeared, he met in Herder his own intellectual destiny. Goethe never lost the impulse and direction then given his genius from Herder's overmastering hand. His stay in Strasburg was for scarcely more than eighteen months; but they were eighteen months to Goethe of the most pregnant experience. It was while a student at Strasburg that this brilliant, gay, and handsome youth, prepared beforehand for it by repeated experiments in love-making and love-breaking, took on himself to act, in real life, almost with conscious self-indulgence, half play, half earnest, the part of Thornhill in Goldsmith's *Vicar of Wakefield*. The circumstances of this case are historic, they likewise belong to literature, and to Goethe's own part in literature; all this, for Goethe has recounted them at length in his autobiography.

We may thus, at the present point, and that in the very act of proceeding with our sketch begun of Goethe's life, enter immediately upon our presentation of Goethe's literary works.

Goethe's autobiography, published under the title of *Truth and Fiction relating to My Life* (so the German expression is usually translated, but *Poetry and Truth out of My Life*, would be more literal), is generally considered, and justly, one of its author's most important productions. It was written in the full mellow ripeness of Goethe's unwithering age, and it constitutes as noteworthy a self-portrayal as exists anywhere in literature. Goethe himself, it must be remembered, is of at least as much consequence in the world of intellect as is the total sum of all the man's writings, apart from the man. The key to Goethe's literary product is Goethe himself. Never was the personality of a man of letters more inseparable than is Goethe's from the books that he wrote. Hence the capital importance, in order to gaining a clear and true idea of Goethe the author, of gaining a clear and true idea of Goethe the man. This we can in no other way so directly do, and do so satisfactorily, as by studying his autobiography.

The autobiography is a work of considerable volume— much larger, for instance, than this entire book. Our only way, then, at once effective and practicable, of proceeding in the business will be to take from that work an important section or episode of it, and, presenting this condensed, let the part thus severed stand imperfectly, but fairly, representative of the whole. There is in the autobiography of Goethe no better episode for our purpose than the famous episode of Frederica, already alluded to. This is extensively and elaborately treated by Goethe; it is highly interesting in itself, and it is, to a singular degree, characteristic, both of the man and of the writer. In it, Goethe will be found, öf course, far from fully, but in unexpectedly large measure, revealed. This, not only because the incident related is such, but, still more, because the incident, being such, is so related by the autobiographer. The incident occurred, it is true, when Goethe was a young man; but Goethe was a man of sixty and upward when he related the incident. We enjoy, therefore, a valuable opportunity to see, first, the man behaving himself in a certain way, and then the man, grown forty years older, deliberately taking a certain view of himself so behaving.

Herder, it seems, had introduced Goethe to Goldsmith's tale, reading it aloud, in German translation, to him, with others, as a study in literary art. Goethe, so Goethe's own narrative informs us, drew on himself the rebuke of Herder for becoming too much interested in the story as story, to pay it due attention as a consummate piece of literary workmanship. He says—but first we need to explain. In connection with the *Vicar of Wakefield*, a companion of Goethe's had spoken of knowing a pastor's family in Sesenheim, a few miles from Strasburg, the exact counterpart of the clergyman's family in the English novel. It was resolved between the two that they pay Sesenheim a visit. Goethe ingratiated himself successfully, and won the heart of the lovely daughter Frederica. This had already happened, when, during a second visit to Sesenheim—which, though unannounced, the girl, wise through the foreboding of love, had expected—some lady guest suggested certain novels. Goethe says:

> I had the *Vicar of Wakefield* on the tip of my tongue; but did not venture to propose it, the similarity of the situations being too striking and too important.

This is one only of many allusions made by Goethe, in the course of his story, to Goldsmith's novel, going to show how conscious all the time he was what part he was playing. If the man of sixty-three had been making late expiation for the errors of youth by telling them now, in bitter confession, to his own shame ! But, alas, there is no such strain of feeling discoverable in his autobiographical warming-over of those experiences of his. This wanton lover—so, from his own expressions, it unmistakably appears—knew that he meant nothing serious for himself, by what was so serious to the girl. Goethe, having just spoken of contemplating at leisure, during his visit to Sesenheim, "the state in which young people are placed *whose early affections can promise themselves no lasting result,*" says:

> My passion increased, the more I learned to know the virtue of the excellent girl; and the time approached when I was to lose, perhaps forever, so much that was dear and good.

On the same page, Goethe indicates his approval of a principle in morals that, if sound, should have made him — for he faithfully carried it out—a happier man in life than, according to his own testimony, he actually was. A man, he says—note this, it is a very important self-disclosure—is always uneasy,

> Until he once for all makes a resolution to declare that *that is right which is suitable to himself.*

How long this "buccaneering bee" remained in the heart of the Sesenheim flower, rifling it of its sweets, it is impossible from the autobiography to determine. Goethe, describing with enthusiasm the beauty of that season of weather "in this noble country," says, "For months together, we were favored with pure ethereal mornings;" as if his sojourn at Sesenheim, interrupted by visits to Strasburg, continued all summer. He says expressly that he and Frederica exchanged assurances of mutual love and confidence. But Goethe—it was Goethe's lips only that spoke; his heart, or at least his conscience and his will, were unsworn. He went away from his " beloved," apparently without explanation. He says:

> When I reached her my hand from my horse, the tears stood in her eyes and I felt very uneasy.

Goethe was doing what was " suitable to himself," and still he felt " very uneasy." His uneasiness, however, he compels us to feel, was more for the pleasure he was himself renouncing, than for the pain he was inflicting on Frederica. For, as to himself, he reassuringly says:

> Having at last escaped the excitement of a farewell, I, on a peaceful and quiet journey, pretty well regained my self-possession.

Goethe thinks that the chastening effect on himself, of the loss he experienced in throwing away Frederica, really improved his manners in society—by making him less stormily and overwhelmingly brilliant than he had been before. He says:

> I had in secret to complain of a love I had lost; this made me mild and pliant, and more agreeable to society than in those brilliant times when nothing reminded me of a want or a fault, and I went storming along completely without restraint.

Such sentiment as reveals itself in the immediately foregoing expression would, in the case of an average man, be termed self-conceit. In the case of Goethe, the usage is to dignify it by the name of egotism.

We shall not have done full justice to Goethe in his relation to Frederica without quoting from him still other expressions on the subject:

> Frederica's answer to my farewell letter rent my heart. It was the same hand, the same tone of thought, the same feeling, which had formed

itself for me and by me. I now, for the first time, felt the loss which she suffered, and saw no means to supply it, or even to alleviate it. She was completely present to me ; I always felt that she was wanting to me; and, what was worst of all, I could not forgive myself *for my own misfortune*. Gretchen had been taken away from me; Annette had left me ; now, for the first time, I was guilty. I had wounded the most lovely heart to its very depths ; and the period of a gloomy repentance, with the absence of a refreshing love, to which I had grown accustomed, was most ago- nizing, nay, insupportable.

Once more. Goethe says :

At the time when I was pained by my grief at Frederica's situation, I again, after my old fashion, sought aid from poetry. I again continued the poetical confession which I had commenced, that, by this self-tor- menting penance, I might be worthy of an internal absolution.

The plan of resort to the " self-tormenting penance " of " poetical confession," by way of deserving " internal abso- lution," was not new with that distinguished French practi- tioner, Lamartine. Before the Frenchman, Goethe had tried it, and it had proved—highly " suitable to himself." For the satisfaction of thoughtful and candid readers, it is proper for us to add that we have given here, not specimens merely of what Goethe had to say in the way of self-blame and re- morse for his behavior, but *every thing* of this sort that he said. Dr. Hedge, in his *Hours with German Classics*, re- marks : " Her [Frederica's] suffering in the separation, great as it was—so great, indeed, as to cause a dangerous attack of bodily disease—could not outweigh the pangs which he [Goethe] endured in his penitent contemplation of the con- sequences of his folly." We must venture to think that Dr. Hedge here came to his conclusion prompted by considering what would have been his own feeling in the case, rather than guided by recent study of the records that fatally reveal Goethe's feeling.

Frederica never married. " To her, perpetual maiden- hood," but unto him—a long dissolving-view of " relations " with women.

We transfer to our pages a touch or two more, bestowed by the lingering and loving hand of the Narcissus-like artist, turning still, as he retires, to survey anew with approval the picture of himself that he has made; and so take our leave of Frederica's story. Goethe had the good taste and fine feel- ing to go and see Frederica, simply pay the heart he had wrung a visit of curiosity! after an interval of years from the time of his abandoning her. He himself, in his autobiography, by way of anticipation, relates the incident—with character- istic self-conceited detail. He relates it in connection with a presentiment and a quasi-ocular illusion experienced by him, as he says, immediately after he had given the poor, tearful child that heartless good-bye from on horseback, and rode off feeling "very uneasy." Speaking of himself, just happily escaped, on that occasion, from the "excitement of a fare- well," he says :

> I now rode along the footpath toward Drusenheim, and here one of the most singular forebodings took possession of me. I saw, not with the eyes of the body, but with those of the mind, my own figure [his own figure, Goethe was very likely at all times to see] coming toward me, on horseback, and on the same road, attired in a dress which I had never worn. It was pike-gray, with somewhat of gold. As soon as I shook myself out of this dream, the figure had entirely disappeared. It is strange, however, that eight years afterward I found myself on the very road, to pay one more visit to Frederica, in the dress of which I had dreamed, and which I wore, not from choice, but by accident. However it may be with matters of this kind generally, this strange illusion in some measure calmed me at the moment of parting. The pain of quitting forever noble Alsace, with all I had gained in it, was softened.

Goethe was a prosperous man in Weimar, at the time when the humor thus took him to see how Frederica would look in his eyes now, after the lapse of eight years. He had meanwhile formed a memorable relation with a distin- guished married woman, Frau von Stein. To that Weimar lady, he promptly wrote an account of this visit of his to Frederica, and added the last insult to an injured memory by saying, with a grossness of gratuitous exoneration of which nothing but dense egotism like Goethe's could render a man unconsciously capable:

> I must do her [Frederica] the justice to say that *she did not attempt, by the slightest allusion, to awaken in my soul the old feeling.*

And that to a woman! Frederica, surviving a nearly fatal illness that followed her betrayal, lived long enough, a ministering angel to the needy, to have read Goethe's story of herself in print; for it did not shame this inconceivable man to publish his autobiography, with the account in it of Frederica, not omitting names for identification, while his victim was still living.

So much for Goethe's autobiography. It would be unjust not to say that many things to be found in the book present the author in an aspect more engaging than that in which he has just now appeared. One such more engaging exhibition of himself, on Goethe's part, we have ourselves already submitted to our readers. We refer to the long passage in which Goethe pays his tribute to Herder. Goethe, we have no doubt, was an agreeable man to know. He was cheerful, obliging, urbane. He was neither jealous nor envious. He seldom contradicted. There is a placid amenity diffused over the pages of his autobiography, by no means unattractive; albeit you feel all the time that this plays, a sheen of iridescence only, on a surface beneath which sink soundless depths of self-complacency imperturbable. We assume it as certain that, in this genial attribute of affability, the autobiographer is a true reflex of the social living Goethe. Whoever wishes to get the most entirely pleasing impression obtainable of this great German, through words proceeding directly from himself, should read Eckermann's *Conversations with Goethe.*

Goethe, after running through who knows how many episodes of love more or less resembling that with Frederica ("Goethe's life was at no time complete without the influence of a noble-hearted woman," is the way in which the tender-footed author of the article on Goethe in the *Encyclopædia Britannica* puts it)—Goethe, we say, well-seasoned with much experience, picked up, at thirty-nine, a girl met casually in the public park, whom, eighteen years after, she having meantime become to him the mother of children, he married. During this long interval of eighteen years, Christiane Vulpius was in Goethe's house, unrecognized by society, as it were a domestic menial. She did not sit at her master's table to meet his company. What we thus set down is inherently so incredible, that, lest we should seem to be wronging Goethe, we transfer to our pages the gentle account of the matter given by the *Encyclopædia Britannica:*

"In the autumn of 1788, walking aimlessly through the park, he met Christiane Vulpius, a young girl, who presented him with a petition in favor of her brother. She had golden curling locks, round cheeks, laughing eyes, a neatly rounded figure; she looked, as has been said, 'like a young Dionysus.' Goethe took her into his house, and she became his wife in conscience, and the mother of his children. He did not marry her till 1806, when the terrors of the French occupation made him anxious for the position of his eldest son. She had but little education, and he could not take her into society; but she made him a good and loving wife, and her quick mother-wit made her available as an intellectual companion. To these days of early married life belong the Roman elegies, which, although Italian and pagan in form, in color, and in sensuality, were written in Germany from home experiences." Is it not curious, by the way, that a woman, through her "quick mother-wit," "available as an intellectual companion" to the first literary man in Europe, should have been unfit for "society" through her "little education?"

Such was the clay and the iron in the mingled image of Goethe; it was, at most, only his head that was of fine gold.

But kindly and thoughtful readers may ask, "Were not the manners of the times such as to constitute a virtual excuse for Goethe?" "The manners of the times" is a phrase better exchanged, in the present case, for "the manners of Weimar." It is Weimar, Goethe's residence, rather than the times in which Goethe flourished, that must be invoked to save Goethe, if he be saved at all. But who made Weimar what it was? Weimar was Goethe. Apropos of this matter, it is mortifying to be obliged to quote Schiller, writing to his friend Körner, as follows:

He [Goethe] is getting old [Goethe was forty-one]. . . . I fear he will be committing an act of folly. . . . He cohabits with a Mamselle Vulpius, who has a child by him. . . . It is very probable that he will marry her in a year or so. I should be sorry to see him finish by such an act of genius—for people will not be wanting to call it such.

Körner's reply shows that Goethe's conduct was of "Weimar," that is, of Goethe himself, rather than of the "times." Körner writes:

At Weimar, the ideas on concubinage seem to differ widely from those in Berlin.

Ten years having passed, and Goethe having not yet committed the "act of genius" deprecated by Schiller, Körner writes again to his friend:

One cannot violate good morals and go unpunished. At the proper time, he [Goethe] could easily have found a loving wife, and what a different existence would then have been his! The other sex has a nobler destiny than to be degraded to be the mere instruments of sensuality. . . . Connections of this description worry a man of the strongest mind to death.

That, in writing such words for virtue as those just given, Körner should stand alone, in this correspondence between him and Schiller, is an immeasurable pity for Schiller's fame.

The thing "suitable to himself" had not, it seems, after all, eventuated very happily for Goethe, in his relation with Christiane Vulpius. The serene Olympian was "worried." He had, together with other things, to justify himself to his friend Charlotte von Stein. Writing to this lady, concerning his relation to Christiane, he begs to know wherein any one was wronged by what he did. He uses this language:

Who claims the feelings which I give to the poor thing?

"*Poor thing!*" This said by him, compassionately perhaps, of the woman he has chosen to make her the mother of his son and heir! Said, too, in self-exculpation; and said to another woman; and that other woman the wife of another man!

In that same year in which he finished his memorable stay at Strasburg, Goethe, now twenty-two years of age, wrote a work destined to render him instantly famous. This

12

was the *Goetz von Berlichingen*—a play which enjoyed the English distinction of being translated by young Walter Scott. Herder inspired Goethe to this production, by making him acquainted with Shakespeare; and it is not impossible that Goethe, in his turn, by the example of this play, may have influenced Scott to undertake those rehabilitations in fiction of vanished times and manners which were soon to make the author of the Waverley Novels one of the universally recognized lords of literature. Goetz von Berlichingen, the hero of Goethe's play, was a sixteenth-century character, a man born out of due time—as it were, the last of the barons. Merck helped Goethe rewrite his play for publication—how much his help may have been worth, we shall never know—and he served Goethe variously in other ways. Goethe rewarded his friend by afterward making him in part the suggestive type of his Mephistopheles (or devil) in the *Faust*. Another friend of Goethe's, Herder, Hermann Grimm thinks, supplied what Merck lacked to complete the poet's diabolic ideal. To make the friendly reward full measure, Goethe, in the case of Merck at least, duly reveals this use of his friend to the public.

Goethe's *Goetz* was emphatically what, in stereotyped phrase, is styled an "epoch-making" production. It took sudden and violent possession of the literary mind of Germany. The press teemed with books reproducing it or imitating it, in form or in spirit. The famous "Storm and Stress" or "Storm and Pressure" (*Sturm und Drang*) period in German literature resulted. This is a title given to express the violence, the excess, the rebellion against law, which characterized the literary spirit of that time. It was not real passion, but it was passion simulated in extravagant travesty. Real power, however, or the promise of real power, there was, in the *Goetz von Berlichingen.* Shakespearean it was not, for it was not action, but only dialogue about action. Still, compared with what before existed in German literature, Goethe's *Goetz* was an approximation to Shakespeare. The play was written in prose. It never, we believe, was acted but once, and then the representation lasted five hours. Of this work of the young Titan, we shall not need to show any specimen to our readers.

There now followed from Goethe's pen a kind of romance, entitled *The Sorrows of Young Werther.* This was a piece of writing so extravagant that no magazine editor of these days in England or America would think of admitting such a contribution to his pages, unless perhaps as an extravaganza confessed. *Werther* is a tale of love, despair, and suicide, told, all but the final act itself, in letters from Werther, the subject; hero certainly we cannot call Werther. The story is founded on fact, is indeed strict fact very thinly disguised. In the fact, Goethe was himself deeply concerned. He loved a woman who was engaged to be another man's wife. That man was his own intimate friend. The betrothed lovers admitted Goethe freely, without jealousy, to share their friendship. But the strain was too much for Goethe, and he— probably, as it is said, well advised by Merck—tore himself away from his dangerous proximity to the object of his improper affection. Coming back again at length, in his wanderings, to Wetzlar, he there found that a tragedy in real life had been enacted, strikingly, in its earlier part, like that late experience of his own. A man by the name of Jerusalem, an acquaintance of Goethe's, had, like himself, loved the beloved (in this case, the wife) of another, and had shot himself in despair. Goethe saw his literary account in the affair, and he immediately wrote his romance, mingling the circumstances of his own case with those of poor Jerusalem. Werther is Goethe *and* Jerusalem, both at once. His two friends, the Lotte whom he had loved and fled from, and Kestner who had now married her, Goethe unhesitatingly put into his literary mill and ground them up for paint, to decorate his romantic canvas withal. They felt it, resented it, complained of it, and—seem finally to have forgiven it, on Goethe's making some sort of apology.

The strange, and, to our modern sense, tasteless, manner in which the realistic and the sentimental are mixed in *Werther*, may be shown by the contrast of the following two passages—which will be felt to be quite sufficient in specimen of such literature.

Werther is made by Goethe to describe the circumstances of his first meeting with Charlotte (for Goethe was little delicate enough even to preserve in his romance the very name of his friend):

> I walked across the court to a well-built house, and, ascending the flight of steps in front, opened the door and saw before me the most charming spectacle I had ever witnessed. Six children, from eleven to two years old, were running about the hall, and surrounding a lady of middle height, with a lovely figure, dressed in a robe of simple white trimmed with pink ribbons. She was holding a rye loaf in her hand, and was cutting slices for the little ones all round, in proportion to their age and appetite. She performed her task in a graceful and affectionate manner, each claimant awaiting his turn with outstretched hands and boisterously shouting his thanks. Some of them ran away at once to enjoy their evening meal, while others, of a gentler disposition, retired to the court-yard to see the strangers and to survey the carriage in which their Charlotte was to drive away. "Pray forgive me for giving you the trouble to come for me and for keeping the ladies waiting; but dressing, and arranging some household duties before I leave, had made me forget my children's supper, and they do not like to take it from any one but me." I uttered some indifferent compliment; but my whole soul was absorbed by her air, her voice, her manner, and I had scarcely recovered myself when she ran into her room to fetch her gloves and fan.

Our readers must know that this bread-and-butter scene has been very much admired. It has been made the subject of paintings—of poems also, probably; of one poem, at least, it is certain. As this poem happens to be in English, and to be from the pen of one well qualified to do his subject justice, we shall presently show it. Meantime, take the contrasted passage. Young Werther has driven fast his acquaintance with Charlotte. He accompanies her to a ball. Here a thunder-storm interrupts the dancing. Werther tells how he and Charlotte occupied themselves together, as the violence of the storm was subsiding:

> We went to the window. It was still thundering at a distance; a soft rain was pouring down over the country and filled the air around

us with delicious odors. Charlotte leaned forward on her arm; her eyes wandered over the scene; she raised them to the sky, and then turned them upon me; they were moistened with tears; she placed her hand upon mine and said, "Klopstock!" At once I remembered the magnificent ode which was in her thoughts; I felt oppressed with the weight of my sensations and sank under them. It was more than I could bear. I bent over her hand, kissed it in a stream of delicious tears, and again looked up to her eyes. Divine Klopstock! why didst thou not see thy apotheosis in those eyes? And thy name, so often profaned, would that I never heard it repeated!

Now for our poem on the bread-and-butter scene of Werther's meeting with Charlotte. It is by Thackeray:

> Werther had a love for Charlotte
>   Such as words could never utter;
> Would you know how first he met her?
>   She was cutting bread and butter.
>
> Charlotte was another's lady,
>   And a moral man was Werther;
> And for all the wealth of Indies
>   Would do nothing for to hurt her.
>
> So he sighed and pined and ogled,
>   And his passion boiled and bubbled,
> Till he blew his silly brains out,
>   And no more by it was troubled.
>
> Charlotte having seen his body
>   Borne before her on a shutter,
> Like a well-conducted person
>   Went on cutting bread and butter.

We may sober ourselves, in dismissing *Werther*, by reflecting that this precious stuff—which nobody with a sense of humor in him could ever, by any possibility, have written, except as an open burlesque—was hailed on its appearance, as a work of deep philosophy, by men like Lavater and Jacobi, and that Napoleon read it, as he read Ossian, with untutored barbarian delight. It should be added that, in one important respect, the *Werther* was a revelation as well as a sensation in German literature—we mean in the ease, the grace, and the harmony, of its style. It was thus, as in

spirit, so also in form, a German echo of the French sentimentalism of Rousseau. It throws, by the way, a curious
light on the literary German's obligingness in indiscreet con-
fidences to his reader, to find a biographer of Goethe making
note of the fact that this poet-lover of another man's wife
wanted "to get Lotte's old comb in exchange for a new
one"! Goethe's choice of keepsake was at least poetically
fit to the whole pretty mess of *Werther*—hero, author, occasion, and all.

Goetz and *Werther* made their author's fame not only, but
his fate. They procured from the young Duke of Weimar
an invitation for Goethe to make him a visit. The visit
made, Goethe was settled for life as a kind of prime minister to the duke, charged with the duty of providing pleasure
for the court. That the pleasure actually provided was in
considerable proportion of a quasi-intellectual sort, may fairly be credited, a share to the minister, a share to the sovereign, a share to the previous influence of Wieland as tutor
to the prince, and a share to the spirit of the time. It had
now become a fashion for German princes to patronize literature.

But Goethe, though seven or eight years older than his
prince, was still a young fellow of only twenty-five. So
youthful a minister of pleasure, to so much more youthful a
prince, by no means committed the mistake of trying to
strain up the enjoyments of the Weimar court to an impossible pitch of sobriety. On the contrary, the riot the two
made together, the minister and the prince, was something
portentous. If unlimited hilarity, with the resources of a
principality to support it, could make truly happy, there
would seem to be no reason why Goethe should not have
had, during these boisterous years, much more than "four
weeks of genuine pleasure."

It was in truth but a melancholy fate, the fortune so generally praised as unique for felicity, that fell on Goethe in
his becoming Petronius Arbiter to the boyish sovereign of
a petty dukedom like Saxe-Weimar. That, in spite of

circumstances so hostile, Goethe should have accomplished so much, is one of the chief things in his praise. Richter said admiringly that only Goethe could have been in such hot sunshine of worldly prosperity without having his wings hopelessly singed. Let us not congratulate, but commiserate, Goethe, that, with endowments pointing him out as manifestly meant for mankind, he should, by his destiny, have been almost inevitably turned inward upon himself, with this for his chief ambition: to present to the world the ideal example—and such was Goethe's confessed ambition and aim—of what "self-culture" could do for its subject! Opening himself on the topic of this his supreme purpose in life, he thus writes to Lavater:

> I wish to act like the greatest men. I wish in nothing to act like the merely greater. This desire—to make the Pyramid of my Being . . . soar as high as can be in air—outweighs all else and permits hardly a momentary forgetting. I may not linger, I am already far in years [Goethe was now thirty-one] and perchance Destiny will come and break me off in the middle of my building, and Babel Tower will stand unfinished, blunt. At least it shall be said, It was a bold design! . . . Very powerful is the talisman of a beautiful love, such as the Stein [Madame Charlotte von Stein, wife of a living husband] seasons life with for me. She has by degrees succeeded to my mother, my sister, and my former loves, and a bond has formed between us as strong as are the bonds of Nature.

Düntzer, in his admiring life of Goethe, quotes the foregoing, and adds, reverently: "Thus was he clear and firm in the consciousness of his striving, and [this in the teeth of Goethe's just-confessed dependence on ' the Stein '] perfectly sufficient to himself"! The same indiscreet biographer notes it that Goethe at eighty years of age recalled with pleasure how a saucy young maid of honor after whom, thirty years before, the great man openly went daft, used archly to call him "Silly Geheimrath." "Silly" Privy Councillor, indeed, Goethe, in undress, was; and to a fund in him, a plenteous fund, of downright soft silliness, much may mercifully be allowed that would have to be charged seriously against him had he been a man of truer manliness, and still been guilty, could that be supposed possible, of the same behavior. Düntzer blabs again, telling of Goethe and Schiller's having a drinking bout together in company with a certain actress, to whom Goethe afterward inscribed a "poem," reminiscent of the occasion, gracefully recalling to that lady how she, though drinking, he admitted, less than "Schiller and he and all," yet "champagne-fuddled on his neck did fall"—namely, on the neck of this truly "silly Geheimrath." By the way, not to treat with any injustice a misguided, indeed, but apparently a pure and noble, woman, it behooves us to say that Madame von Stein seemed to have conceived the disinterested and romantic idea that she might save Goethe from himself by giving him her friendship. Repeatedly she was obliged to deny herself to him, in order to chastise and repress his improprieties toward her, and still she kept him her friend—until he, by forming his "relation" with Christiane Vulpius, broke some promise of his to her, probably that of behaving himself in a manner worthy of his genius.

Amid the roystering pleasures that he created to share with his young master, Karl August, Goethe teemed with literary plans and undertakings. But as he could not get on well with piling up the "Pyramid of his Being," so neither could he coax any thing entirely satisfactory out of his genius—except on condition that he had a woman to love. "In what," he, in his autobiography, appealingly asks—the man of sixty-four asks:

In what can young people take the highest interest, how are they to excite interest among those of their own age, if they are not animated by love, and if affairs of the heart, *of whatever kind they may be*, are not living within them?

He needed to *grow* his subjects for poetry, and he found nothing that made these thrive and blossom so freely as to feed them with the fresh first affection of a young maiden heart. He has himself testified that every thing he wrote was from actual experience of his own. His love-songs are no exception to the rule. These, generally speaking at least, have their costly fragrance from the expressed and subtilized life-juice of a beating human heart. The egotism of the poet, too absolute to feel constraint from any claims of delicacy, has prompted him to give to the public, in one way or another, the natural history of many of his amatory poems. This one was inspired by his experience with Annette, this one by his experience with Kitty, this one by his experience with Frederica, this one by his experience with Lotte, this one by his experience with Lili, and so on and on.

The songs of Goethe are very famous, and the reader will wish to see specimens of them. We feel obliged, however, to give him due notice that, in their English form, they will prove somewhat disappointing. Probably, even in their German form, the average student, though adequately conversant with the language, would still miss the spell found in them by some. You must be steeped in knowledge and in admiration of Goethe in order to enjoy Goethe's songs, especially his love-songs, up to the measure of their fame. It is not enough that you admire Goethe, the poet and the man. You must *know* him, and admire him, in both these characters. The songs, and again we have to say, especially the love-songs, are of himself, nay, are himself. Self-felicitation, self-pity, are alternately the key in which most of them are written.

Take, for one of the more intelligible of Goethe's love-ditties, the following, much admired, entitled *New Love, New Life*. The author is about leaving "Lili" (the name is a poetical pseudonym for a real personage), not without backward-looking regret (for his own sake), to seek "fresh woods and pastures new", in which to browse his heart and his genius. The old man of sixty and upward, in his autobiography, tells us all about it, kindly adding these words :

To make this merely imaginary contemplation of a living experience come nearer to a youthful sympathy, I may insert some songs, well known, indeed, but perhaps more impressive in this connection.

The autobiographer then inserts the following song:

Heart, my heart, O, why this sadness?
  What doth weigh on thee so sore?
Changed so from thy wonted gladness,
  ' That I scarcely know thee more.
Gone is all which thou held dearest,
Gone the care which thou kept nearest,
   Gone thy toils and after-bliss.
   Ah! how couldst thou come to this!

Binds thee here her bloom so youthful—
  That divine and lovely form—
That sweet look, so good and truthful,
  With its all-subduing charm?
If I swear no more to see her,
If I man myself and flee her,
   In a moment more, alack!
   Straight to her I hie me back.

She with magic net enfolds me,
  That defies my utmost skill;
Lovely, wanton maid—she holds me,
  Holds me fast against my will.
In her magic ring who finds him,
After all her ways must mind him.
   Ah! how great the change to me!
   Love! when wilt thou set me free!

One more of the Lili poems, whereof the poet himself shall
tell the occasion and the motive.   He says:

A little golden heart which I had received from her in those fairy hours
still hung by the same little chain to which she had fastened it, love-
warmed, about my neck.   I seized hold of it, and kissed it.

Here are the lines:

Remembrancer of joys long passed away,
  Relic, from which as yet I cannot part,
O, hast thou power to lengthen love's short day?
  Stronger thy chain than that which bound the heart?

Lili, I fly!—yet still thy fetters press me
  In distant valley, or far lonely wood;
Still, with a struggling sigh of pain, confess thee
  The mistress of my soul in every mood.

> The bird may burst the silken chain which bound him,
>> Flying to the green home which fits him best;
> But, ah! he bears the prisoner's badge around him,
>> Still by the piece about his neck distressed.
> He ne'er can breathe his free, wild notes again;
> They're stifled by the pressure of his chain.

Goethe's father had given him the privilege of visiting Italy, and his fellow-tourists urged him to the journey; but the luxury of love and "renunciation" was too sweet not to be tasted all over again afresh, and he let Lili draw him back to her side.

All except the last of the foregoing poetical translations are from the hand of Mr. John S. Dwight; the last is by the celebrated Margaret Fuller. Margaret Fuller, in her time, edited the *Dial*, the famous organ of New England "Transcendentalism." She evidently it is who, in this periodical, uses, concerning Goethe, the following language:

"That Goethe as a man was selfish to a very high degree, a debauchee, and well-bred epicurean, who had little sympathy with what was highest in man so long as he could crown himself with rose-buds, we are willing to admit. But let him have justice none the less."

To both the admission and the exhortation, we heartily agree. Here is a song of Goethe's, certainly sweet in itself, and not less sweet enjoyed without flavor of any specific personal association. Mr. Dwight translates:

> I think of thee, when the bright sunlight shimmers
>> Across the sea;
> When the clear fountain in the moonbeam glimmers,
>> I think of thee.

> I see thee, if far up the pathway yonder
>> The dust be stirred:
> If faint steps o'er the little bridge to wander
>> At night be heard.

> I hear thee, when the tossing waves' low rumbling
>> Creeps up the hill;
> I go to the lone wood and listen, trembling,
>> When all is still.

I am with thee, wherever thou art roaming,
        And thou art near!
The sun goes down, and soon the stars are coming.
        Would thou wert here!

Goethe's short, sweet sentiments in verse are so fine, so famous, and withal so representative of his character, his genius, and his art, that we must give a few more of them. The two following we have been drawn to try translating ourselves. The first is entitled "Found." Some readers may like to associate it with Goethe's finding of the woman that was eventually to be his wife; but it will then not bear close study without revealing traits rather repellent than attractive. The best way to take it, is the child's way, that is, not to find allegory in it; though, on the other side, that makes the poem too trifling. We have sought to give exactly the metre, the rhyme, and the rhythm of the original; the grace of utter simplicity in it, reconciled with ideal perfection in form—that, it would need the hand of a Goethe, working freely in first creation, to produce for the English reader:

Alone I wandered
    Amid the wood,
To look for nothing,
    In listless mood.

I saw in shadow
    A floweret there,
Like star it glittered,
    Like eye was fair.

I thought to pluck it,
    When soft it spoke,
"So, then, to wither
    Must I be broke?"

With all its rootlets,
    I delved it out,
To garden bore it
    Fair house about.

There new I set it,
    In sheltered place;
Now still it bourgeons
    In blooming grace.

The next piece is of course allegory again; and allegory—
as is to be looked for in Goethe—not without its pain suggested to the thoughtful mind. But the dainty touch in it
of the artist in verse, how inimitable it is! We try to represent in translation all the metrical traits of the original,—
it bears the title, "Heath-rose," or "Brier-rose":

> Saw a youth a brier-rose blow,
>   Brier-rose on the heather,
> Young and morning-lovely so,
> Straight he ran to see the show,
>   Gladsome altogether.
> Brier-rose, brier-rose, brier-rose red,
>   Brier-rose on the heather.
>
> Quoth the youth: "I sever thee,
>   Brier-rose on the heather."
> Quoth the rose: "Forever thee
> Sting I to remember me,
>   And to know thy tether."
> Brier-rose, brier-rose, brier-rose red,
>   Brier-rose on the heather.
>
> And the willful youth he brake
>   Brier-rose on the heather,
> Brier-rose fought and wound did make,
> Her bestead not cry of ache,
>   And he knew no tether.
> Brier-rose, brier-rose, brier-rose red,
>   Brier-rose on the heather.

Yet two delicious morsels of sentiment in song from
Goethe, and we go to other, more weighty, if not more admirable, work of his pen. The two pieces proposed are
entitled, "Wanderer's Night-songs." They are no doubt
autobiographical; and, besides that, they are symbolical.
But "liberal applications lie in art, as nature," and these two
exquisite songs we will leave to the untrammeled imagination
of the reader:

> Thou that from the heavens art
>   Every pain and sorrow stillest,
> And the doubly wretched heart
>   Doubly with refreshment fillest,—

> I am weary with contending !
>> Why this rapture and unrest ?
> Peace descending,
>> Come, ah, come into my breast !

The foregoing translation lacks little of being as sweet as its original, and it clings close to the letter of that. But in the piece following, the translator—Longfellow, as before—had a more difficult task; and he has used greater freedom, without attaining equal felicity:

> O'er all the hill-tops
>> Is quiet now,
> In all the tree-tops
>> Hearest thou
> Hardly a breath;
>> The birds are asleep in the trees;
> Wait, soon like these
>> Thou too shalt rest.

Gems, exquisitely wrought, of literary workmanship, these pieces, in the original, are; and, moreover, as absolutely simple and natural as if they were indeed nature, not art. Heine said, " Nature wanted to see how she herself looked, and so she made Goethe." Nature it was, then, let us say, and not art, that wrote these songs.

Little remains that need be told of the outward fortune of Goethe. It was a prolonged and repeated experience with him of " new love, new life." At sixty-three, writing in his autobiography, he could still say appreciatively:

" It is a very pleasant sensation when a new passion [of love] begins to stir in us, *before the old one is quite extinct.*"

At Weimar, from his twenty-fifth year, he lived and labored until, in his eighty-third year, he died. During the long placid interval he made a memorable journey to Italy, spending about two years there, or on the way thither and thence. This journey and sojourn he celebrated in a book of travels, one of his highly prized productions. Italy had a profound influence on Goethe's subsequent intellectual life, furnishing one of the chief foods to his ever-hungering self-culture. It gave him the subject and the inspiration for his dramatic poem, *Torquato Tasso.* His so-styled classic poem of *Iphigenia in Tauris* was also written in Italy. (A prose form of this poem the author had previously prepared.)

The *Iphigenia*, whatever its faults and short-comings, is, in the opinion of the present writer, on the whole the clearest and noblest monument of the poet's genius. As Schiller well pointed out, it is not really classic in motive; but it is exquisitely classic in form. The modern spirit—everywhere, of course, an importunate atmosphere about the poet—pressed its way resistlessly in and profoundly affected the entire conception of the poem. Goethe was a remarkably successful pagan—"the old pagan" was one of the hard names his contemporary enemies called him; but it was not in the nature of things that a man of the eighteenth Christian century could be wholly a pagan of the third or fourth century before Christ. If, therefore, the poem be strictly considered as an attempted reproduction of the ancient classic age of Greece, the character justly attributed to it by Schiller is undoubtedly an artistic imperfection; the sentiment of the *Iphigenia* is not ancient and pagan, but modern and, in a sense, Christian. What, however, is, relatively, a fault, is, absolutely, a virtue, in the poem. We repeat that the *Iphigenia*, both negatively, that is, by the absence from it of things exceptionable, and positively, that is, by the presence in it of a sentiment purifying and ennobling, seems to us to be the work of its author worthiest to make his name a name to be praised.

To render apprehensible and enjoyable, to the reader not versed in Greek history (or Greek tradition) and Greek literature, the peculiar beauty and merit of this modern antique of Goethe's, is well-nigh out of the question. The conception of the poem presupposes two things; namely, first, a distinctively ancient and pagan myth, one quite outside the range of modern and Christian ideas, and, second, a well-known previous poetic treatment of that myth, proceeding from the hand of a great Greek master in tragedy, Euripides. The myth is, that Iphigenia, youthful daughter to Agamemnon, leader-in-chief of the Greeks mustered to the siege of Troy, was offered at Aulis a sacrifice to Diana, in order, by appeasing that virgin goddess, to secure a long-delaying favorable wind for the Grecian fleet. At the instant of the descent of the sacrificial knife, the maiden victim was caught away by the relenting goddess and borne far thence to the savage region of Tauris, there to become priestess in her temple. (A beautiful hind, bleeding from the blow that had missed Iphigenia, was substituted as victim at the altar in Aulis.) So much for the myth concerning Iphigenia.

The Euripidean tragedy of *Iphigenia in Tauris* makes it the bloody custom of the realm so named, to sacrifice all strangers arriving in it as victims to Diana. There Orestes, brother to Iphigenia, arrives, in company with his bosom friend Pylades. Orestes and Iphigenia meet without recognizing each other. She, however, learning that he is from Argos, undertakes to save his life, on condition that he will bear for her a letter to her native city, Mycene—whither she is perpetually homesick to return. Orestes will not consent to be separated from his friend Pylades; and Pylades makes a fine start to be equally magnanimous. Orestes, however, prevails upon him to yield the point of honor, when, behold—Iphigenia producing the letter for him to carry—the letter is addressed, to whom but to Orestes? This, of course, brings about a mutual recognition, and the three join in plotting a common escape for all.

So far, the myth and the treatment of the myth are substantially the same for both Euripides and Goethe. At this point begins the divergence. For, whereas Euripides makes the plot for escape, with the success of the plot, turn on a deep deception practiced by the three Greeks—in excellent accord with the Greek national repute for duplicity—Goethe makes his plot with its success turn on the ultimate beautiful truthfulness of Iphigenia, held to by her against the strongest temptation to falsehood. Iphigenia, under Goethe's hand, is transfigured from a heathen to a Christian woman. She becomes a figure resplendently fair. The moral sense is satisfied with her behavior; more than satisfied—braced, lifted, purified. We give a brief passage from the conclusion of the poem—a conclusion which has been led up to by the poet in approaches admirable for their simplicity of art. It ought to be explained additionally that Thoas, the monarch of Tauris, is deeply in love with Iphigenia. He, too, barbarian as he is, feels the effect of such clear virtue beheld. Buoyed by noble admiration of the noble in Iphigenia, he rises to the height of renunciation, and lets his beloved go, with blessing, from his hands, she taking both her brother and his friend back with her to Argos. Let readers understand that a scheme of escape had at first been agreed upon, with Iphigenia's consent, involving deception. That first scheme was that the three Greeks should steal and carry off from Tauris the precious image of Diana. Iphigenia, recovering her virtue of truth, had thought better of this plan. She voluntarily divulged all to the king. An encounter occurs, angry at first, between Orestes and Thoas—Iphigenia mediatrix. We give the closing scene of the poem, presenting this encounter together with its issue:

Iphigenia. Relieve my cares ere ye begin to speak.
     I fear contention, if thou wilt not hear
     The voice of equity, O king—if thou
     Wilt not, my brother, curb thy headstrong youth!
Thoas. I, as becomes the elder, check my rage.
     Now answer me; how dost thou prove thyself
     The priestess' brother, Agamemnon's son?
Orestes. Behold the sword with which the hero slew
     The valiant Trojans. From his murderer
     I took the weapon, and implored the gods
     To grant me Agamemnon's mighty arm,
     Success, and valor, with a death more noble.
     Select one of the leaders of thy host,
     And place the best as my opponent here.
     Where'er on earth the sons of heroes dwell,
     This boon is to the stranger ne'er refused.
Thoas. This privilege hath ancient custom here
     To strangers ne'er accorded.

13

Orestes.   Then from us
               Commence the novel custom! A whole race
               In imitation soon will consecrate
               Its monarch's noble action into law.
               Nor let me only for our liberty—
               Let me, a stranger, for all strangers fight.
               If I should fall, my doom be also theirs;
               But, if kind fortune crown me with success,
               Let none e'er tread this shore, and fail to meet
               The beaming eye of sympathy and love,
               Or unconsoled depart!
Thoas.   Thou dost not seem
               Unworthy of thy boasted ancestry.
               Great is the number of the valiant men
               Who wait upon me; but I will myself,
               Although advanced in years, oppose the foe,
               And am prepared to try the chance of arms.
Iphigenia.   No, no! such bloody proofs are not required.
               Unhand thy weapon, king! my lot consider;
               Rash combat oft immortalizes man;
               If he should fall, he is renowned in song:
               But after ages reckon not the tears
               Which ceaseless the forsaken woman sheds;
               And poets tell not of the thousand nights
               Consumed in weeping, and the dreary days,
               Wherein her anguished soul, a prey to grief,
               Doth vainly yearn to call her loved one back.
                .   .   .   .   .   .
               See here, the mark on his right hand impressed
               As of three stars, which on his natal day
               Were by the priest declared to indicate
               Some dreadful deed therewith to be performed.
                .   .   .   .   .   .
               Shall I adduce the likeness to his sire,
               Or the deep rapture of my inmost heart,
               In further token of assurance, king?
Thoas.   .   .   .   .   .   .
               Their purpose, as thou didst thyself confess,
               Was to deprive me of Diana's image.
               And think ye I will look contented on?
               The Greeks are wont to cast a longing eye
               Upon the treasures of barbarians—
                .   .   .   .   .   .
Orestes.   The image shall not be a cause of strife!
               We now perceive the error which the god—

Our journey here commanding—like a veil,
Threw o'er our minds. His counsel I implored,
To free me from the Furies' grisly band.
He answered, "Back to Greece the sister bring,
Who in the sanctuary on Tauris' shore
Unwillingly abides; so ends the curse!"
To Phœbus' sister we applied the words,
And he referred to thee. . . .
Like to a sacred image, unto which
An oracle immutably hath bound
A city's welfare, thee she bore away,
Protectress of our house, and guarded here
Within this holy stillness, to become
A blessing to thy brother and thy race.

O king, incline thine heart to thoughts of peace!

Requite the blessing which her presence brought thee,
And let me now my nearer right enjoy!
Cunning and force, the proudest boast of man,
Fade in the lustre of her perfect truth;
Nor unrequited will a noble mind
Leave confidence so child-like and so pure.

Iphigenia. Think on thy promise; let thy heart be moved
By what a true, an honest tongue hath spoken!
Look on us, king! an opportunity
For such a noble deed not oft occurs.
Refuse thou canst not—give thy quick consent.

Thoas. Then, go!

Iphigenia. Not so, my king! I cannot part
Without thy blessing, or in anger from thee:
Banish us not! the sacred right of guests
Still let us claim; so not eternally
Shall we be severed. Honored and beloved,
As mine own father was, art thou by me;
And this impression in my soul abides.
Let but the least among thy people bring
Back to mine ear the tones I heard from thee,
Or should I on the humblest see thy garb,
I will with joy receive him as a god,
Prepare his couch myself, beside our hearth
Invite him to a seat, and only ask
Touching thy fate and thee. Oh, may the gods
To thee the merited reward impart

> Of all thy kindness and benignity!
> Farewell! Oh, turn thou not away, but give
> One kindly word of parting in return!
> So shall the wind more gently swell our sails,
> And from our eyes with softened anguish flow
> The tears of separation. Fare thee well!
> And graciously extend to me thy hand,
> In pledge of ancient friendship.
>
> *Thoas* (*extending his hand*).   Fare ye well!

Miss Anna Swanwick, an English lady, has performed the part of translator for this poem of Goethe's—as also for his *Tasso*, another unexceptionable work of the poet—with singular taste and skill. We have made use of her version.

It seems a pity not to have presented more in full the poem that, for us, as we have confessed, is, on the whole, its author's greatest, or, if not his greatest, his highest, poetical achievement. But a modern antique is at best an artificial thing. The interest one feels in it is derivative and indirect, not original and immediate. One enjoys it, primarily, because it resembles something else that one enjoys; and, secondarily, because, while resembling, it differs. On either side, it is an associative, dependent enjoyment. The secondary pleasure becomes, in the case of the *Iphigenia*, the principal; in other words, we enjoy an ostensible antique most of all wherein it is not a true antique. The greatest success, that is to say, of the poem, paradoxically lies in its failure to be what it purports to be. The *Samson Agonistes* of Milton is a less pleasing, but it is a truer work of literary art than the *Iphigenia* of Goethe. That poem is (if the solecism will be allowed) a real modern antique. Its motive, its sentiment, its interest, every thing of it, in short, except its form, belongs to the date supposed, and to the ethnic conditions, of the occurrences given. The work is, indeed, a mixture of elements, in that the tragic form is Greek, while the whole tragic spirit is Hebrew. But there is no fundamental anachronism in the *Samson Agonistes* of Milton, as in the *Iphigenia* of Goethe there is. "[Milton's] *Samson* has more of the spirit of ancient times than any production of any other modern

poet ; he [Milton] is great indeed," was Goethe's own judgment, pronounced to Eckermann. Our extract from the
Iphigenia, probably the finest continuous passage of equal
length that the drama contains, falls short of indicating fairly
the beauty and the power of the poem. The poem is great
for itself, and not simply for striking passages in it.

Soon after his return to Weimar from the Italian journey, Goethe published a second "historical" drama, the *Egmont*. This, as its name would indicate, deals with incidents
in the famous revolt of the Netherlands against the cruel,
despotic, and persecuting Roman Catholic sway of Charles V.
of Spain. The poet, in constructing his drama, departs
widely, and, as it seems to us, needlessly, unwisely, and even
unjustly, from the truth of history. The departure is in
one respect highly characteristic of the man, as well as of
the poet. He represents Egmont as a reckless gallant having for mistress a girl whom he has betrayed. The historic
fact is that Egmont, at the date of the action treated by
Goethe, was a staid married man with a large family of
children. The fabricated mistress, however, is one of the
most celebrated creations, in human character, of Goethe's
genius. Goethe knew well enough where his strength lay.
He could write best such things as his own experience furnished him. Egmont's "Clärchen," we need not doubt, was
a portrait from the life.

"Many-sidedness" was a capital objective point in Goethe's life-long sedulous self-culture. Art was almost as
much to him as was literature. He even thought that perhaps his vocation was to be a painter. The doubt was to
this great philosophical genius a problem which he found no
better way of solving than to fling his pocket-knife, a "handsome" one, into the river, while he said to himself, If I see
it enter the water then I will be a painter; but if the bush-
es on the bank hide it, when entering, from my view, then
not. He did not devote himself to painting as a profession;
but to painting (and indeed to every form of art) as a study,
he did. His house in Weimar became an art museum. In

his latter years he was the recipient of many gifts from many lands, in the form of works of art, which materially helped him enrich his collection.

Science, too, Goethe cultivated. And his addiction to science revealed at once a singular sagacity and a singular fatuity in his intellectual character. It was a conceit of Goethe's that he had made original scientific investigations of his own which overthrew Newton's theory of colors. This mistake, on his part, stares posterity in the face, not only in the form of dreary tomes filled with futile dissertation (or with preposterous vituperation, directed against Sir Isaac Newton), from the author of *Faust ;* but also in the form of petulant oral expressions from the serene master of smiling wisdom, preserved for us all in the printed recollections of his personal friends. To Eckermann, for instance, Goethe talked in this flatulent fashion:

> That a man should be able to make an epoch in the world's history, two conditions are essential—that he should have a good head and a great inheritance. Napoleon inherited the French Revolution; Frederick the Great, the Silesian War; Luther, the errors of the popes; and I, those of the Newtonian theory of colors. My own time has no conception of what I have accomplished; but posterity will know.

Posterity indeed knows; not exactly, however, what Goethe, in his enormous self-confidence, imagined.

On the other side of the balance, Goethe is to be credited with two contributions, solid, if not very important, to science; one is his discovery of the intermaxillary bone in man, and the other is a point relating to the metamorphoses of plants in the process of growth. Professor Tyndall, it may be added, in a late painstaking monograph of his on Goethe's *Theory of Colors,* delivered it as his opinion that the great German, besides being wrong utterly in his conclusions, was also — herein contrasting with Sir Isaac Newton — utterly wrong and unscientific in his methods and in his spirit.

It is one of the commonplaces of remark about Goethe, that self-culture was the great aim of his life; that in this aim is to be found the true unity of his career. Some say

this in praise, some say it in blame; but all say it, and it must be regarded as true. To us, we confess, it seems an infinite pity that there did not come to this "divinely gifted man" some high call of duty outside himself to which he could in no wise refuse to respond. What might not such a great mind have done for his fellows, if he had been a Great-heart as well? And perhaps there lacked only the fit opportunity. One feels like saying this, and then one remembers that the Germany of Goethe's time was trodden under foot of strangers, as never was any great country in the world before, and that Goethe shut himself up to study Chinese, while his countrymen were struggling in that great war of liberation for Germany on the altar of which young Körner offered up his genius and his life. And the battle-fields of his country afforded Goethe means to make osteological investigations among the bones of his perished brethren! Börne, a German patriot Jew, says bitterly of Goethe, in contrast with a long list of other great poets named by him:

> But how has Goethe exhibited himself to his countrymen and to the world? As the citizen of a free city he merely recollected that he was the grandson of a mayor who, at the coronation of the Emperor of Germany, was allowed to hold the temporary office of chamberlain. As the child of honest and respectable parents he was delighted when once a dirty boy in the street called him a bastard; and he wandered forth in imagination (the imagination of a *future poet*) the son of some prince, questioning himself as to *which* he might perchance belong to. Thus he *was*, and thus he *remained*. Not once has he ever advanced a poor, solitary word in his country's cause—he who, from the lofty height which he had attained, might have spoken out what none other but himself could dare to pronounce. Some few years since, he petitioned "their high and highest mightinesses" of the German Confederation to grant his writings their all-powerful protection against piracy; but he did not remember to include in his prayer an extension of the same privilege to his literary contemporaries.

Goethe's defense of himself against the charge of want of patriotism was substantially that he had devoted himself to encouraging sound culture among his countrymen, and that he had "uniformly refused to mix himself up with party politics." When, however, the tide of French invasion rolled its waves up to the door of his own house in Weimar, and his patron duke was made to feel the weight of Napoleon's displeasure, then at length Goethe had something to say, which he said with sighs and tears, against the ruthless invader. But again, Goethe, about this time, had a personal interview with Napoleon, and that conqueror quite won the late indignant and lachrymose poet's heart, by telling him that he had read *Werther* seven times, and saying to him, with characteristic brutality of compliment, *Vous êtes un homme* ("You are a man"). The conqueror decorated the poet with the cross of the Legion of Honor, and the poet wreathed the conqueror with the laurel of his song. And such was Goethe.

The poet's genius was growing dull and barren under too much self-culture on his part, or under too little exercise of outward expression, when there happened to Goethe one of the great felicities of his life. Schiller, in 1794, made discreet and wary advances toward friendly relation with Goethe, the speedy fruit of which was a solid alliance, offensive and defensive, between the two men, lasting till Schiller died. "You have given me a second youth and refashioned me into a poet, which I may be said to have ceased to be," Goethe generously wrote to Schiller in 1798. Schiller's reciprocal debt to Goethe was perhaps greater.

The volumes of published correspondence between Goethe and Schiller constitute a remarkable monument of the mutual friendship of these two illustrious men—by common consent the most illustrious in German literary history. Friendship, we may justly call their reciprocal relation to each other; but it was an affair between them much more of the head than of the heart. The word league, or alliance, would better suit the fact that existed. Each had his personal reason for wishing the literary support of the other, and a treaty was accordingly negotiated between them. The letters they exchanged are noteworthy for the strict decorum of punctilious respect invariably paid by each to the other. There is never the self-forgetting, the self-disclosing, the self-surrendering, of trustful familiarity. Addressing Zelter—with whom, also, Goethe maintained a long correspondence—the great man sometimes condescended to say "Thou." ("Thou" is the note, with a German, of familiar friendly affection.) Goethe nowhere to Schiller writes "Thou." Very different in this respect is, on both sides, the tone of the correspondence between Schiller and Körner from that of the correspondence between Schiller and Goethe. Five years before the treaty of alliance was finally concluded by him with Goethe, Schiller had written bitterly of the latter to Körner. The poor and proud young poet had been waiting, and waiting in vain, for some response from Goethe to earlier overtures, ventured by him, looking toward the establishment of personal relation between himself and that literary lord of Weimar. Bringing himself at length to the point of trying again, Schiller wrote to Goethe an extremely skillful diplomatic letter, begging the latter's collaboration in support of a magazine, the *Hours,* which he was about to start. The moment was lucky, and that skillful letter accomplished its purpose; Goethe and Schiller were thenceforward allies. But the Goethe-Schiller correspondence contains no evidence that the high contracting parties to this famous treaty of alliance ever got on any different footing with each other from that of mutual complaisance dictated by mutual self-interest.

Goethe, previously to the formation of his friendship with Schiller, had begun his "novel" of *Wilhelm Meister,* as also his poem of *Faust.* These works were, both of them, the fruit of slow, long, and intermittent activity on the part of their author. There was nothing external to make Goethe work hard and continuously ; and that inward "spur which the clear spirit doth raise" had, in Goethe's case, been, by many diversions, much hindered from pricking effectively. Now, however, Schiller became a spur to Goethe which for ten years did not let him rest. Goethe in return became, to Schiller, a curbing and a guiding rein, which,

during the same period, did what was possible to bring that
essentially youthful and essentially immature, though noble
and lofty, genius into the right law and habit of movement
for finishing successfully his brief and brilliant career.

Goethe's *Wilhelm Meister* is fundamentally German in
quality and spirit. To enjoy it thoroughly, you must be
yourself a German. For imagining that you thoroughly
enjoy it, it might be enough for you to be profoundly persuaded that Goethe was too great a genius and too mighty
a mouth of wisdom not to make his prose masterpiece a book
worthy of your studious heed. The present writer well
remembers how he himself, years ago, in the hopeful, credu-
lous blood of youth, undertook the reading of *Wilhelm
Meister*—having heard that herein was reposed the sum of
the wisdom reaped by one of the wisest of men during half
a century or more of the rich experience of life. What was
his surprise, and what his dazed and dismayed disgust, to
find himself plunged almost at once into a reek of animalism,
open, contented, cheerful, unashamed animalism, only to be
likened to the fable of Circe's sty ! He revolted, and gave
up his reading; but such was the spell still upon him of
prevalent conventional opinion, that he remained in a com-
fortless feeling that he was himself somehow at fault, in not
having yet been educated up to the proper point for making
that sort of thing food for his soul. As in duty bound, he has,
of late, for the purpose of this book, gone, with open mind,
resolutely through, from beginning to end, not, he believes,
skipping a page, the whole story of the "Apprenticeship"
of Wilhelm Meister. Of that worthy's "Travels"—for the
work is divided into parts thus named—he dare not testify
but he may have spared himself here and there a paragraph.
Thus qualified to form his own opinion, the writer ventures
to sum up the good and the bad of this noted production,
by describing the *Wilhelm Meister* as a tissue of smoothly,
suavely, harmoniously woven German prose, constituting a
dull, slow, prolix, low, groveling, fleshly, ill-schemed, loose-
jointed, invertebrate, dim, beclouded, enigmatical, self-com-

placently autobiographic "novel" — with episodes, or at least passages in it, worthy of the fame of its author.

By immemorial custom, the German mechanic goes through two stages of experience; one in which he is an " apprentice," and one, subsequent, in which he makes a round of " travel," as a journeyman. Wilhelm Meister, Goethe's hero, is " apprenticed " to life, in the first part of the story; and in the second part, he is supposed to have become a " master." The idea of the book was expressly adapted for enabling the author, on a thread of disguised and freely modified autobi-ography, to string the pearls of wisdom that he had gathered from the observation and reflection of his life. Wilhelm Meister (that is, Goethe himself), after an early youth of sensuality—so described by the author that Thomas Carlyle in translating felt compelled to abate at points the incredibly vulgar details into which the original enters—young Wil-helm Meister, we say, runs dishonorably away from home and joins a strolling band of play-actors and actresses, with whom he spends the whole time of his " apprenticeship." Of the incidents naturally composing the experience of such a wandering company, the plot of the story, if plot it can be called, is made up. Remarks and criticisms on dramatic writing and on dramatic representation are interspersed— remarks and criticisms having certainly their value, but also certainly having no proper place in a " novel." One whole " book " of *Wilhelm Meister* consists of a narrative, purport-ing to be given by herself in writing, of the religious experience of a female character incidentally introduced into the story. The title of this " book " is, *The Confessions of a Fair Saint.* The evident purpose of the author was, simply to make literary use of some material that he had acquired through acquaintance once enjoyed with a lovely Christian woman who had sought to win the wayward and brilliant young Goethe to Christ. This episode, if it were not so manifestly a piece of mere literary practice on the part of the author, would seem to possess a certain charm of spiritual refinement. Lest, to some reader of ours, graciously willing to think the best that is possible of every man, we seem to be judging Goethe at this point with too little charity, we quote here some expressions from our author on the subject of his own personal relation to God, which will be sufficient to indicate how far from the Christian spirit he consciously and deliberately was:

> I had believed from my youth upward that I stood on very good terms with my God—nay, I even fancied to myself, according to various experiences, that he might even be in arrears to me; and I was daring enough to think that I had something to forgive him. This presumption was grounded on my infinite good-will, to which, as it seemed to me, he should have given better assistance.

The foregoing is indeed told as a course of thought belonging to the author's youth ; but the autobiographer, now sixty-three years old, neither expresses nor implies any repudiation or any disapproval of these youthful sentiments of his. Nay, at seventy-three years of age, writing to a lady who had addressed to him an earnest Christian expostulation, he expresses himself, in almost the same tone of religious self-complacency, as follows:

> All my life I have meant honestly toward myself and others, and in all my earthly action have looked to the highest. . . . Let us remain untroubled about the future [that is, the future following death].

The one really beautiful thing—this is by no means wholly a beautiful thing—in creation of character and in imagination of fate, is the interwoven episode of Mignon. This we must show in just a glimpse or two, to our readers, and therewith dismiss the *Wilhelm Meister* to the limbo in which it belongs.

Mignon is the name of a mysterious child dropped into the hands of Wilhelm, as fruit of his experience with the strolling players. An Italian gentleman of rank had, by sad fatality, without knowing the truth of that lady's relation to him, fallen in love with his own sister. He is under vows as a priest, and he cannot marry; but this child Mignon is born to the pair out of wedlock. (The base and the beautiful are so mingled in Goethe's work, that pure beauty it is often impossible to get, without displeasing adhesion of baseness.) The mother dies, and the crazed father, at rest in mind, but in body restless, wanders about the world leading his daughter, and carrying a harp, on which he makes weird music. Wilhelm falls in with this strange pair, and Mignon, child as she is, conceives precociously a passion for him. There is not a little detail about the child's conduct in her relation to Wilhelm which, though for this "novel" comparatively unobjectionable, will not bear reproducing. The end is, that Mignon, grown old enough at length to have the woman's feeling, goes distraught with hopeless love for Wilhelm, dies, and is buried with beautiful exequies. It is not till after her death and burial that the secret of her birth and the mystery of the harper, her father, are explained—as we have explained them.

Succeed in dissociating what disgusts from the story of Mignon, and the cleansed remainder you find pure and beautiful. There was real genius at work in the creation and display of this character and fate.

Mignon sings a pathetic song, mingled of love-sick longing unconfessed toward Wilhelm, and of home-sick longing toward Italy—her native land, dimly remembered by the child—and toward that mansion which had been the home of her infancy. This melody is one of the loveliest of Goethe's lyrics; and here it is, sympathetically translated by **Mr. W. H. Channing**:

> Know'st thou the land, where flowers of citron bloom,
> The golden orange glows through leafy gloom,
> From the blue heavens the breezes float so bland,
> The myrtle still, and tall the laurels stand?
> Know'st thou the land?
>
> > O there, O there!
> Loved one, with thee I long to wander there.
>
> Know'st thou the house? Its roof the columns bear—
> The polished floors, the halls so bright and fair,
> Where marble figures standing look on me:
> "Thou poorest child, what have they done to thee?"

Know'st thou the house?
> O there, O there!
With thee, kind guardian, O could I be there!

Know'st thou the mountain peak?—the airy bridge,
Where loaded mules climb o'er the misty ridge?
In hollows dwell the serpent's ancient brood;
The rent crag rushes down the foaming flood.
Know'st thou the mount?
> O there, O there
Leadeth our way—O, father, let us there!

The exequies of Mignon are, in conception, at once pagan and beautiful. They are thus described:

The company proceeded to the Hall of the Past; they found it magnificently ornamented and illuminated. The walls were hung with azure tapestry almost from ceiling to floor, so that nothing but the friezes and socles, above and below, were visible. On the four candelabra in the corner, large wax lights were burning; smaller lights were in the four smaller candelabra placed by the sarcophagus in the middle. Near this stood four boys dressed in azure with silver; they had broad fans of ostrich-feathers, which they waved above a figure that was resting upon the sarcophagus. The company sat down; two invisible choruses began in a soft, musical recitative to ask, "Whom bring ye us to the still dwelling?" The four boys replied with lovely voices, "'Tis a tired playmate whom we bring you; let her rest in your still dwelling, till the songs of her heavenly sisters once more awaken her."

CHORUS. Firstling of youth in our circle, we welcome thee! with sadness welcome thee! May no boy, no maiden, follow! Let age only, willing and composed, approach the silent hall, and in the silent company repose this one dear child!

BOYS. Ah, reluctantly we brought her hither! Ah, and she is to remain here! Let us, too, remain; let us weep, let us weep upon her bier!

CHORUS. Yet look at the strong wings; look at the light, clear robe. How glitters the golden band upon her head! Look at the beautiful, the noble, repose!

BOYS. Ah! the wings do not raise her; in the frolic game, her robe flutters to and fro no more; when we bound her head with roses, her looks on us were kind and friendly.

CHORUS. Cast forward the eye of the spirit. Awake in your souls the imaginative power, which carries forth what is fairest, what is highest, life, away beyond the stars.

BOYS. But, ah! we find her not here; in the garden she wanders not; the flowers of the meadow she plucks no longer. Let us weep, we are leaving her here! Let us weep, and remain with her!

CHORUS. Children, turn back into life! Your tears let the fresh air dry, which plays upon the rushing water. Flee from night! Day and pleasure and continuance are the lot of the living.

BOYS. Up! Turn back into life! Let the day give us labor and pleasure, till the evening gives us rest, and the nightly sleep refreshes us.

CHORUS. Children! hasten into life! In the pure garments of beauty, may Love meet you with heavenly looks and with the wreath of immortality!

An abbé, after the boys retire, makes an appropriate little pagan address, and the occasion is over.

Here is a sentence on *Wilhelm Meister* from Carlyle himself, pronounced by him when fresh from his labor and his disgust in getting well acquainted with the production, through translating it for the publishers: "There is not, properly speaking, the smallest particle of historical [narrative] interest in it except what is connected with Mignon. Meister himself is perhaps one of the greatest *ganaches* [blockheads] that ever was created by quill and ink. I am going to write a fierce preface disclaiming all concern with the literary or the moral merit of the work. . . . What a work! Bushels of dust and straw and feathers, with here and there a diamond of the purest water."

When he was a man sixty years old, Goethe wrote a second "novel," entitled *Elective Affinities.* The idea of this is to exhibit the principle of free love working to separate married pairs and to join them anew in other alligation, according to their natural "elective affinities."

Attention has yet to be paid to that selected work of Goethe which is universally esteemed the crowning achievement of his genius ; we mean, of course, the *Faust.* Briefly, however, meantime, of a purer, if less aspiring, poem of his, the *Hermann and Dorothea.*

This is perhaps the most strictly popular of Goethe's longer pieces in verse. It is what the author himself styles an "epic" poem; though the extremely humble tone of it is such that we English-speakers should more naturally describe

it as an idyll. The story is a story of love, love complicated
with various domestic passions sufficiently plebeian. The
local color is inimitably German. Goethe hits in it an idiom
of expression felicitously faithful to the dialect of common
village life in Germany. The thinking, and the feeling too,
of the poem are as faultlessly real as is the language in
which they speak. The keeping, the harmony, is throughout almost ideal. In short, the *Hermann and Dorothea*
is an eminently successful piece of poetic art. The artist
performs for poetry the part that Socrates is said to have
performed for philosophy. He brings her down from the
clouds and makes her walk on the ground.

For it is walking, not flying, that Goethe's muse does in
the *Hermann and Dorothea.* Scarcely once does she balance her wings and lift herself free in the air. She walks,
she ambles, in hexameters. Very softly flowing hexameters
they are, the perfection of what the German language in
that verse admits. The constraint of effort disappears in the
ease of triumphant execution.

There is a very satisfactory English hexameter version of
the *Hermann and Dorothea.* From this we give a single
very brief extract, an extract sufficient, however, to indicate
the character of the whole poem. The story, in short, of
the idyll is that Hermann, son of an inn-keeper who feels
the dignity of his calling, falls in love with a girl met by
him as she goes, in company with a caravan of refugees
from war's alarms, to some unknown place of refuge. The
young fellow makes a confidant of his mother, who undertakes hopefully to bring round his highly opinionated father,
at present much set on a different match for his son. Several
villagers are taken into counsel on the subject—in a manner
decidedly German as distinguished from American.

The village pastor and the village apothecary undertake,
on the general family behalf, to go and view the maiden
and report results. They do this, and, to make assurance
doubly sure, the shame-faced young man engages the maiden
out-of-hand—as his wife? no, he dared not yet risk refusal

at her hands, but as a servant in his father's house. She frankly
accepts the proffered place and comes home accordingly with
the bashful youth. But the youth's father very nearly spoils
his son's prudent plan. Coarsely, on her first arrival, he
rallies the modest young creature as his son's " bride " full
easily won. The pastor intervenes, however, and the maiden,
who was about to go away cruelly wounded in feeling, is then
and there, the crisis having been so precipitated, indeed
wooed and won. There is nothing better in the poem than
the management on Goethe's part of this sudden development of plot. The full text of the passage is leisurely and
long drawn out. We shall have to condense our extract.
The father, mistaking the situation, addresses the girl :

" Ay, this is pleasant, my child ! I am glad to see that my son is
Blessed with good taste, like his sire. . . .
And you required, I suppose, but a short time to form your conclusion,
For, sure, it seems to me that he's not such a hard one to follow."

Hermann but slightly caught these words, but his limbs to the marrow
Quivered, and all at once the whole circle was hushed into silence.

But the excellent maiden by words of such cruel mocking
(As they appeared), being hurt and deeply wounded in spirit,
Stood there, her cheeks to her neck suffused with quick-spreading blushes ;
Yet her feelings she checked, and her self-possession regaining,
Though not entirely concealing her pain, thus spake to the old man :

" Truly, for such a reception your son quite failed to prepare me,
Painting to me the ways of his father, that excellent burgher.

Is it noble to make me at once the butt of such mocking
As, on the very threshold, well-nigh from your house drove me back-
    ward ? "

Much was Hermann alarmed, and made signs to his good friend the pastor,

Who upon that thus addressed her with words of searching intention :

" Surely, thou foreign maiden, thou didst not wisely consider,
When with all haste thou resolvedst to be a servant to strangers.

Truly, thou seem'st not well-suited for this, since the jokes of the father
Wound thee so deeply at once ; and yet there is nothing more common
Than to tease a girl about finding a youth to her fancy."

14

Thus with hot gushing tears she at once addressed him in answer:

" Happy are ye, and glad; and how should a joke then e'er wound you?

Let me again begone! In the house no more may I tarry.
I will away, and go to seek my poor people in exile,
Whom I forsook in their trouble, to choose for my own profit only.
This is my firm resolve; and now I may dare to acknowledge
That which else in my heart full many a year had lain hidden.
Yes, the father's mocking hath deeply wounded me; not that
I am peevish and proud (which would ill become a poor servant),
But that, in truth, I felt in my heart a strong inclination
Tow'rd the youth who to-day had appeared as my saviour from evil.

And when I found him again at the well, the sight of him pleased me
Not at all less than if I had seen an angel from heaven;
And my consent was so glad, when he asked me to come as a servant! "

Now for the first time I feel how far a poor maiden is severed
From the youth who is rich, although she were never so prudent,
All this now have I told, that you may not my heart misinterpret.

And I will now go forth again, as I've long been accustomed,
Caught by the whirlwind of time, to part from all I could cherish.
Fare ye well! I can stay no longer, but all is now over."

Thus she spoke, and again to the door was quickly returning,
Still keeping under her arm the little bundle brought with her.
But with both her arms the mother laid hold of the maiden,
Clinging round her waist, and cried in wondering amazement:
" Say, what meanest thou by this, and these tears now shed to no purpose?
No, I will not permit thee, thou art my son's own betrothed one."

But the father stood there displeased with what was before him,
Eying the weeping women, and spoke with the words of vexation:
" This, then, befalls me at last, as the greatest test of forbearance,
That at the close of the day what is most unpleasant should happen!
For I find nothing so hard to bear as the weeping of women,
And the passionate scream, that with eager confusion commences,
Scenes which a little good sense might soften down with more comfort.
Irksome is it to me still to look on this wondrous beginning;
Ye must conclude it yourselves, for I to my bed am now going."

The retiring father is detained by the son and all is happily concluded by a betrothal, duly, on the spot, sealed and

witnessed between the youth and the maiden. The actual marriage is left to anticipation.

Voss (Johann Heinrich: 1751–1826), an important German literary figure, was beforehand with Goethe in the species of poetry of which the *Hermann and Dorothea* became immediately and permanently the most illustrious German exemplar. That writer's *Luise* it was, which led to Goethe's *Hermann and Dorothea*. It would be a nice attempt of poetic taste— poetic taste, it would need to be, conversant with German life and with the German language—to feel and to state the difference in quality which creates the contrast between the foregoing from the *Hermann and Dorothea*, and the following from the *Luise*, for which we use a fragment of translation found in *Fraser's Magazine* for April, 1849.

It was Luise's birthday. The family in honor of the occasion take their noon-day meal, German fashion, out-of-doors. The lines we first extract describe the scene and then hint how the good old pastor is disposed of by his wife, to give Luise and her lover their chance together. Voss:

Under the sweet, cool shade of two umbrageous lime-trees,
Which, with their gold bloom gay, with the bees' song drowsily ringing,
Shading the parlor front, o'er the mossed roof whisperéd waving,
Cheerfully held his feast the worthy Pastor of Grünau,
For his Louisa's sake—domestic, yet grand, in his nightgown.

    .   .   .   .

"Sleep thou cool in the chamber. Already has housemaid Susannah
Drugged the flies with pepper and milk; and caught in the mousetrap
Him that we saw, and made the alcóve all pleasant and airy."
Thus spake she, and drew her loved spouse into the chamber,

    .   .   .   .

While the maid the remains of the meal and the festival glasses
Carried away, with the diapered cloth that covered the table."

How evidently is this in the Homeric manner humiliated! (Voss translated Homer into German hexameters.) The lines following show what Goethe's teacher in "epic" poetry could do in a higher mood—a mood of gentle, pensive pathos. The pastor of Grünau blesses his daughter, a wife about departing with her husband, to leave her father lonely:

May the blessing of God, my dearest and loveliest daughter,
Be with thee! yea, the blessing of God on this earth and in heaven!
Young have I been, and now am old, and of joy and of sorrow,
In this uncertain life, sent by God, much, much have I tasted:
God be thanked for both! O, soon shall I now with my fathers
Lay my gray head in the grave! how fain! for my daughter is happy;
Happy, because she knows this, that our God, like a father who watches
Carefully over his children, us blesses in joy and in sorrow.

. . . .

Soon, soon my daughter's chamber, soon 't will be desolate to me,
And my daughter's place at the table! In vain shall I listen
For her voice afar off, and her footsteps at distance approaching!
When with thy husband on that way thou from me art departed,
Sobs will escape me, and thee my eyes bathed in tears long will follow.

Voss's poem is less happily transferred to English than is Goethe's. But what our readers have seen may serve to help them judge for themselves the extent to which Goethe was pupil to Voss in the line of "epic" poetry.

Now for the *Faust*. This is a tragedy founded on the familiar myth of a man's selling himself to the devil—for an appropriate consideration. The name "Faust" is the name, shortened, of a real person, Doctor Johannes Faustus, professor of magic and of black arts, who lived in Germany, a contemporary of Luther and Melanchthon.

The legend of Faust has for three centuries haunted the German imagination, and, indeed, the imagination of Europe. It has been often treated in literature. Lessing tried his hand on it. But, before Lessing, an experiment more noteworthy still than his had been made. The English poet Marlowe was a precursor of Shakespeare. He died prematurely, by violence, at twenty-nine, but he had then already, by performance, proved himself a genius of such power as to make it not presumptuous for us to say that Shakespeare would have had a fellow, had Marlowe lived. Marlowe wrote a great play, entitled *Faustus*, on the same subject. This is now, together with Goethe's *Faust* translated, published, as a companion piece to that, in one of the volumes of "Morley's Universal Library." It may thus be bought for a trifle, and readers will do well to get it for the sake of the interesting comparison it will enable them to make. The English handling will be found more entertaining, as a piece to read throughout, than the German; but the German, on the other hand, reaches a much more exciting pitch of tragedy at the close. The Englishman's work is as clear as light, and the progress is straightforward from the starting-point to the goal. The German's work plunges you not seldom into cloud, and the path you follow winds, digresses, and delays. The difference between these two productions answers to the difference between the two national types of genius. Goethe evidently is deep in debt to Marlowe, whose play he, in fact, at one time seriously thought of translating into German.

Both Marlowe and Goethe make their hero Faustus a laborious student who has drained dry the sources of satisfaction to the mind found in the various ordinary departments of human knowledge. Wearied and worried, but unsated, the voracious student turns to magic lore. The result is that Mephistophilis (so Marlowe, but Goethe spells "Mephistopheles") appears in answer to incantation, and a compact is settled by him with Faust binding the man to surrender himself in the end to the devil, and reciprocally binding the devil to be at the man's command meantime. So far the two poets coincide with each other, and, we believe, with the legend. But whereas Marlowe has a definite limit of time fixed—twenty-four years—for Mephistophilis's service to Faust, Goethe, more subtly, has Faust agree to be the devil's at any moment whatsoever, at which he, Faust, shall be brought to the point of saying, "There, now, this is so good that I should like to have it indefinitely continue."

Goethe had his *Faust* on the stocks no less than sixty years before it was finally dismissed as a finished work; he began it at twenty years of age, and he did not round it to completion till within about a year of his death. There is probably no parallel in literary history to this long term of labor on a single work—if single work be, indeed, the *Faust* of Goethe, which exists in two parts so different from one another that had they belonged to a period of time as remote as that of the *Iliad*, Wolf, iconoclast to Homer, would have found it easy to frame, from internal evidence, a quite irrefragable argument against identity of authorship for them. The "Second Part" of Goethe's *Faust* is generally conceded to be a "land of darkness as darkness itself." When the *Faust* is spoken of, you may safely, as a rule, assume it to be the "First Part" only that is meant. We shall limit ourselves here strictly to the First Part.

Critical students of the *Faust* are all forced to admit that the work is wanting in such perfect fusion of parts into unity as might have been looked for had it been written at one heat, long-continued, of the imagination, instead of being composed, as it was, in fragments, to be, with much after beating on the anvil, welded into one. Goethe was, fundamentally, rather an artist than a poet. But Goethe's art was not equal to the task of making a whole great poem of the *Faust*. Mr. Emerson, in his *Representative Men*, showed fine instinct in having Shakespeare, rather than Goethe, stand for "the Poet." Goethe he made stand for "the Writer." Mr. Hermann Grimm's courage is greater, or his taste less sure. Emboldened perhaps by the late step to the front which Germany as a nation has taken, this critical biographer of Goethe claims for his idol the solitary first place, without fellow, among the poets of all nations and of all times. We quote Professor Grimm's words. He is, with confident prediction, speaking of the future of the *Faust:*

> This career of this greatest work of the greatest poet of all nations and times has just begun, and only the leading steps have been taken toward bringing to light the value of its contents.

There is a confession of faith for you! The master himself was contented with less tribute than the disciple is eager to pay. Goethe intimated that it was as absurd to equal him with Shakespeare as it was to equal Tieck with him. Surely

the god herein was as much wiser, as he was more modest,
than his worshiper. Mr. Hermann Grimm's work, entitled
Life and Times of Goethe, has been admirably translated
by an American lady, who, in a prefatory note, speaks of
Goethe as " at once the most real, as well as the most ideal,
man and poet that ever lived." This language does not
over-express the sentiment concerning Goethe that is tending to establish itself as one of the unquestionable postulates
of literary criticism. The connection between character and
genius is vital. It is vivisection to sever one from the other.
" *Man* and poet " are indissolubly joined. Like man, like
poet ; also, like poet, like man. Dr. Hedge virtually confesses this in his avowed willingness to argue from the greatness of the poet to the goodness of the man, in the case of
Goethe. Indeed, he makes his formula general. He says :
" I do not envy the mental condition of those who can rest in
the belief that a really great poet can be a bad man." Such a
mode of establishing moral excellence for Goethe will not be
satisfactory to all. Some will still inquire, " How did Goethe
behave himself ? " At any rate, our readers will see that it
behooved their author to do as he has done, namely, show
them Goethe the man while showing them Goethe the poet.
And at no other time is knowledge of Goethe's character,
in connection with knowledge of his genius, more necessary
than when one is seeking to form a just estimate of the
Faust.

Of the *Faust* of Goethe, as a whole, it must be said that
it is dull reading, very dull reading, to the average English-
speaker. That episode in it, however, which at last swallows up the play, is interesting; we refer to the episode of
Margaret or Gretchen. Interesting this is, exciting even
and powerful; but disagreeably, as well as painfully, so.
Margaret is a young girl—" past fourteen," as Faust is made,
with repulsive arithmetic, to say—whom that gentleman, a
" doctor " of mature age, seduces from virtue. About the
character and the fate of Margaret centres whatever of
popular human interest the poem provides.

In keeping with the patch-work poetic art exemplified in *Faust,* the drama is introduced by two prologues. A "Dedication," full of self, but full of beauty, was finally prefixed. The first prologue is sufficiently mundane; the second is styled the "Prologue in Heaven." The idea of this latter is suggested by the opening of Job. A feature in it, however, that is not of Job, is the song of three archangels who chant the praises of God. We give this, in the rendering of Mr. C. T. Brooks, whose translation of the *Faust* was the first to reproduce in English all the diversified metres of the original. Mr. Bayard Taylor followed Mr. Brooks, and did the same work over again, with less scholarship and with less felicity. The poet Shelley rendered this prologue well, but on the whole not so well as Mr. Brooks did it after him. *Faust* (the First Part only, remember, we speak of here) has been done into English probably not less than fifty times. Miss Anna Swanwick's is perhaps the most entirely pleasing version of all.

Here, then, is the song of the three archangels, according to Mr. Brooks:

Raphael. The sun, in ancient wise, is sounding,
  With brother-spheres, in rival song;
  And, his appointed journey rounding,
   With thunderous movement rolls along.
  His look, new strength to angels lending,
   No creature fathom can for aye;
  The lofty works, past comprehending,
   Stand lordly, as on time's first day.

Gabriel. And swift, with wondrous swiftness fleeting,
   The pomp of earth turns round and round,
  The glow of Eden alternating
   With shuddering midnight's gloom profound;
  Up o'er the rocks the foaming ocean
   Heaves from its old, primeval bed,
  And rocks and seas, with endless motion,
   On in the spheral sweep are sped.

Michael. And tempests roar, glad warfare waging,
   From sea to land, from land to sea,
  And bind round all, amidst their raging,
   A chain of giant energy.

There, lurid desolation, blazing,
    Foreruns the volleyed thunder's way:
Yet, Lord, thy messengers are praising
    The mild procession of thy day.
All Three. The sight new strength to angels lendeth,
    For none thy being fathom may,
The works no angel comprehendeth
    Stand lordly as on time's first day.

The effect of the versification is here remarkably re-echoed from the German original. To a listening ear not accustomed to either German or English, the sound, we imagine, would seem much the same for Goethe and for Brooks. Still, Goethe's stanzas are, no doubt, far finer to the German, than Brooks's are to the Englishman or the American. Klopstock was before Goethe in conceiving the course of the sun as accomplished with "thunder-sound." To us, the accompaniment of noise seems to degrade, instead of elevating, the idea of the motion of celestial bodies. It is, however, perhaps the pagan notion of a sun-chariot driven with whirl and rumble of wheels, that Goethe incongruously mixes with the Christian representation of God and archangels. What motion it is of the sun to which Goethe refers, we find it hard to determine. If the apparent motion, diurnal or annual, of the sun about the earth—but we must not stay to criticise. Let leisurely and curious readers study the conception, or conceptions, involved in this famous song of the archangels, and see if they can successfully adjust and reconcile the different parts one to another. Is there a point of view, for the archangels to be supposed occupying, that will yield the proportion and perspective of vision attributed by the poet? Or, is there, in short, nothing left of the song, when fairly analyzed, but a *caput mortuum* of ringing rhyme and rhythm? Still, if Goethe is ever sublime, as Milton has taught us to know sublimity, it is in this song of the archangels that he is so. But Urania was not Goethe's muse.

The rest of the " Prologue in Heaven " is irredeemably profane. The vindication attempted, namely, that it is not more audaciously free than the beginning of Job, breaks down under the weight of the sentiment blasphemously imputed by Goethe to God, in these words addressed by God to Mephistopheles: "The like of thee I never yet did hate; of all spirits that deny, the scoffing scamp is the one to me least offensive," etc. Goethe, no doubt, meant here to keep just within bounds; but it was a case in which Mephistopheles, urging from behind, pricked Faust resistlessly forward to take the step beyond. This figurative mode of speaking is justified by the fact that Faust is really Goethe himself. Goethe said :

> The marionette [puppet] fable of Faust murmured with many voices in my soul. I, too, had wandered into every department of knowledge, and had returned early enough satisfied with the vanity of science. And life too I had tried under various aspects, and always came back sorrowing and unsatisfied.

The *Faust* is a highly composite piece of literary art. The most diverse and heterogeneous materials, wrought into the most diverse and heterogeneous forms, are built into the edifice. We shall not conceal our own confident opinion that the time will come when men will wonder that ever such a heteroclite production imposed itself on several generations of readers, or rather of critics, as a true triumph of genius and of art. The atmosphere of a mocking worldly wisdom pervades the work. There are reliefs in it of beauty and of pathos; there are passages of power. But if we were challenged to produce from the *Faust* a single lofty or noble sentiment, one generous expression, such as "makes a man feel strong in speaking truth," we should be obliged to confess ourselves at a loss. The very versification—with brief intervals, and rare, of exception—moves as if animated, or galvanized rather, with mockery. Masterly, no doubt, the versification is; and its masterliness is in nothing else more strikingly felt than in the jerky and jiggish responsiveness it shows to the jeering spirit it prevailingly has to express. *Faust* is a piece of almost pure *diablerie* from beginning to end. By authoritative critics it is considered a great poem. To us it seems far more like an ironical retribution which the outraged spirit of truth and nobleness wreaked, in Goethe's case, on selfish self-culture, by simply leaving that unworthy ideal of life wholly to itself—and to the devil—to work out its own legitimate result.

We feel no disposition to prove our point, even partially, by citations. On the contrary, we pass over what would tend to prove it, and select instead our specimens from the small best part of the *Faust.*

Here is Faust's first meeting with Margaret. Mephistopheles has previously primed and preened his man to fall in love with the child and to win her love for him:

A STREET.

FAUST. MARGARET [*passing over*].

Faust   My fair young lady, will it offend her
        If I offer my arm and escort to lend her?
Margaret. Am neither lady, nor yet am fair!
        Can find my way home without any one's care.
           [*Disengages herself and exit.*]
Faust.   By heavens, but then the child *is* fair!
        I've never seen the like, I swear.
        So modest is she and so pure,
        And somewhat saucy, too, to be sure.
        The light of the cheek, the lip's red bloom,
        I shall never forget to the day of doom!
        How she cast down her lovely eyes,
        Deep in my soul imprinted lies;
        How she spoke up, so curt and tart,
        Ah, that went right to my ravished heart!

The details that follow will not bear reproducing. Faust goes, conducted by Mephistopheles, to Margaret's bed-chamber (she absent), there to pasture his prurient imagination on what he sees. A little mawkish sentiment, as if of reaction on his part from evil intent, uttered by Faust, serves only to make the whole thing more insufferably nauseous. In another scene, Margaret is shown us singing a song which Goethe, having it already on hand, thriftily worked into his play, about the "King of Thule"—a song well enough in its way, not a very admirable way, but in obvious ill-keeping as

sung by sweet, innocent, young Margaret; who, however—
sweet and innocent, though evidently the author purposed to
have us regard her as being—is, curiously enough, made by
him to accuse her own mother of overworking her through
stinginess, and this to her stranger lover !

More in character, and more nearly worthy, though far
from worthy, of its fame, is Margaret's song at the spinning-
wheel.   In this, the maiden confesses her love—by the way, a
disagreeably precocious, ungrounded, and ill-assorted love—
for Doctor Faust. Here is the song—in Brooks's translation:

> My heart is heavy,
> My peace is o'er;
> I never—ah! never—
> Shall find it more.
>   While him I crave,
> Each place is the grave;
> The world is all
> Turned into gall.
>   My wretched brain
> Has lost its wits,
> My wretched sense
> Is all in bits.
>   My heart is heavy,
> My peace is o'er;
> I never—ah! never—
> Shall find it more.
>   Him only to greet, I
> The street look down;
> Him only to meet, I
> Roam through town.
>   His lofty step,

> His noble height,
> His smile of sweetness,
> His eye of might,
>   His words of magic,
> Breathing bliss,
> His hand's warm pressure,
> And, ah! his kiss.
>   My heart is heavy,
> My peace is o'er;
> I never—ah! never—
> Shall find it more.
>   My bosom yearns
> To behold him again.
> Ah, could I find him,
> That best of men!
> I'd tell him then
> How I did miss him,
> And kiss him
> As much as I could.
> Die on his kisses
> I surely should!

The fatal objection to this song, as sung, by such a sweetheart, of such a lover, is that it sings a sentiment which, supposed, on the one hand, to arise under purely natural conditions,
is without warranting motive—exercised by a mere child
toward a mature prig like Faust—or, on the other hand,
supposed to arise under conditions of diabolic interference,
loses its human interest and becomes either a tediously improbable, or a positively repulsive, conception.   In all the

artistic accidents of form, Goethe here, as is usual with him in such versifications, is triumphant. Obviously, in describing for Margaret the personal appearance of her lover, the poet drew from his looking-glass. He "saw his own figure." The effect of egotism forces itself irresistibly into the song.

The end, of course, is ruin for the child. Her brother, Valentine, Faust kills in a duel—a duel occasioned by the young fellow's taking up a championship for his sister. Margaret's mother dies from a deadly potion given her by her daughter, to make her sleep while Faust and his victim are meeting each other. The child did not mean harm to her mother; Faust supplied her with the potion. Margaret herself, her wits crazed, drowns her babe, and is imprisoned, to die by being beheaded. The prison scene between the girl and her seducer is celebrated. It is the most really moving thing that Goethe ever wrote. Here it is condensed from Brooks's version. (We ought to say that, to make the variety of form in his work complete, Goethe has a short prose scene preceding this.) Faust, having through Mephistopheles secured the gaoler's keys, enters the dungeon to rescue Margaret. Margaret mistakes him for the executioner. Now Goethe:

Margaret [*burying herself in bed*]. Woe! woe!
          They come. O death of bitterness!
  Faust [*softly*]. Hush! hush! I come to free thee; thou **art** dreaming.
Margaret [*prostrating herself before him*]. Art thou a man? then feel
          for my distress.
  Faust. Thou'lt wake the guards with thy loud screaming!
          [*He seizes the chains to unlock them.*]
Margaret [*on her knees*]. Headsman, who's given thee this **right**
          O'er me, this power!
          Thou com'st for me at dead of night;
          In pity spare me, one short hour!
          Will 't not be time when matin bell has rung?
                  [*She stands up.*]
          Ah, I am yet so young, so young!
          And death pursuing!
          Fair was I, too, and that was my undoing.
          My love was near, far is he now!

Torn is the wreath, the scattered flowers lie low.

　　　　.　　　　.　　　.　　　　.

But first I'd nurse my child—do not prevent me.
I hugged it through the black night hour;
They took it from me to torment me,
And now they say I killed the pretty flower.
I shall never be happy again, I know.
They sing vile songs at me!　'Tis bad in them to do it!
There's an old tale that ends just so.
Who gave that meaning to it?

Faust [*prostrates himself*].　A lover at thy feet is bending,
Thy bonds of misery would be rending.

Margaret [*flings herself beside him*].　O let us kneel, the saints for aid
　　　　invoking!
See! 'neath the threshold smoking,
Fire-breathing,
Hell is seething!
There prowling,
And grim under cover,
Satan is howling!

Faust [*aloud*].　Margery!　Margery!

Margaret [*listening*].　That was the voice of my lover!

　　　　[*She springs up.　The chains fall off.*]

Where is he?　Where?　He calls.　I hear him.
I'm free!　Who hinders?　I will be near him.
I'll fly to his neck!　I'll hold him!
To my bosom I'll enfold him!
He stood on the threshold—called Margery plainly!
Hell's howling and clattering to drown it sought vainly—
Through the devilish, grim scoffs that might turn one to
　　　　stone,
I caught the sweet, loving, enrapturing tone.

Faust.　'Tis I!

Margaret.　'Tis thou!　O say it once again!

　　　　[*Clasping again.*]

'Tis he!　'tis he!　Where now is all my pain?
And where the dungeon's anguish?　Joy-giver!
'Tis thou!　And come to deliver!
I am delivered!
Again before me lies the street,
Where for the first time thou and I did meet;
And the garden-bower,
Where we spent that evening hour.

Faust [*trying to draw her away*]. Come! Come with me!

Margaret.   O tarry!
   I tarry so gladly where thou tarriest.
      [*Caressing him.*]

Faust. Hurry!
   Unless thou hurriest,
   Bitterly we both must rue it.

Margaret. Kiss me! Canst no more do it?
   So short an absence, love, as this,
   And forgot how to kiss?
   What saddens me so as I hang about thy neck?
   When once, in thy words, thy looks, such a heaven of blisses
   Came o er me, I thought my heart would break,
   And it seemed as if thou wouldest smother me with kisses.
   Kiss thou me!
   Else I kiss thee!
      [*She embraces him.*]
   Woe! woe! thy lips are cold,
   Stone dumb.
   Where's thy love left?
   O! I'm bereft!
   Who robbed me?
      [*She turns from him.*]

Faust.   O come!
   Take courage, my darling! Let us go;
   I clasp thee with unutterable glow;
   But follow me! For this alone I plead!

Margaret [*turning to him*]. Is it then thou?
   And is it thou indeed?

Faust. 'Tis I! Come, follow me!

Margaret. Thou break'st my chain,
   And tak'st me to thy breast again!
   How comes it, then, that thou art not afraid of me?
   And dost thou know, my friend, who 'tis thou settest free?

Faust. Come! come! The night is on the wane.

Margaret. Woe! woe! My mother I've slain!
   Have drowned the babe of mine!
   Was it not sent to be mine and thine?
   Thine, too—'tis thou! Scarce true doth it seem.
   Give me thy hand! 'Tis not a dream!
   Thy blessed hand! But ah! there's dampness here!
   Go, wipe it off! I fear
   There's blood thereon.
   Ah, God! what hast thou done!

Put up thy sword again;
I pray thee, do!

Faust.   The past is past—there leave it then;
Thou kill'st me too!

Margaret.   No, thou must longer tarry!
I'll tell thee how each thou shalt bury;
The places of sorrow
Make ready to-morrow;
Must give the best place to my mother,
The very next to my brother,
Me a little aside,
But make not the space too wide!
And on my right breast let the little one lie.
No one else will be sleeping by me.
Once, to feel *thy* heart beat nigh me,
O, 'twas a precious, a tender joy!
But I shall have it no more—no, never!

   . . . . .

Make haste! make haste!
No time to waste!
Save thy poor child!
Quick! follow the edge
Of the rushing rill,
Over the bridge
And by the mill,
Then into the woods beyond
On the left where lies the plank
Over the pond.
Seize hold of it quick!
To rise 'tis trying,
It struggles still!
Rescue! rescue!

Faust.   Bethink thyself, pray!
A single step amd thou art free!

Margaret.   Would we were by the mountains!   See!
There sits my mother on a stone,
The sight on my brain is preying!
There sits my mother on a stone,
And her head is constantly swaying;
She beckons not, nods not, her head falls o'er;
So long she's been sleeping, she'll wake no more.
She slept that we might take pleasure.
O that was bliss without measure!

Faust.	Since neither reason nor prayer thou hearest, I must venture by force to take thee, dearest.
Margaret.	Let go! No violence will I bear! Take not such a murderous hold of me! I once did all I could to gratify thee.
Faust.	The day is breaking! Dearest! dearest!
Margaret.	Day! Ay, it is day! the last great day breaks in! My wedding-day it should have been! Tell no one thou hast been with Margery! Alas for my garland! The hour's advancing! Retreat is in vain! We meet again, But not at the dancing. The multitude presses, no word is spoke. Square, streets, all places— A sea of faces— The bell is tolling, the staff is broke. How they seize me and bind me! They hurry me off to the bloody block.

Faust.	O had I ne'er been born!
Meph.	[*appears without*]. Up! or thou'rt lost! The morn flushes the sky. Idle delaying! Praying and playing! My horses are neighing, They shudder and snort for the bound.
Margaret.	What's that comes up from the ground? He! He! Avaunt! that face! What will he in the sacred place? He seeks me!
Faust.	Thou shalt live!
Margaret.	Great God in heaven! Unto thy judgment my soul have I given!
Meph.	[*to Faust*]. Come! come! or in the lurch I leave both her and thee!
Margaret.	Thine am I, Father! Rescue me! Ye angels, holy bands, attend me! And camp around me to defend me! Henry! I dread to look on thee.
Meph.	She's judged!
Voice	[*from above*]. She's saved!
Meph.	[*to Faust*]. Come thou to me.
	[*Vanishes with Faust.*]
Voice	[*from within, dying away*]. Henry! Henry!

15

So ends the *Faust*—the *Faust,* that is to say, as it stands without that afterthought of the author, the Second Part.

What we have given, certainly is conceived and written with power. How—not simply by imagination born in the soul of the poet, but through experience acquired by the man of the world—Goethe was qualified to write it, one does not like to conjecture. There it is, however produced ; it is far from pleasing poetry, but that it has a degree of passion in it is, we think, beyond gainsaying. The very end of it all, however, seems to us weak and unsatisfactory. The first part so ending did leave a kind of demand for a second part—to supply a completion that was lacking. But the completion that was lacking, the second part actually added does not supply ; the sense of want remains. Faust, in the second part, becomes still more obviously Goethe—and still more obviously an irredeemable egotist. He marries Helen, her of Troy, revived ! This strange phantasmagoric contrivance of the author's seems to have been intended as an allegory vaguely shadowing forth the idea that Goethe united in himself the romanticism of the middle ages with the classicism of antiquity.

We have expressed and implied a low æsthetic and ethical estimate of the *Faust.* Some readers may naturally question with themselves : " Has not our author been unduly influenced by Philistine or Puritan narrowness ? Has he capacity enough of liberal comprehension to judge justly the masterpiece of a genius like Goethe ?" We may properly, therefore, support ourselves by citing two authorities not to be suspected of Hebraistic perverseness.

Coleridge, under the immediate imminency of Goethe's living renown, spoke severely as follows (he had been urged to translate the *Faust*) :

" I debated with myself whether it became my moral character to render into English—and so far, certainly, lend my countenance to—language, much of which I thought vulgar, licentious, and blasphemous. I need not tell you that I never put pen to paper as a translator to *Faust.*"

Emerson, while living, was reported in the newspapers as expressing distaste for the *Faust* on the ground of its moral offensiveness.

Is the *Faust*, then, not a great poem? To pronounce it, as we do, the unworthy work of a great poet, honors Goethe more. A great poet, then, Goethe was? One who might have been a great poet, let us, correcting ourselves, rather say. Goethe needed only to be a great man; and it was goodness that chiefly lacked to greatness in Goethe. He loved not wisely but too well—HIMSELF. His life was a reduction to absurdity of the idea of self-culture as a proper supreme aim of human endeavor. The "Pyramid of his Being" was a stately structure, but it was founded on sand. Faust had been overreached by Mephistopheles.

X.

SCHILLER.

1759–1805.

FEW men probably ever have had a hungrier " avidity of fame " than that which all his life long stung the soul of Friedrich Schiller. Few, again, are the men whose posthumous satisfaction of desire has been as ample as his. To be permanently the favorite poet of a great historic nation, a nation constantly growing greater, is surely an overflowing reward of endeavor ; and this reward is Schiller's. But his reward, large as it is, is not larger than was his endeavor. He died prematurely at forty-five, almost literally self-consumed with the ardors of his own inextinguishable spirit.

Johann Christoph Friedrich von Schiller was born the son of a gardener. His father was the highly loyal servant of a German duke, the Duke of Würtemberg. This duke patronized the elder Schiller, together with the hopeful boy, Friedrich—in a manner much to the distaste and discomfort of the latter. He had founded a military academy; and in this he graciously offered gratuitous education for the lad. Such an offer from such a source was equivalent to a mandate, and it had to be accepted. Young Schiller was, therefore, duly immured in the ducal military school, and there subjected to the cast-iron regimen which then usually prevailed in establishments of the sort. The eager bird beat hard against the bars of his cage—in vain. Some eight dreary years were thus passed, and the boy became a man of twenty-one, when, having previously tried and abandoned the study of law for a profession, he took unwilling degree as army surgeon.

But he had meantime cultivated literature in secret. It was pitiful, the starvation diet of books on which the poor young student was fain to feed his hungry mind. Out of these, and out of his own soul, with experience of life and observation of life so narrow and so small, he had excogitated a work which was to set all Germany in a blaze. His first draft of this, written as it were in blood and fire, he finished when he was nineteen years of age. It was not till two years after that the drama referred to, *The Robbers*, was published. Two years again elapsed, and this play was put upon the stage at Mannheim. The youthful author went clandestinely to see it, and, being detected, was placed under military arrest for a fortnight in consequence. That duke's government was watchfully paternal. All German conservatism was shocked by *The Robbers*. One functionary solemnly declared that had he been the Supreme Being, and had he foreknown that the world, if created, would have *The Robbers* written in it, he should never have created the world ! But young Germany gave a great leap of the heart in response to *The Robbers*.

From so much painstaking patronage on the part of his ducal lord, Schiller was ungrateful enough to abscond. Taking refuge, under a feigned name, in a neighboring principality, he went on producing plays in somewhat the same line of literary art with *The Robbers*.

The fugitive young author soon got back to Mannheim. Here he found employment somewhat to his taste, in connection with the theatre. This was for a short time only, but the experience was highly useful to him in a practical way; it helped him adapt his productions to the actual requirements of stage representation. He could henceforth better write plays to be acted, instead of plays simply to be read. Finding at Mannheim no satisfactory settled way of life, Schiller wandered to Leipsic. At Leipsic he formed that acquaintance with Körner (father of the poet) which was to be so important to his future career. Körner proved a wise and generous friend to the poor and struggling poet. He undertook, out of his own pocket, to keep Schiller going one whole year, without the poet's distracting himself in any way to earn a livelihood; Schiller might devote his energies exclusively to bringing out that which was most within him into literary expression. For such kindness Schiller had nothing with which to repay his friend, except gratitude—gratitude, and a share in his own confidently expected future renown. These commodities were, both of them, lavishly forthcoming. Witness the following letter:

> Your friendship and your kindness open up to me an Elysium. Through you, my beloved Körner, I may perhaps yet become what I despaired of ever being. As my powers ripen, so will my happiness increase, and near you, through you, I look to develop them. These tears that here, on the threshold of my new career, I shed in gratitude, in honor, to you, will fall again when that career is ended. If I should become that of which I now dream, who, then, happier than you? . . . Do not destroy this letter. Ten years hence it may be you will read it with strange emotion, and in the grave you will softly slumber thereon.

Schiller, with all his genuine scorn of the mercenary motive, yet was a thrifty soul. It is to us clear, from the Schiller-Körner correspondence, as well as from the Schiller-Goethe, that Schiller was always, even in his most enthusiastic expressions, likely to have a worldly-wise eye to his own advantage. This advantage, however, he desired, nobly and purely, for the sake of the service that he felt himself capable, with opportunity, of rendering to literature. To that cause no man ever yielded himself up with more absolute, more burning devotion than did Schiller. What he enjoyed of success he fairly earned with endeavor. His fame he bought with his life.

The force that you feel throbbing in Schiller's work was not wholly a healthy natural force. It was partly artificial, fed with stimulation as well as with food. Schiller drank strong coffee, and drank it to excess. He also used too much wine. Worse, perhaps, he used his nights for labor instead of for sleep. Nor was this all. He wrought himself up with will to a high pitch of mental excitement, that so he might write with power. Standing at his desk to write, he would frequently meantime declaim aloud with fury what he wrote, stamping and raving like a pagan prophet of old in order that so the demon of poetic prophecy might indeed usurp and possess his soul. The fuel that he burned for his fire was thus supplied from his very life. No wonder that a flame forced to rage so fiercely raged itself out in forty-five years.

The Robbers, Love and Intrigue, Fiesco, Don Carlos, dramas all of them, with a prose romance entitled the *Ghost-seer* had already been produced when, in 1787, Schiller went by invitation to Weimar. But the hopes with which he went of there achieving personal relation to Goethe were destined yet for some years to be disappointed. Not without bitterness, he uttered himself to Körner on this defeat of desire. Here, for instance, is one of his expressions:

> I doubt if we [Goethe and himself] shall ever draw very near to each other. . . . His world is not my world; our ideas on some points are fundamentally opposed.

Under the influence, perhaps, of disappointment at his own reception, he looked at Goethe with cold eyes, and saw him as follows :

> His appearance considerably lowered the idea I had conceived from hearsay of his imposing and handsome person. He is of middle size, and he looks and walks stiff. His countenance is not open, but his eye is very full of expression. . . . The expression of his countenance is serious, at the same time that it is benevolent and kind.

But a little uneasily, in recollection of the various things that he has suffered to escape him, reflecting on Goethe, or

revealing his own disposition to envy that more fortunate
man, he writes again to Körner :

> I cannot help laughing when I t'.nk over all I have written to you
> about Goethe. You will have a·quired a deep insight into my weak
> points, and have inwardly chuckled at me; but let it be so. I wish you
> to know me as I am. This man, this Goethe, is in my way; and he
> reminds me so often how hard fate has been upon me. How tenderly
> was his genius nursed by fate, and how must I to this very moment still
> struggle !

Does that seem querulous? A little below heroic pitch,
no doubt ; but Schiller was very free to Körner. Perhaps,
too, he was thriftily not unwilling to excite Körner's valuable sympathy in his own behalf. One cannot help feeling
a little regret to find Schiller, in the same letter, making so
hard-headed, not to say so hard-hearted, a suggestion of the
practical sort as this following :

> If you could procure me within a year a wife with twelve thousand
> dollars (thalers), with whom I could live and to whom I could become
> attached, I could then in five years write you a Frederickiad [an epic on
> Frederick the Great], a classic tragedy, and, as you so insist upon it, half
> a dozen fine odes.

But that matrimonial hint from Schiller to his friend is not
really so bad as it looks. If, in the making of it, some good
earnest did mingle with the playful, still all Schiller wanted
was his chance to work for literature and for fame ; or,
rather, he wanted that in the form of a home and a com-
petence, to put him at ease and at leisure. And perhaps he
was not without his hope that Körner himself might be
incited to keep on being his Mæcenas.

Schiller never got what he wanted. He lived narrowly,
and died poor. But he found in due time a true wife, and his
work was to him more than wealth. Perhaps if he had been
more comfortable he would not have been more productive;
and he might not have lived so close to the heart of the
people. He might also not have been happier. That
" Frederickiad," by the way, was never written. But it was
sufficiently talked of between the two friends for Schiller to

give Körner some of his ideas on the subject of it.   **Schiller** writes :

Whatever it might cost me, I should place the freethinker, Voltaire, in a glorious light, and the whole poem should bear that stamp.

This eager expression recalls Goethe's word about **Voltaire**. It was hardly possible, Goethe said, to conceive the influence exerted by the brilliant Frenchman on the young minds of that generation.   The language just quoted from Schiller, he used when he was thirty years old.   He seems never to have been other than a deist of the Voltairean type.   No scoffer, however, was he, like Voltaire.   His contrasted spirit of earnestness is favorably shown in his poem, *The Words of Faith*, which we may appropriately introduce at the present point.   The poet here confesses his own quasi-religious creed, in verse :

> Three words I utter, of priceless worth;
>   They are the wide world's treasure;
> Yet never on earth had they their birth,
>   And the spirit their depth must measure.
> Man is ruined—poor—forlorn—
> When his faith in these holy words is gone.
>
> Man is *Free* created—is *Free*—
>   Though his cradle may be a prison;
> Mobs are no plea for tyranny,
>   Nor rabble bereft of reason.
> Fear not the free man; but tremble first
> Before the slave, when his chain is burst.
>
> And *Virtue*—is Virtue an empty sound?
>   Man's life is to follow her teaching;
> Fall as he may on the world's rough ground,
>   To the Godlike he still may be reaching.
> What never the wise by his wisdom can be,
> The childlike becomes in simplicity.
>
> And *God*, in holy, eternal love,
>   Reigns when humanity falters;
> Through limitless being his energies move,
>   His purpose of good never alters;
> Though changes may circle all matter and time,
> God dwells in the peace of perfection sublime.

> O, trust in these words of mightiest power;
> They are the wide world's treasure;
> Through ages they've been man's richest dower,
> And the spirit their depth must measure.
> Never is man of good bereft
> If his faith in these holy words is left.

Mr. W. H. Channing supplies us our translation. Such words as those from Schiller are tonic words. It is occasion of rejoicing that Schiller's work, though he did write some things that ought never to have been written, is on the whole so clear and so friendly to virtue.

It will have been gathered from our sketch of Schiller's fortunes that he never enjoyed the highest advantages for thorough education. His lack of generous early culture always somewhat hampered his genius. He had to make up as best he could, by study for each emerging occasion, what might have been in good degree supplied to him through wide general fitting and furnishing of his mind, had that inestimable good from fortune fallen betimes to his lot.

But to know Goethe, as Schiller came at length to know him, was perhaps better than the average university education of those days. For the very best results, however, to Schiller, this came to him too late. There were but ten years left now for him to live—years he will make them of strenuous and of fruitful activity, his really greatest works being all of them still to write. The best lyrical pieces that he produced, and his noblest, ripest dramatic creations, belong to the period of his alliance with Goethe, the last ten years of his life. The *Song of the Bell, The Walk,* among his minor poems; the *Wallenstein,* the *Mary Stuart,* the *Maid of Orleans,* the *Bride of Messina,* the *William Tell,* among his dramas, were the fruit of these final glorious years.

In the interval of about five years, between his first disappointing encounter with Goethe and the eventual cementing of his alliance with that illustrious man, there was interposed a stage of transition in development for Schiller, during which it seemed half doubtful whether he might not get transformed from poet into philosopher. He fell under the sway of the Kantian metaphysics, and he exercised himself in prose more than in verse. It was now that he wrote his *History of the Thirty Years' War.* Of his own success in the historical line, Schiller thought favorably enough to write to his friend Körner as follows:

> I do not see why I should not be the first historical writer in Germany, if I were to set earnestly to work; and surely then there would be some prospects opening before me.

A little while before, he had written:

> I am, and shall remain, a poet, and shall die a poet.

The sense of vocation to poetry wavered only, it never quite intermitted, with Schiller.

Besides his *Thirty Years' War,* Schiller wrote an historical fragment, the *Revolt of the Netherlands.* He also composed a series of letters on "æsthetical culture," in which he set forth his ideas of literary art. Schiller always possessed what you might call the courage of his own literary achievements. He expressed boldly his confidence that the prose style in which he composed his *Æsthetic Letters* was alone enough to make them immortal. Ill equipped in scholarship as he was, Schiller undauntedly attacked the choruses in the *Iphigenia* of Euripides, for translation. Very cheerful he felt over his results. To Körner he wrote:

> The choruses gain by my translation, that is to say, what they would not have gained by another translator; for the diction in the original imparts great beauty to them. I challenge many of our poets, who pride themselves upon their Greek and Latin, to do what I have done from so cold a subject. It was not in my power, like them, to make use of the niceties of the Greek text. I was obliged to guess at my original, or, rather, to create a new one.

Again, of his finished *Wallenstein,* Schiller writes to Körner:

> I cannot deny that I feel well satisfied with my own work, and that I admire it. You will not miss any of the fire and energy of my best years [Schiller was now forty years old] without their roughness.

Such confidence, on his own part, in himself was a great stay and a great spur to Schiller's genius. Besides this, it kept up the confidence of his friends.

The standing-place for life and livelihood which Schiller finally secured was a professorship of history in the University of Jena. The labor was great and the emoluments were small; but it was a reliance, and he was brought within a few miles of Weimar. Karl August became his patron, when Goethe became his friend.

It was in magnanimous rivalry of genius and of art with Goethe that Schiller did a large part of his best work as lyrical poet. The two poets prompted, spurred, curbed, applauded each other. Goethe rejoiced when a poem of his own in the lyrical line—a " ballad," as he called it—published anonymously, was by some attributed to Schiller. He accepted it as a sign that, in approximating one another, each poet was ridding himself of manner and possessing himself of style.

A far less worthy work it was, to engage this noble pair of brothers, when they set themselves to a warfare of squibs in verse, under the title of *Xenien* (epigrams)—a warfare waged against the whole generation of literary men espousing ideas fundamentally different from their own. Such epigrams must be very salt with wit to keep sapid, even a decade of years. And many, very many, of the Goethe-Schiller effusions lost, like champagne, what sparkle they had, the instant they were opened to the public. Very stale, flat, and unprofitable they mostly are now. One is sorry that Goethe and Schiller ever condescended to such use of their gifts. But the immortals are mortal as long as they live. They become immortal only by dying.

The one most massive, mightiest work, the most mature, and the loftiest too, of Schiller's genius is, in our own opinion, beyond peradventure the *Wallenstein*. This, therefore, we select for our chief subject of present exhibition. Before proceeding, however, to that, we must show some specimens of Schiller's minor poems; and then, too, besides, our readers will hardly content themselves without a taste of that redoubtable work, that *enfant terrible*, of the author's barmy youth, *The Robbers*.

We begin with our own individual first choice among the short poems of Schiller. This is entitled, *The Division of the Earth*. Mr. C. P. Cranch translates it well, leaving a touch or two of infelicity which, with sincere modesty, we try to amend. In one stanza he says "bawl," where that word goes beyond the original in expressing unseemly or unmanly outcry. Will "call" do better?

"Here, take the world!" cried Jove, from his high heaven,
    To mortals—"Take it; it is yours, ye elves;
'Tis yours, for an eternal heirdom given;
    Share it like brothers 'mongst yourselves."

Then hasted every one himself to suit,
    And busily bestirred them old and young—
The farmer seized upon the harvest fruit;
    The squire's horn through the woodland rung.

The merchant grasped his costly warehouse loads,
    The abbot chose him noble pipes of wine,
The king closed up the bridges and the roads,
    And said, "The tenth of all is mine."

Quite late, long after all had been divided,
    The Poet came, from distant wandering;
Alas! the case was everywhere decided—
    Proprietors for every thing!

"Ah, woe is me! shall I alone of all
    Forgotten be—I, thy most faithful son?"
In loud lament he thus began to call,
    And threw himself before Jove's throne.

"If in the land of dreams thou hast delayed,"
    Replied the god, "then quarrel not with me;
Where wast thou when division here was made?"
    "I was," the Poet said, "with thee;—

"Mine eyes hung on thy countenance so bright,
    Mine ear drank in thy heaven's harmony;
Forgive the soul which, drunken with thy light,
    Forgot that earth had aught for me."

> " What shall I do ?" said Zeus, " the world's all given:
> The harvest, chase, or market, no more mine ;
> If thou wilt come and live with me in heaven,
> As often as thou com'st, my home is thine."

Very prettily conceived, it seems to us. Mr. Cranch follows Schiller in the irregularity of making his last line a foot longer, for the closing stanza, than for the others. We have only to suggest that a slight seeming inconsistency might easily have been avoided by the author—the inconsistency, that is, of making his Poet account as he does for his failure to be on hand at the division. The Poet explains that he was with Jove, at that important moment. But how, if he was with Jove, should not he have heard the proclamation to divide given out in Jove's own voice ? Equally well Schiller might have had the proclamation sent forth silently by messengers going to all quarters—which would have left the Poet's excuse unassailably good.

By the side of Schiller's *Words of Faith*, already given, we might have placed his hymn of *Hope*, which prophesies to the soul its own immortality—the translation is Mr. J. S. Dwight's:

> A still small voice in every soul
>   Of happier days keeps chanting ;
> And eagerly on to the golden goal
>   We see men running and panting.
> The world grows old and grows young again ;
> Still this hope of improvement haunts man's brain.
>
> Hope welcomes to life the smiling child ;
>   Her light shapes round the school-boy swim ;
> Hope fires the young man with visions wild ;
>   And she goes not under the earth with him,
> When his race is run, and the grave doth ope ;—
> On the brink of the grave he planteth—Hope.
>
> It is not an empty, flattering dream,
>   Offspring of idle thought ;
> Through every heart it sendeth a gleam
>   Of that better world we've sought.
> And what the voice within us speaks
> Deceives not the soul that trustingly seeks.

In *The Ideal and Life*, Schiller gives us a confession of his own poetical faith. He always, in principle as in practice, was a poet of the ideal. Whereas Goethe aimed to hold his mirror up to the world and to life, so as to reflect that which is, Schiller was ever seeking to catch in his mirror an image of the unseen ideal, that he might show it to men, and inspire them with a view of that which ought to be. Here, in the rendering of Mr. J. S. Dwight, are the first three stanzas of the poem—there are fifteen stanzas in all :

> Ever clear, and mirror-pure, and even,
> Zephyr-light flows life in heaven,
> Where th' Olympians spend their blessed days.
> Moons keep changing, race on race keep flying ;
> But the roses of their youth, undying,
> Changeless blossom, while all else decays.
> 'Twixt the soul's repose and joys terrestrial,
> Man must hesitate and choose alone ;
> On the lofty brows of the celestial
> Both do glitter, blent in one.

> Would ye here on earth the gods resemble,
> And at death no longer tremble ?
> Of his garden's fruit, then, never taste.
> On the show the eyes may feed at leisure ;
> But enjoyment's transitory pleasure
> Soon by sick satiety is chased.
> E'en the Styx, which nine times winds around her,
> Chains not Ceres' daughter to that shore ;
> For the apple grasped she, and then bound her
> Orcus' claim for evermore.

> *Flesh* alone is subject to those powers
> Weaving this dark fate of ours ;
> While above the reach of time or storm,
> Playmate of the blessed ones up yonder,
> *She* amid the flowers of light doth wander,
> Godlike 'mid the gods, undying FORM.
> Would ye soar aloft on her strong pinion ?
> Fling away all earthly care and strife !
> Up into th' Ideal's pure dominion
> Fly from this dull, narrow life !

Enough of Schiller's quasi-moralizing songs. His celebrated *Song of the Bell* is a song moralized, rather than moralizing. That is to say, the direct ostensible intention is not to inculcate a moral; but indirectly, and as it were by occasion, a moral is conveyed. The poem describes the process of founding or casting a bell. The really descriptive part is, however, shorter and less important than the part which, by association of some sort, treats of human life. The poem is one of considerable length—too long to be given entire. A section cut out from the heart of it will very well exemplify the spirit and the method of it all. The process of the founding has reached a point at which the melted amalgam presents to fracture a certain appearance. This the poet describes, and then passes, with sudden, surprising association of thought, to the idea of a conflagration which, at the critical moment of transfer to the mold, miscarriage with the fiery molten mass might produce:

> Well—we may begin to pour;
>   Pointed hard the edges are
> Where we break it. But before
>   Offer up a pious prayer.
>   Out the stopples stave!
>   God the building save!
> Roaring, smoking through the pass,
> Shoots the fiery, swelling mass.
>
> An instrument of good is fire,
> With man to watch and tame its ire;
> And all he forges, all he makes,
> The virtue of the flame partakes;
> But frightfully it rages when
> It breaks away from every chain,
> And sweeps along its own wild way,
> Child of Nature, stern and free.
> Woe if once, with deafening roar,
>   Naught its fury to withstand,
> Through the peopled streets it pour,
>   Hurling wide the deadly brand!
> Eager the elements devour
>   Every work of human hand.

From the cloud, to bless the plain,
Pours the rain;
From the cloud, our hopes to dash,
Darts the flash!
Hear'st that moaning from the tower?
  'Tis the tempest dread!
  Bloody red
The heavens glour;
'Tis not daylight's steady glow!
Hark, what tumult now
Rends the sky!
Lo! the smoke up-rolling high!
Flickering mount the fiery shafts:
Where the wind its wild wave wafts,
Onward through the street's long course
Rolls the flame with gathering force;
As in an oven's jaws, the air
Heated glows with ruddy glare;
Falling fast the rafters shatter,
Pillars crash and windows clatter,
Children scream and mothers scatter;
Beasts to perish, left alone,
'Mid the ruins groan.
All is hurry, rescue, flight;
Clear as noon-day is the night;
Through the hands, in lengthened rows,
  Buckets fly;
Through the air, in graceful bows,
  Shoots the watery stream on high.
Fierce the howling tempest grows;
Swiftly, borne upon the blast,
Rides the flame, devouring fast;
Roaring, crackling, it consumes
All the crowded granary rooms;
All the rafters blaze on high;
And, as if 'twould tear away
Earth's foundations in its flight,
On it mounts to heaven's height,
  Giant-tall!
  Hope hath all
Man forsaken; helpless now
He to heavenly might must bow,
  Idly musing o'er his fall,
Wondering at his work laid low.

Burnt to ashes
  Lies the town,
Like a desert spread
For the wild storm's bed.
Through the dreary window-holes
Darkness lurks and boding owls ;
  Through bare walls the clouds look down.
Lingering yet,
One look he casts
O'er the tomb
Where his hopes were wont to bloom ;
Then takes up the wanderer's staff:—
Now at Fortune he may laugh ;
For one, his sweetest, purest joy,
The cruel flame could not destroy ;
Where are those lives, than life more dear ?
His little innocents ? Are they here ?
He numbers o'er his little band,
And all his dear ones round him stand.

To the earth now we've consigned it,
  Safely lodged within the clay :—
Beautiful, as we designed it,
    Will it now our toil repay ?
      Should the cast go wrong ?
      Or burst the model strong ?
    Ah ! perhaps while we were working,
    Mischief has been near us lurking.

We appended the strophe in which Schiller describes the stage thus accomplished in the bell-founding, so that our readers might the better see how transition is effected from point to point of the process The poet proceeds to compare the depositing of the bell in a mold of earth to the consigning of seed to the soil. Then with a touch of human feeling, such as is Schiller's and such as is not Goethe's, he adds these lines:

    But costlier seed we bury, weeping,
      While in meek faith to heaven we pray,
    That from the coffin's loathsome keeping
      It may spring forth to brighter day.

No wonder that Schiller has, far beyond Goethe, the heart of the German fatherland.

16

Of the minor poems of Schiller, having narrative interest
in them—his "ballads" more properly so-called—the *Diver*
and the *Knight Toggenburg* are probably as good examples as
any. Schiller's productions of this sort are very popular in
Germany. They are highly charged with sentiment, or they
are fervid with lyrical movement. Take first the *Diver*.
This ballad was founded on a legend the story of which
Schiller has modified to suit his own ideas. The hero of the
old legend was a professional diver, and there was no romance of love involved. With Schiller it is an interesting
young page who does the dangerous feat, and, by way of
afterthought, love is introduced as a motive. The changes
add to the interest, but they take away from the verisimili-
tude, of the story. In reading Schiller's *Diver*, you feel that
the action of the cup-throwing, on the part of the king, is too
wanton, is not supplied with motive enough. Equally you
feel to be not adequately warranted the gallant young page's
first willingness to venture himself for the prize. But
one's instinctive sense of the vivid force of the narrative
and the description, such critical considerations hardly
affect. As to how Schiller prepared himself for describing
the whirlpool, a note of his to Goethe supplies an interesting
indication. Goethe had written some complaisance to Schiller about the agreement he found to exist between the
Diver and something that he had himself actually seen in his
travels—the Falls of Schaffhausen, we think it was. Schiller
replied:

> I am not a little glad that, according to your observation, my description
> of the whirlpool should correspond with the actual phenomena; my only
> opportunity of studying this bit of nature was at a mill, but I also carefully
> studied Homer's description of the Charybdis, and that perhaps may have
> helped me to keep to nature."

Here is the poem retrenched of five stanzas—Mr. Dwight
translates again :

> " Who dares it ?   What knight or squire so brave
>   Will dive for this golden cup ?
> See, I cast it into the whirling wave—
>   See, the chasm's black throat has swallowed it up.

'Tis gone—whoever now will show it,
On the venturous seeker I'll freely bestow it."

The monarch speaks, and away he throws
   From the cliff, that, rough and steep,
Out over the boundless ocean rose,
   The cup to the whirlpool's howling deep.
" Now, who's the firm-hearted—again I speak it—
In the Charybdis's jaws to seek it ?"

   .   .   .   .

But all, as before, dead silence kept;
   When a youth, right gentle to view,
From the trembling crowd of pages stepped,
   And his belt and mantle behind him threw.
And the knights and ladies stood wondering there
To see what a beardless youth would dare.

As he stepped to the brink to take one look o'er
   On the whirling gulf below,
The Charybdis was just giving back with a roar
   The floods it had swallowed but even now ;
And, like the far thunder's awful rumbling,
From its gloomy lap they came foaming and tumbling.

And it whirled, and it boiled, and it roared, and it hissed,
   As when water and fire contend ;
It sprinkled the skies with its scattering mist,
   And flood on flood crowded on without end,
As 'twould never go dry—you could fancy rather
That one ocean was giving birth to another.

But its angry heavings at length subside,
   And black, through the foam-crests white,
Down cleaves a yawning crevice wide,
   Deep down to the heart of night ;
And the roar of the waves grows dead and hollow,
As down through the gurgling tunnel they follow.

Now swift, ere the flood rolls back, he springs,
   Commending to God his soul,
And a shriek of terror above him rings ;
   He's swept away in the billowy roll ;
And away from all eyes, with a moment's glimmer,
The black gulf snatches the hardy swimmer.

Not a sound o'er the watery gulf is heard,
  Save the murmuring, deep sea-swell;
Or when mouth to mouth faint whispers the word:
  "Thou high-hearted youth, fare thee well!"
And more and more hollow its howling they hear—
'Tis a moment of breathless suspense and fear.

    .   .   .   .   .

And it whirled, and it boiled, and it roared, and it hissed,
  As when water and fire contend;
It sprinkled the skies with its scattering mist,
  And flood on flood crowded on without end;
And, like the far thunder's awful rumbling,
From its gloomy lap they came foaming and tumbling.

And see! from the blackening billows there
  What lifteth itself so white?
Now an arm, now a swan-like neck, is bare;
  And it struggles up with a swimmer's might;
And—'tis he! in his left hand holding up,
With a flourish of triumph, the glittering cup.

    .   .   .   .   .   .

And he comes; they crowd round him with jubilee peals;
  At his monarch's feet he sinks,
And presents him the cup, as he humbly kneels;
  And the king to his beautiful daughter winks;
She fills it with sparkling wine to the edge,
And the brave youth turns his monarch to pledge.

"Long life to the king! And enjoy him well,
  Who here breathes in the rosy light;
But under there it is terrible;
  O tempt not the gods, nor their warning slight,
And never, O never desire to see
What they've graciously hid in night from thee.

"It hurried me under, lightning-swift;
  Then up through the tunnel of rock
An opposite current took me adrift,
  Till the two streams met in furious shock,
And kept me poised like a spinning top
Dizzily whirled, with no power to stop.

"But God was there in my hour of fear,
  As I prayed with half-spent breath,
And showed me a ledge that jutted near,
  And I clasped it quick and escaped my death;

And there hung the cup on a coral tree,
Else had it gone down eternally ;—

" For below me it lay there, mountains deep,
   In purple darkness spread;
And though to the ear all seemed to sleep,
   Yet the eye could see far down with dread,
How the huge salamanders, and dragons with **claws,**
Groped about there within its hellish jaws.

" All knotted together, in uneasy play
   They nestled, a hideous swarm—
The swift sword-fish and the prickly ray,
   And the heavy hammer's misshapen form,
And, gnashing his teeth with angry motion,
I saw the grim shark, the hyena of ocean.

     •   •   •   •   •   •

" O, then I shook—for they crawled up near,
   A hundred at once, where I hung,
As if they would snap at me; all in my fear
   I let go the coral to which I had clung ;
When, with deafening roar, the whirlpool caught me :
But it caught to save—for to light it brought me."

In sheer amazement stood the king,
   And said : " The beaker's thine own ;
And I'll give thee moreover this golden ring,
   Gleaming with costliest diamond stone,
If thou'lt tempt it again, and bring word to me,
What thou saw'st on the lowermost bed of the sea."

That heard the fair daughter with dismay,
   And she pleaded most winningly :
" O father, enough of the terrible play !
   He hath stood what no other hath stood for thee !
If thy heart's cruel craving thou canst not tame,
Let one of thy knights put the boy to shame."

But the monarch snatched at the glittering cup,
   And he hurled it with all his might :
" Now dive, my brave youth, and bring me it up,
   And thee will I name my most excellent knight ;
And to her thou this day shalt wedded be,
Who pleads for thee now so tenderly."

Then with heavenly force o'er his soul it swept,
    And it flashed from his eyes, like fire;
And he saw where the blushing maiden wept,
    And he saw her sink trembling before her sire;
Then it moves him, the heavenly prize to win,
For life or for death he plunges in.

Full soon come the breakers, full plainly they hear,
    Back rolling with thundering brawl;
All fondly bend over to see him appear:
    They're coming, they're coming, the waters all!
They come and they go with a fiendish glee;—
But the youth—why comes not he?

The "Knight Toggenburg," is softly sentimental, rather than lyrically swift and bold. Here it is; our translation is from the *Edinburgh Review:*

"Knight, to love thee like a sister
    Vows this heart to thee;
Ask no other warmer feeling—
    That were pain to me.
Tranquil would I see thy coming,
    Tranquil see thee go;
What that starting tear would tell me
    I must never know."

He with silent anguish listens,
    Though his heart-strings bleed;
Clasps her in his last embraces,
    Springs upon his steed,
Summons every faithful vassal
    From his Alpine home,
Binds the cross upon his bosom,
    Seeks the Holy Tomb.

There full many a deed of glory
    Wrought the hero's arm;
Foremost still his plumage floated
    Where the foemen swarm;
Till the Moslem, terror-striken,
    Quailed before his name.
But the pang that wrings his bosom
    Lives at heart the same.

One long year he bears his sorrow,
    But no more can bear:
Rest he seeks, but, finding never,
    Leaves the army there; .
Sees a ship by Joppa's haven,
    Which, with swelling sail,
Wafts him where his lady's breathing
    Mingles with the gale.

At her father's castle portal,
    Hark! his knock is heard;
See! the gloomy gate uncloses
    With the thunder-word:
"She thou seek'st is veiled forever,
    Is the bride of heaven;
Yester eve the vows were plighted—
    She to God is given."

Then his old ancestral castle
    He forever flees;
Battle-steed and trusty weapon
    Never more he sees.
From the Toggenburg descending,
    Forth unknown he glides;
For the frame once sheathed in iron
    Now the sackcloth hides.

There beside that hallowed region
    He hath built his bower,
Where from out the dusky lindens
    Looked the convent tower;
Waiting from the morning's glimmer
    Till the day was done,
Tranquil hope in every feature,
    Sat he there alone.

Gazing upward to the convent,
    Hour on hour he passed,
Watching still his lady's lattice,
    Till it oped at last—
Till that form looked forth so lovely,
    Till the sweet face smiled
Down into the lonesome valley,
    Peaceful, angel-mild.

Then he laid him down to slumber,
    Cheered by peaceful dreams,
Calmly waiting till the morning
    Showed again its beams.
Thus for days he watched and waited,
    Thus for years he lay,
Happy if he saw the lattice
    Open day by day—

If that form looked forth so lovely,
    If the sweet face smiled
Down into the lonesome valley,
    Peaceful, angel-mild.
Then a corse they found him sitting
    Once when day returned;
Still his pale and placid features
    To the lattice turned.

We shall not deny that to us the foregoing celebrated poem seems too feeble and improbable in motive to be deserving of its celebrity. The story is perhaps as well told as so extremely lackadaisical a story admitted of being; the trouble is that it was hardly worth being told at all. But at points where motive, or probability, or consistent conception of character are in question, Germans are less exacting literary judges than we English-speakers; or else a lack existing at such points, in a literary production, they are better able to supply from the resources of their own imagination, or their own sensibility.

It will be a fairly sharp change now, but a stimulating, to revert for a moment to that Titan offspring of Schiller's youth, *The Robbers.* The hero of this play is a well-born wild young fellow who takes to the road, or rather to the woods—that is, becomes a robber. The occasion is, his being disowned and cast off by his father, or his supposing himself to be so—this, and general dissatisfaction with the existing state of society; in reality, his being disowned is a vile plot laid against him by his younger brother at home, who traduces him, absent, to his father as a reckless and graceless spendthrift. Charles von Moor is the gentleman robber's name. Charles becomes the leader of an organized band of like-minded companions, who make themselves the terror of the country-side. The upshot is that Charles leads his troop to the neighborhood of his own old home, and there learns that his father is in a dungeon dying of starvation under the cruel tyranny of his wicked brother; while his sweetheart too is persecuted by that same brother's loathsome suit for her hand. He frees his father, but almost immediately, by disclosing himself to him as a robber and a murderer, causes the old man's death through grief, he drives his wicked brother to suicide, stabs with his own hand his beloved to the heart, to attest his loyalty to the robber band—he had sworn a great oath to them that he would never forsake them—and finally gives himself up to justice, as his sacrifice laid on the altar of law. Absurd enough, you will say; but it was not so absurd as not to fire well-nigh to madness the inflammable heart of that generation of young men. The prose style in which the play is written well comports with the spirit in which it is conceived; it is to the last degree extravagant and wild. The author seems to have had little other aim than to seek everywhere the very strongest expression of which language admitted. The result would be pure burlesque, but for the strange heart of sincerity that beats and burns under the beating and burning words. You feel the unmistakable pulse of power. As performance, worth nothing at all, this drama, as promise, was worth something incalculable. The stormy vehemence of *The Robbers* contrasts with the effeminate intensity of *Werther* about as the moral vigor of Schiller's character contrasted with the emasculated softness of Goethe's. There was traceable to the last, in either author's work, something of the quality that those two youthful pieces severally revealed.

A fragment condensed from that closing scene in which Charles strikes his Amelia dead, and then announces his purpose of giving himself up to justice, will satisfy most readers. The scene is laid in a forest near Charles's ancestral castle. Amelia, unrecognized, of course, by her captors, is brought in, a prize, to Charles. She, as Schiller's stage directions describe it, "rushes upon Charles and embraces him in an ecstasy of delight." We condense:

Charles. Tear her from my neck! Kill her! Kill him! Kill me—yourselves—every body! Let the whole world perish! [*About to rush off.*]

Amelia. Whither? what? Love! eternity! happiness! never-ending joys! and thou wouldst fly? . . .

C. Too late! In vain! Your curse, father! . . . Die, father! Die, for the third time, through me! These, thy deliverers, are robbers and murderers! Thy Charles is their captain! [*Old Moor expires.*]

[*Amelia stands silent and transfixed like a statue. The whole band are mute. A fearful pause.*]

C. [*rushing against an oak*]. The souls of those I have strangled in the intoxication of love—of those whom I crushed to atoms in the sacredness of sleep—of those whom—Ha! ha! ha! do you hear the powder-magazine bursting over the heads of women in travail? Do you see the flames creeping round the cradles of sucklings? That is our nuptial torch; those shrieks our wedding music! . . .

A. . . . What have I done, poor innocent lamb? I have loved this man!

C. This is more than a man can endure. Have I not heard death hissing at me from more than a thousand barrels, and never yet moved a hair's breadth out of its way. And shall I now be taught to tremble like a woman? tremble before a woman? No! a woman shall not conquer my manly courage! Blood! blood! 'tis but a fit of womanish feeling. I must glut myself with blood; and this will pass away. [*He is about to fly.*]

A. [*sinking into his arms*]. Murderer! devil! I cannot—angel—leave thee!

C. [*thrusting her from him*]. Away! insidious serpent! . . . Dost thou remember whom thou art embracing, Amelia?

A. My only one, mine, mine forever.

C. [*recovering himself in an ecstasy of joy*]. She forgives me, she loves me! Then am I pure as the ether of heaven, for she loves me! With tears I thank thee, all-merciful Father! [*He falls on his knees and bursts into a violent fit of weeping.*] . . . O Amelia! Amelia! Amelia! [*He hangs on her neck, they remain locked in a silent embrace*].

A Robber [*stepping forward enraged*]. Hold, traitor! This instant come from her arms! . . .

An Aged Robber. Faithless man! where are thy oaths? Are wounds so soon forgotten? . . . Base, perfidious wretch! and wouldst thou now desert us at the whining of a harlot?

A Third Robber. Shame on thy perjury! . . .

The Robbers [*all in disorder, tearing open their garments*]. See here! and here! Dost thou know these scars? Thou art ours! With our hearts' blood we have bought thee, and thou art ours bodily, even though the archangel Michael should seek to wrest thee out of the grasp of the fiery Moloch! Now! March with us! Sacrifice for sacrifice, Amelia for the band!

C. [*releasing her hand*]. It is past! I would arise and return to my father; but Heaven has said, "It shall not be!" . . . Come along, comrades!

A. [*pulling him back*]. Stay, I beseech you! One blow! one deadly blow! Again forsaken! Draw thy sword and have mercy upon me!

C. Mercy has taken refuge among bears. I will not kill thee!

A. [*embracing his knees*]. O for heaven's sake! . . . All I ask is death. See, my hand trembles! I have not courage to strike the blow. I shrink from the gleaming blade! To thee it is so easy, so very easy; thou art a master in murder—draw thy sword, and make me happy!

C. Wouldst thou alone be happy? Away with thee! I will kill no woman!

A. Ha! destroyer! thou canst only kill the happy; those who are weary of existence thou sparest! [*She glides toward the robbers.*] Then do ye have mercy on me, disciples of murder! There lurks a blood-thirsty pity in your looks that is consoling to the wretched. Your master is a boaster and a coward.

C. Woman, what dost thou say? [*The robbers turn away.*]

A. No friend? No; not even among these a friend? [*She rises.*] Well, then, let Dido teach me how to die! [*She is going; a robber takes aim at her.*]

C. Hold! dare it! Moor's Amelia shall die by no other hand than Moor's. [*He strikes her dead.*]

Some alteration follows between Charles and his companions, and finally Charles decides on surrendering himself to the officers of the law. It was apparently Schiller's idea that he might relieve himself of the reproach of immorality by this method of concluding the play.

Schiller's *Wallenstein* is a work of immense volume, for a play; the full text of it would nearly or quite fill such a book as this. It exists in three parts, thus constituting what is, technically as it were, called a trilogy. The tripartite division, however, of the drama was an afterthought with the poet. The original conception was that of one play.

The first part bears the title, "The Camp of Wallenstein." The idea of this is to accomplish the purpose which, in ancient tragedy, the prologue was devised to serve; Schiller wished to instruct and prepare his spectators for the tragedy he would present to them. That such elaborate preparation was by him deemed to be necessary, naturally suggests that his choice of subject was not wholly felicitous. The interest of Wallenstein, as a possible character in tragedy, was in fact too remote, and too pale through remoteness. We do not mean too remote by distance in time, but too remote by popular unfamiliarity. Wallenstein had never taken supreme possession of the imagination of men. Schiller had to create that general interest in his hero which, properly, should have existed already prepared to his hand. Besides this, the action which he had to treat was highly complex, and difficult to concentrate within manageable limits. That, in the face of conditions so little friendly to success, Schiller should have succeeded, and succeeded magnificently, was a true triumph of genius; of genius, and also of character no less.

For it was not genius alone that here accomplished the apparently impossible; it was genius, by that best of earthly taskmasters, character, put under the yoke, and kept under the yoke, of long and strenuous toil. The Schiller-Goethe correspondence, for the period during which its author was struggling with his Herculean task of the *Wallenstein,* forms an instructive and an inspiring record of intellectual hard work, done by high-born genius loyally obeying the prick of conscience and of will. Here is one cry of straitness and travail for his *Wallenstein,* uttered by Schiller in the ears of Goethe, under date November, 1796:

[In Wallenstein] I have to deal with the most refractory subject, from which I cannot extract any thing except by heroic perseverance. And as, in addition to this, I have not the commonest opportunities for coming into closer contact with life and men, and hence of getting out of my own narrow existence into a wider sphere, I am forced to make my feet take the place of hands, like an animal that lacks certain organs. But truly I lose an incalculable amount of strength and time by having to overcome the barriers of my accidental position, and in having to prepare my own instruments in order to comprehend so foreign a subject as the living world, and more especially the political world, is to me.

Schiller, under the influence of Goethe, was constantly struggling to get outside of himself and become "objective," as the word is. That was Goethe's own idea in literary character for himself; and the general opinion seems to be that Goethe succeeded in realizing his ideal. At any rate, he urged and encouraged Schiller to strive after it. Schiller made occasional cheerful and hopeful note of his own conscious growth in ability to show things, rather as he saw them about him, than as he felt them within him—in short, to be an objective instead of a subjective poet, an artist instead of a sentimentalist, in literature. He writes to Goethe :

> As regards the spirit in which I am working [in the *Wallenstein*], you will probably be satisfied with what I have done. I shall have no difficulty in keeping my subject outside of myself and with only giving the objective. . . . The principal character, as well as most of the secondary ones, I have as yet really treated with the pure love of an artist. It is only the character next to the chief one—the younger Piccolomini—in whom I feel any personal interest.

Seldom have men of letters more diligently studied the principles of literary art than did Schiller and Goethe together. Their published correspondence is one almost continuous record of their experiences, observations, reflections, discoveries, experiments, and guesses, in this line. Schiller, still in connection with his *Wallenstein,* writes to Goethe:

> I have, during these last days, been reading [certain Greek tragedies]. . . . It struck me that the characters in the Greek tragedy are more or less ideal masks, and not actual individuals, such as I find in Shakespeare's, and also in your, dramas. . . . Truth does not suffer at all by this.

Wallenstein, the protagonist in Schiller's play, was a believer and a practitioner in astrology. How to introduce the astrological element effectively into his drama was a serious problem with Schiller. In attempting the solution, he by no means depended solely on his own genius; he read for his purpose. He writes to Goethe :

> Among some cabalistic and astrological works, [I found one that] helped me considerably in my astrological studies. . . . I am not without hopes of being able to give this astrological matter poetical dignity.

The following report of progress, under date subsequent, has its implication of the sometimes vain labor involved in producing a great poetical work. To Goethe:

> All is still going on quite satisfactorily with the work [*Wallenstein*], and although a poet cannot set any more value upon his first draught than a merchant upon such of his goods as are at sea, still I nevertheless think that I have not been wasting my time.

Of a later practical problem with the *Wallenstein*, Schiller announces thus to Goethe his success in finding a solution:

> I have fortunately at last been able so to arrange things that it [the "Death of Wallenstein" the third and last part] has five acts also.

The last two parts were both thus made to conform to the conventional rule for tragedy. The first part, the prologue, so to style it, was simply a succession of scenes, not divided into acts. It was near three years after the date of the first note given here from Schiller about his *Wallenstein*, that the poet wrote (one can imagine with what a sigh!) as follows to Goethe—the date is March 19, 1799:

> The mass which has hitherto drawn and held me to it has now gone, and I feel as if I were hanging indefinitely in empty space. At the same time I feel also as if it were absolutely impossible for me ever to produce any thing again.

Schiller was not the man to abide long in a feeling of impotence such as he thus described. He rallied from that exhaustion, and produced within the two succeeding years three new dramas, besides other poems. Schiller was a tireless spirit. Nothing short of death could quench his ardor for achievement.

The subject of the *Wallenstein* is the treason and the death of the hero. Wallenstein—or Waldstein, as exact historical scholars now spell the name—was a conspicuous figure in the Thirty Years' War. He seems to have been a truly great man—great, but selfish. In Schiller's drama, he commands your admiration, without commanding your sympathy. Dramatic literature hardly contains a finer exhibition of haughty dominating power in character, than Schiller has given us in his representation of Wallenstein. There must have been something great in the soul of the poet who was capable of such a conception.

The historic Waldstein may be studied to advantage in Gindely's *History of the Thirty Years' War*, recently, with general applause from the critics, translated from German into English by the veteran Professor Ten Brook, formerly of the University of Michigan.

Whether Wallenstein was really guilty or not of the treason with which he was charged, is one of the vexed questions of history. The tendency of opinion has been to acquit him. But Gindely condemns him, intimating that he holds in reserve for future use documentary evidence that will close the question, and close it against Wallenstein, forever. Schiller, we think, was sufficiently justified in treating his subject as he did. He treats the treason of Wallenstein against his emperor as a thing thought of by him, dallied with, but finally resolved upon only through stress of outward circumstance. All accounts agree that Wallenstein was from boyhood of a peculiarly heady and ungovernable spirit. "Why was I not born a prince? Nobody should punish me then," the boy of seven indignantly exclaimed to his mother, when she was correcting him for some fault. His parentage was Protestant; but, left early an orphan, he became a Catholic, under the influence of an uncle whose ward he was. His greed of power was insatiable, and the power he gained was incomparably greater than that of any other subject of the emperor. He was able to dictate conditions to his sovereign, who actually allowed him to levy troops and wage war independently of himself. Wallenstein reached a pitch of pride and power so high that to his emperor proposing to him a command under the archduke, the emperor's own son, he haughtily replied, with blasphemy, "I would not serve under Almighty God." Against Wallenstein, as the right arm of the Roman Catholics, was pitted Gustavus Adolphus, of Sweden, as the Protestant champion. Of Gustavus Adolphus, and of Gustavus Adolphus alone, Wallenstein stood in some wholesome awe. Gustavus had at length fallen in battle, when Wallenstein, disaffected toward the emperor, made his treasonable advances toward the Swedes. The latter were wary and suspicious; for Wallenstein had in stratagem made feints of such disposition before. The following soliloquy, attributed by Schiller to Wallenstein, will at the same time sketch strikingly to the reader the previous course of this man's history, and display the poet's conception of his character. The situation has grown desperate for Wallenstein. There has been, most unexpectedly, a general defection from his cause, on the part of leaders profoundly trusted by him. Octavio Piccolomini, the chief of these, has accused him to the emperor of meditated treason. Wallenstein, thus deserted and thus endangered, strengthens himself by recalling his own achievements in the past. Here is his soliloquy:

[*Scene—a spacious room in the* DUKE OF FRIEDLAND'S *palace.*]

Wal. [*in armor.*]   Thou hast gained
    Thy point, Octavio! Once more am I
    Almost as friendless as at Regensburg.
    There I had nothing left me, but myself—
    But what one man can do you have now experience.
    The twigs have you hewed off, and here I stand
    A leafless trunk. But in the sap within
    Lives the creating power, and a new world
    May sprout forth from it. Once already have I
    Proved myself worth an army to you—I alone!
    Before the Swedish strength your troops had melted;
    Beside the Lech sank Tilly, your last hope;
    Into Bavaria, like a winter torrent,
    Did that Gustavus pour, and at Vienna
    In his own palace did the emperor tremble.
    Soldiers were scarce, for still the multitude
    Follow the luck; all eyes were turned on me,
    Their helper in distress; the Emperor's pride
    Bowed himself down before the man he had injured.
    'Twas I must rise, and with creative word
    Assemble forces in the desolate camps.
    I did it. Like a god of war, my name
    Went through the world. The drum was beat—and lo!
    The plough, the workshop is forsaken; all

Swarm to the old familiar long-loved banners;
And as the wood-choir, rich in melody,
Assemble quick around the bird of wonder,
When first his throat swells with his magic song,
So did the warlike youth of Germany
Crowd in around the image of my eagle.
I feel myself the being that I was.
It is the soul that builds itself a body,
And Friedland's camp will not remain unfilled.

"Friedland," of course, is Wallenstein, who was Duke, or Prince, of Friedland. The "bird of wonder" is the phœnix, a fabled fowl, sole of its kind, and, when appearing, an object of general admiration. Milton (*Paradise Lost*, V., 268, *ff.*) likens to a phœnix the descending archangel Raphael, in the lines,

Sails between worlds and worlds . . .

. . . till within soar
Of towering eagles, to all the fowls he seems
A phœnix, gazed by all as that sole bird,
Etc.

Two subordinate officers of Wallenstein—as the plot against plot ripens, and as the hero unconsciously nears his own doom of death by traitorous assassination—talk with each other. One of them recalls his old master's youth and manhood, as familiar to him through former approximately equal fellow-ship with Wallenstein. The following lines, from this man's half-relenting reminiscence of the past, dash off a rapid and vivid sketch of powerful character. Butler, who interrupts Gordon with a question, is an Irishman, once wounded in his pride by Wallenstein, and now ready to revenge himself by compassing his chieftain's death:

Gordon. A youth who scarce had seen his twentieth year
Was Wallenstein, when he and I were friends:
Yet even then he had a daring soul;
His frame of mind was serious and severe
Beyond his years; his dreams were of great objects.
He walked amidst us of a silent spirit,
Communing with himself: yet I have known him
Transported on a sudden into utterance

17

Of strange conceptions; kindling into splendor
His soul revealed itself, and he spake so
That we looked round perplexed upon each other,
Not knowing whether it were craziness,
Or whether it were a god that spoke in him.

Butler. But was it where he fell two story high
From a window-ledge, on which he had fallen asleep;
And rose up free from injury?   From this day
(It is reported) he betrayed clear marks
Of a distempered fancy.

Gordon.   He became
Doubtless more self-enwrapt and melancholy;
He made himself a Catholic. Marvellously
His marvellous preservation had transformed him.
Thenceforth he held himself for an exempted
And privileged being, and, as if he were
Incapable of dizziness or fall,
He ran along the unsteady rope of life.
But now our destinies drove us asunder:
He paced with rapid step the way of greatness,
Was Count, and Prince, Duke-regent, and Dictator.
And now is all, all this too little for him;
He stretches forth his hand for a king's crown,
And plunges in unfathomable ruin.

Another soliloquy of Wallenstein's gives us the working
within his breast of doubtful thought and motive, while,
caught in the current of circumstance—a current fast rushing on into resistless rapids of destiny—he revolves the question, like, but so unlike, Hamlet's: "To do or not to do."
The passage is a powerful one :

Wal. [*in soliloquy.*]   Is it possible?
Is't so?   I *can* no longer what I *would?*
No longer draw back at my liking!   I
Must *do* the deed because I *thought* of it,
And fed this heart here with a dream?   Because
I did not scowl temptation from my presence,
Dallied with thoughts of possible fulfillment,
Commenced no movement, left all time uncertain,
And only kept the road, the access open?
By the great God of heaven! it was not
My serious meaning, it was ne'er resolved.
I but amused myself with thinking of it.

The free-will tempted me, the power to do
Or not to do it. Was it criminal
To make the fancy minister to hope,
To fill the air with pretty toys of air,
And clutch fantastic sceptres moving toward me?
Was not the will kept free? Beheld I not
The road of duty close beside me—but
One little step, and once more I was in it!
Where am I? Whither have I been transported?
No road, no track behind me, but a wall,
Impenetrable, insurmountable,
Rises obedient to the spells I muttered
And meant not—my own doings tower behind me.
    [*Pauses and remains in deep thought.*]
A punishable man I seem; the guilt,
Try what I will, I cannot roll off from me;
The equivocal demeanor of my life
Bears witness on my prosecutor's part
And even my purest acts from purest motives
Suspicion poisons with malicious gloss.
Were I that thing for which I pass, that traitor,
A goodly outside I had sure reserved,
Had drawn the cov'rings thick and double round me,
Been calm and chary of my utterance.
But being conscious of the innocence
Of my intent, my uncorrupted will,
I gave way to my humors, to my passion:
Bold were my words, because my deeds were *not*.
Now every planless measure, chance event,
The threat of rage, the vaunt of joy and triumph,
And all the May-games of a heart o'erflowing,
Will they connect, and weave them all together
Into one web of treason; all will be plan,
My eye ne'er absent from the far-off mark,
Step tracing step, each step a politic progress;
And out of all they'll fabricate a charge
So specious, that I must myself stand *dumb*.
I am caught in my own net, and only force,
Naught but a sudden *rent* can liberate me.
    [*Pauses again.*]
How else! since that the heart's unbiased instinct
Impelled me to the daring deed, which now
Necessity, self-preservation, *orders*.
Stern is the on-look of Necessity;

Not without shudder may a human hand
Grasp the mysterious urn of destiny.
My deed was mine, remaining in my bosom,
Once suffered to escape from its safe corner
Within the heart, its nursery and birthplace,
Sent forth into the foreign, it belongs
Forever to those sly, malicious powers
Whom never art of man conciliated.

[*Paces in agitation through the chamber, then pauses, and, after the pause, breaks out again into audible soliloquy.*]

What is thy enterprise? thy aim? thy object?
Hast honestly confessed it to thyself?
Power seated on a quiet throne thou'dst shake,
Power on an ancient consecrated throne,
Strong in possession, founded in old custom;
Power by a thousand tough and stringy roots
Fixed to the people's pious nursery-faith.
This, this will be no strife of strength with strength.
That feared I not.   I brave each combatant,
Whom I can look on, fixing eye to eye,
Who, full himself of courage, kindles courage
In me too.   'Tis a foe invisible,
The which I fear—a fearful enemy,
Which in the human heart opposes me,
By its coward fear alone made fearful to me.
Not that, which full of life, instinct with power,
Makes known its present being, that is not
The true, the perilously formidable.
O no! it is the common, the quite common,
The thing of an eternal yesterday,
What ever was, and evermore returns,
Sterling to-morrow, for to-day 'twas sterling!
For of the wholly common is man made,
And custom is his nurse!   Woe then to them
Who lay irreverent hands upon his old
House furniture, the dear inheritance
From his forefathers.   For time consecrates;
And what is gray with age becomes religion.
Be in possession, and thou hast the right,
And sacred will the many guard it for thee!

[*To the page who here enters.*]

The Swedish officer?—Well, let him enter.

[*The page exit*, WALLENSTEIN *fixes his eye in deep thought on the door.*]

Yet is it pure—as yet!—the crime has come

> Not o'er this threshold yet—so slender is
> The boundary that divideth life's two paths.

Our readers will perceive how it was that the *Wallenstein* grew to such volume under the author's hands. Schiller had what one dislikes to call the national fault of prolixity. His intensity he maintains, but it is a prolix intensity. If somehow the *Wallenstein* could be condensed one half, or even more, what a gain there would be in impression and in power !

The characters in the drama are mostly historical; but Max Piccolomini, son to Octavio, and Thekla, Wallenstein's daughter, loved by Max and loving him, are exceptions. These are imaginations of the poet's brain. The mutual relation of the two, and their tragic fate, constitute an episode in the drama, which the action could have spared, perhaps even with gain to the unity and the progress of the plot; but to part with the episode would be a loss to the poetry. Our readers will remember that Schiller, trying hard against himself to regard his personages all with the indifference of the artist, acknowledged that, in the case of Max Piccolomini, he had not succeeded. Max, the poet loved as the child of his own imagination. A high, heroic, chivalrous, ideal character Schiller had to gratify himself with introducing into nearly every one of his dramas. The noblest success in this kind that he ever achieved, it seems to us that he achieved in his Max Piccolomini. Max is so entirely the soul of truth and honor that he will not believe his father telling him that Wallenstein is a traitor to the emperor. His master has, he insists, been misrepresented, maligned, to his father. Wallenstein, in order to attach the young officer more securely to his own interest, had allowed Max to hope that he might eventually win the hand of his daughter. Secretly, the father's ambition for her aspired to nothing beneath a royal bridegroom. Max at last has an interview with Wallenstein, in which that chieftain himself unfolds to the young man his treasonable purposes. In the dialogue that follows Max's pure heart speaks out nobly. Surely it was a fine

self-gratification that the poet insisted upon from the artist,
when Schiller would be "subjective" enough to write this
dialogue.   Wallenstein has bidden Max take time to recollect
himself before choosing his part.   Now Schiller:

[WALLENSTEIN *rises and retires at the back of the stage.*   MAX *remains for*
a long time motionless, in a trance of excessive anguish.   At his first motion
WALLENSTEIN *returns and places himself before him.*]

Max. My General, this day thou makest me
Of age to speak in my own right and person,
For till this day I have been spared the trouble
To find out my own road.   Thee have I followed
With most implicit unconditional faith,
Sure of the right path if I followed thee.
To-day, for the first time, dost thou refer
Me to myself, and forcest me to make
Election between thee and my own heart.

Wal. Soft cradled thee thy Fortune till to-day:
Thy duties thou couldst exercise in sport,
Indulge all lovely instincts, act forever
With undivided heart.   It can remain
No longer thus.   Like enemies, the roads
Start from each other.   Duties strive with duties.
Thou must needs choose thy party in the war
Which is now kindling 'twixt thy friend and him
Who is thy Emperor.

Max.   War! is that the name?
War is as frightful as heaven's pestilence.
Yet it is good, is it heaven's will as that is.
Is that a good war, which against the Emperor
Thou wagest with the Emperor's own army?
O God of heaven! what a change is this.
Beseems it me to offer such persuasion
To thee, who like the fixed star of the pole,
Wert all I gazed at on life's trackless ocean?
O! what a rent thou makest in my heart!
The ingrained instinct of old reverence,
The holy habit of obediency,
Must I pluck live asunder from thy name?
Nay, do not turn thy countenance upon me—
It always was as a god looking at me!
Duke Wallenstein, its power is not departed:
The senses still are in thy bonds, although,
Bleeding, the soul hath freed itself.

Wal.   Max, hear me.
Max. O! do it not, I pray thee, do it not!
       There is a pure and noble soul within thee,
       Knows not of this unblest, unlucky doing.
       Thy will is chaste, it is thy fancy only
       Which hath polluted thee—and innocence,
       It will not let itself be driven away
       From that world-awing aspect.   Thou wilt not,
       Thou canst not, end in this.   It would reduce
       All human creatures to disloyalty
       Against the nobleness of their own nature.
       'Twill justify the vulgar misbelief,
       Which holdeth nothing noble in free will,
       And trusts itself to impotence alone
       Made powerful only in an unknown power.
Wal. The world will judge me sternly, I expect it.
       Already have I said to my own self
       All thou canst say to me.   Who but avoids
       Th' extreme,—can he by going round avoid it?
       But here there is no choice.   Yes—I must use
       Or suffer violence—so stands the case,
       There remains nothing possible but that.
Max. O that is never possible for thee!
       'Tis the last desperate resource of those
       Cheap souls, to whom their honor, their good name,
       Is their poor *saving*, their last worthless *keep*,
       Which, having staked and lost, they stake themselves
       In the mad rage of gaming.   Thou art rich,
       And glorious; with an unpolluted heart
       Thou canst make conquest of whate'er seems highest;
       But he, who once hath acted infamy,
       Does nothing more in this world.
Wal. [*grasps his hand*].   Calmly, Max!
       Much that is great and excellent will we
       Perform together yet.   And if we only
       Stand on the height with dignity, 'tis soon
       Forgotten, Max, by what road we ascended.
       Believe me, many a crown shines spotless now,
       That yet was deeply sullied in the winning.
       To the evil spirit doth the earth belong,
       Not to the good.   All, that the powers divine
       Send from above, are universal blessings:
       Their light rejoices us, their air refreshes,
       But never yet was man enriched by them:

In their eternal realm no *property*
Is to be struggled for—all there is general.
The jewel, the all-valued gold we win
From the deceiving Powers, depraved in nature,
That dwell beneath the day and blessed sun-light;
Not without sacrifices are they rendered
Propitious, and there lives no soul on earth
That e'er retired unsullied from their service.

Max. Whate'er is human, to the human being
Do I allow—and to the vehement
And striving spirit readily I pardon
The excess of action; but to thee, my General!
Above *all* others make I large concession.
For thou must move a world, and be the master—
He kills thee, who condemns thee to inaction.
So be it then! maintain thee in thy post
By violence. Resist the Emperor,
And if it must be, force with force repel:
I will not praise it, yet I can forgive it.
But not—not to the *traitor*—yes!—the word
Is spoken out—
Not to the *traitor* can I yield a pardon.
That is no mere excess! that is no error
Of human nature—that is wholly different;
O that is black. black as the pit of hell!
    [WALLENSTEIN *betrays a sudden agitation.*]
Thou canst not hear it *named*, and wilt thou *do* it ?
O turn back to thy duty. That thou canst,
I hold it certain. Send me to Vienna.
I'll make thy peace for thee with th' Emperor.
He knows thee not. But I do know thee. He
Shall see thee, Duke! with my unclouded eye,
And I bring back his confidence to thee.

Wal. It is too late.   Thou know'st not what has happened.

Max. Were it too late, and were things gone so far,
That a crime only could prevent thy fall,
Then—fall! fall honorably, even as thou stood'st,
Lose the command. Go from the stage of war.
Thou canst with splendor do it—do it, too,
With innocence. Thou hast lived much for others,
At length live thou for thy own self.   I follow thee.
My destiny I never part from thine.

Wal. It is too late ! Even now, while thou art losing
Thy words, one after the other are the mile-stones

Left fast behind by my post couriers,
Who bear the order on to Prague and Egra.

Thé agony of resolution is after all not over for Max. A subsequent scene brings Max and Thekla together, with the countess, Wallenstein's sister, of course aunt to Thekla. Max, torn with suspense and despair, cries out for an angel from heaven to show him what he ought to do. Then he bethinks him of Thekla. What other angel than Thekla does he need? Now follows a device highly characteristic of Schiller. Max devolves on Thekla the burden of deciding whether he shall go—that is, to the emperor; or stay—that is, with Wallenstein, her father. At first blush, this seems a flaw of imperfect in the heroic character of Max. But it at least brings out the heroic in Thekla. And perhaps the dramatist could in no other way better relieve his hero of the imputation of sacrificing Thekla, than by affording her the opportunity of sacrificing herself. The two together are equal to their duty and their fate. Or shall we have to say almost equal? Max, self-taught, and taught by Thekla, abides, indeed, by his faith to the emperor. But is it a perfect triumph of truth and nobleness that he should put himself, as he does, at the head of his devoted followers, and, leading them, purposely, in an attack, foreknown by him to be hopeless, on the Swedes, perish by a kind of suicide, buried under mounds of the dead immolated with their leader, and, as it were, immolated by him? Thekla, too, escapes out of life by the gate of suicide. This is commonplace tragedy, rather than triumphant imagination of virtue strong enough still to live when to die was much more desirable.

Max, yet trustingly and affectionately loyal to Wallenstein, had spoken in the following beautiful strain of that great man's addiction to astrology. The passage we are now about to quote is a celebrated one. We have been using, and we still use, Coleridge's translation of the *Wallenstein*, a work not without its faults of inexactness, but on the whole unapproachably noble. By singular exception, Coleridge has made, in the present passage, an original interpolation of his own, extending to several lines. These we designate to the reader by printing them in italics. The separation, however, between what is Coleridge and what is Schiller is not sharp; the two interlace each other, both at the beginning and at the end. Now Max on Wallenstein as astrologer:

> O never rudely will I blame his faith
> In the might of stars and angels! 'Tis not merely
> The human being's Pride that peoples space
> With life and mystical predominance;
> Since likewise for the stricken heart of Love
> This visible nature, and this common world,
> Is all too narrow: yea, a deeper import
> Lurks in the legend told my infant years
> Than lies upon that truth, we live to learn.
> For fable is Love's world, his home, his birthplace:
> Delightedly dwells he 'mong fays and talismans,
> And spirits; and delightedly believes
> Divinities, being himself divine.
> *The intelligible forms of ancient poets,*
> *The fair humanities of old religion,*
> *The power, the beauty, and the majesty,*
> *That had their haunts in dale, or piny mountain,*
> *Or forest by slow stream, or pebbly spring,*
> *Or chasms, and wat'ry depths, all these have vanished;*
> *They live no longer in the faith of reason!*
> But still the heart doth need a language, still
> Doth the old instinct bring back the old names,
> And to yon starry world they now are gone,
> Spirits or gods, that used to share this earth
> With man as with their friend; and to the lover
> Yonder they move, from yonder visible sky
> Shoot influence down: and even at this day
> 'Tis Jupiter who brings whate'er is great,
> And Venus who brings every thing that's fair!

An interpretation thus gentle given by Max to Wallenstein's superstitious study of the stars—this, together with that high-hearted youth's tragic end in suicidal battle, imparts an indescribable pathos to the following passage, which, besides, is brooded over, deep and dark, with the shadow of Wallenstein's own now imminent doom. It is the night in which Wallenstein will fall under the stabs of assassins. His sister is with him, and he is watching the sky. Jupiter is his star; but the gloomy duke's words at one time wander, without notice, from speaking of Jupiter to speaking of young Piccolomini, whom this stern man really did love as with a father's affection. We know of nothing in dramatic poetry pitched in a key of loftier pathos than is the following :

> *Wal.* [*moves to the window*]. There is a busy motion in the heaven,
> The wind doth chase the flag upon the tower,
> Fast sweep the clouds, the sickle of the moon,
> Struggling, darts snatches of uncertain light.
> No form of star is visible! That one
> White stain of light, that single glimmering yonder,
> Is from Cassiopeia, and therein
> Is Jupiter. [*A pause.*] But now
> The blackness of the troubled element hides him!
> [*He sinks into profound melancholy, and looks vacantly into the distance.*]
> *Coun.* [*looks on him mournfully, then grasps his hand*].
> What art thou brooding on?
> *Wal.*   Methinks,
> If I but saw him, 't would be well with me.
> He is the star of my nativity,
> And often marvellously hath his aspect
> Shot strength into my heart.
> *Coun.*   Thou 'lt see him again.
> *Wal.* [*remains for a while with absent mind, then assumes a livelier manner, and turns suddenly to the countess*].
> See him again? O never, never again.
> *Coun.* How?
> *Wal.*   He is gone—is dust.
> *Coun.*   Whom meanest thou then?
> *Wal.* He, the more fortunate! Yea, he hath finished!
> For him there is no longer any future,
> His life is bright—bright without spot it *was*,
> And cannot cease to be. No ominous hour
> Knocks at his door with tidings of mishap.
> Far off is he, above desire and fear ;
> No more submitted to the change and chance
> Of the unsteady planets. O 'tis well
> With *him !* but who knows what the coming hour
> Veiled in thick darkness brings for us!

Coun.   Thou speak'st
Of Piccolomini.   What was his death ?
The courier had just left thee as I came.
[*Wallenstein by a motion of his hand makes signs to her to be silent.*]
Turn not thine eyes upon the backward view,
Let us look forward into sunny days,
Welcome with joyous heart the victory.
Forget what it has cost thee.   Not to-day,
For the first time, thy friend was to thee dead ;
To thee he died, when first he parted from thee.

Wal. I shall grieve down this blow, of that I'm conscious :
What does not man grieve down ?   From the highest,
As from the vilest thing of every day
He learns to wean himself; for the strong hours
Conquer him.   Yet I feel what I have lost
In him.   The bloom is vanished from my life.
For O ! he stood beside me, like my youth,
Transformed for me the real to a dream,
Clothing the palpable and familiar
With golden exhalations of the dawn.
Whatever fortunes wait my future toils,
The *beautiful* is vanished—and returns not.

We need only indicate the catastrophe by giving a fragment of dialogue between the conspirators.   The actual
assassination takes place unseen, but it treads immediately
on the heels of the following significant exchange of sentiment between an assassin who halts and an assassin who
urges.   It is Butler who urges, and it is Gordon who halts :

Gor. He sleeps !   O murder not the holy sleep !
But. No ! he shall die awake.   [*Is going.*]
Gor.   His heart still cleaves
To earthly things : he's not prepared to step
Into the presence of his God !
But. [*going*].   God's merciful !
Gor. [*holds him*].   Grant him but this night's respite.
But. [*hurrying off*].   The next moment
May ruin all.
Gor. [*holds him still*].   One hour !—
But.   Unhold me !   What
Can that short respite profit him ?
Gor.   O—Time
Works miracles.   In one hour many thousands

Of grains of sand run out; and quick as they,
Thought follows thought within the human soul.
Only one hour !   *Your* heart may change its purpose,
His heart may change its purpose—some new tidings
May come: some fortunate event, decisive,
May fall from Heaven and rescue him.   O what
May not one hour achieve !

The very end of the drama consists in a stroke of expression designed by the author to suggest a mercenary interest as having animated the elder Piccolomini in his fidelity to the emperor against Wallenstein. A letter comes from the emperor addressed to Octavio under a significant title, indicating that the faithful informer has received his reward. The superscription reads: "To the PRINCE Piccolomini." With those words uttered aloud, the curtain drops, and the long trilogy of the *Wallenstein* is ended.

We ought to say that of the two latter divisions of the trilogy the first is called *The Piccolomini*, and the last *The Death of Wallenstein*. The matter of these is, in various editions, variously distributed. We have ourselves, in our citations, drawn from both the two final parts as these appear in the arrangement of Coleridge's translation.

No Shakespeare was Schiller. The German does not, like the Englishman, cut you out as it were a section from the real world of men and of events and transplant this, living and breathing, into literature. There is always a sentimental, a romantic, an idealizing, haze hung over the stage on which Schiller's personages move and speak. You see his men and women somewhat as if they walked in buskins and wore masks. A drama thus very different in kind from the *King Henry VIII.* of Shakespeare is the *Wallenstein* of Schiller. It comes nearer in type to the epic style of Lucan's *Pharsalia;* or to that style dramatized in the *Polyeucte* of Corneille. But the *Wallenstein* is purer and nobler, because more genuine, than the *Polyeucte*, and it is purer and nobler, because less pagan, than the *Pharsalia*. Schiller understood the art of theatric effect, and there is therefore real interest of action in the *Wallenstein ;* but the author's highest power, as also his highest pleasure, is rather to be oratoric than to be dramatic. In this Schiller resembles Corneille. But in this Schiller surpasses Corneille. There are no speeches in the *Polyeucte,* for instance, comparable, for true eloquence, with the speeches of the *Wallenstein.* Not on the whole adapted to be a popular drama, the *Wallenstein* is, for thoughtful and elevated minds, as inexhaustibly ministrant to a certain pathetic and lofty delight as any thing we know in dramatic literature. You need long leisure for it, with a mood disengaged; and then the solemn mystery of power and pathos in the play weaves an extraordinary spell of dominance over your imagination and your heart. If it was not written by the greatest poet, it at least is for us the greatest poem in German literature.

When Schiller and Goethe are brought together in thought with a view to the gauging of their comparative greatness, it should always be remembered that, for Schiller, twenty-five embarrassed and impoverished years constituted his whole term of literary activity; while Goethe, after he began to produce, enjoyed ease and affluence for more than sixty years. Consider duly all that this enormous disparity of chance for the two men imports, and, comparing then the actual achievement of the one with the actual achievement of the other, assuredly you will feel that Schiller rendered a full better account of himself than did Goethe.

Narrowness, with intensity, was contrasted in Schiller against breadth, with repose, in Goethe. Schiller's end in life was literature, and fame through literature. Goethe's end in life was the culture of himself. Of neither was the end in life the noblest that might have been; but surely Schiller's was nobler than Goethe's. Correspondingly, too, the gain to the world, alike through literary product bequeathed, and through example exhibited of aim and of character, was, as we think, more from the less of the two than it was from the greater. For Goethe was undoubtedly planned to be both a greater man and a greater poet than Schiller.

XI.

THE ROMANCERS AND THE ROMANTICISTS.

WE devote the present chapter to an assemblage of writers whom we may call the Romancers and the Romanticists. We shall be able, under this twofold title, to group a number of literary names, most of whom are very naturally associated, though as to some of them we may have to use a little gentle force to bring them thus kindly together.

A " Romancer " is not of course the same thing as a " Romanticist." A Romanticist is one who adopts, or who favors, a certain taste and style in literary composition; a free, subjective taste and style, best understood by the contrast of that stricter, severer form and spirit which we call the classic. A Romancer, as we choose now to use the term, is one who tells stories of a peculiar sort, stories in which popular legend and a weird supernatural enter as a considerable element.

Let us begin here with an author who unites in himself the character of Romancer with the character of Romanticist—Ludwig Tieck (1773–1853.)

While Tieck's living fame was yet in its most vivid freshness and brilliancy, Goethe, talking with Eckermann, said :

> Tieck has a talent of great importance, and no one can be more sensible than myself to his extraordinary merits. Only when they [the more extravagant Romanticists] raise him above himself, and place him on a level with me, they are in error.

Tieck still remains for us a sufficiently important name to deserve respectful, though it must be hastening, attention at our hands.

This writer was not only a romanticist in literary taste and principle, but in his time the acknowledged head of the romantic school in German literature. It was easier for him to be vague than it was to be definite, and he liked it better. Moonlight was sweeter than sunlight to Tieck. Scherer quotes his lines :

> Magical moonlit night,
> Holding the senses fettered,

Wonderful fairy world,
Arise in thy glory—

and not unaptly calls them the "manifesto of Romanticism."
This romanticist, however, was capable of the most homely
realism in fiction; and such, in fact, was the cast of his later
imaginative work.

Tieck was both poet and prose writer. It is as prose writer
that he will most interest our readers. From among Tieck's
short stories, the happiest of which are probably those embraced in the volume entitled *Phantasus*, we select *The Fair-
haired Eckbert* to exhibit in abridgement here. Carlyle has
translated this in his *German Romance*. We use his translation.

The scene of the story is laid in the Hartz region. The hero is
a knight, familiarly called the Fair-haired Eckbert, who lived
in seemingly contented retirement with his wife, lamenting
only that she gave him no children. His quiet home was seldom visited by guests. But there was one man, Walther, with
whom Eckbert formed a close relation of friendship—so
close, in fact, that one evening, in a burst of confidence, he
begged his wife Bertha to tell their trusted guest the singular
story of her own maiden life. This she did. Having run
away from her childhood's home, she had been welcomed,
after wanderings many and wide, into the hospitality of a
withered old woman's lonely cottage, where she long abode.
The old woman had in her cottage two pet familiars—a bird
and a dog. In this company, and seeing no other, Bertha lived
and was happy. Let her now herself take up her story, as
Tieck supplies her with words. Remember that Bertha is
telling the tale, at her husband's wish, to Walther the guest:

I am surprised that I have never since been able to recall the dog's
name, a very odd one, often as I then pronounced it.

Four years I had passed in this way (I must now have been nearly
twelve) when my old dame began to put more trust in me, and at length
told me a secret. The bird, I found, laid every day an egg, in which there
was a pearl or a jewel. I had already noticed that she went often to fettle
privately about the cage, but I had never troubled myself further on the

subject. She now gave me charge of gathering these eggs in her absence, and carefully storing them up in the strange-looking pots. She would leave me food, and sometimes stay away for weeks, for months.

The child Bertha had her books to read, and, quickened by these, she peopled her solitude with company born of her brooding brain. The bird was a weird one that could sing a song with words, as follows:

> Alone in wood so gay
> 'Tis good to stay,
> Morrow like to-day,
> Forever and aye:
> O, I do love to stay
> Alone in wood so gay.

Bertha continues her tale, Walther listening:

I was now fourteen; it is the misery of man that he arrives at understanding through the loss of innocence. I now saw well enough that it lay with me to take the jewels and the bird in the old woman's absence, and go forth with them to see the world which I had read of. Perhaps, too, it would then be possible that I might meet the fairest of all knights, who forever dwelt in my memory.

Bertha dallied with her thought of taking the bird and the jewels and going away with them—but now Tieck once more, through his Bertha proceeding with her story:

One day she [the old woman] went out again, telling me that she should be away on this occasion longer than usual; that I must take strict charge of every thing, and not let the time hang heavy on my hands. I had a sort of fear on taking leave of her, for I felt as if I should not see her any more. . . .

I knew not what to make of it; the dog leaped up continually about me; the sunshine spread abroad over the fields; the green birch-trees glittered; I always felt as if I had something I must do in haste; so I caught the little dog, tied him up in the room, and took the cage with the bird under my arm. The dog writhed and whined under this unusual treatment; he looked at me with begging eyes, but I feared to have him with me. I also took one pot of jewels, and concealed it by me; the rest I left.

The bird turned its head very strangely when I crossed the threshold; the dog tugged at his cord to follow me, but he was forced to stay. . . .

. . . In a pleasant town I hired a small house and garden, and took

18

to myself a maid.   I forgot the old woman and my former way of life
rather more, and, on the whole, I was contented.

For a long while the bird had ceased to sing; I was, therefore, not a
little frightened when one night he suddenly began again, and with a different rhyme.   He sang:

> Alone in wood so gay,
> Ah, far away!
> But thou wilt say
> Some other day,
> 'Twere best to stay
> Alone in wood so gay.

The aspect of the bird distressed me greatly; he looked at me continually, and his presence did me ill.   There was now no end to his song;
he sang it louder and more shrilly than he had been wont.   The more I
looked at him the more he pained and frightened me; at last I opened
the cage, put in my hand, and grasped his neck; I squeezed my fingers
hard together, he looked at me, I slackened them; but he was dead.   I
buried him in the garden.

After this there often came a fear over me for my maid; I looked back
upon myself, and fancied she might rob or murder me.   For a long while
I had been acquainted with a young knight whom I altogether liked; I
bestowed on him my hand, and with this, Sir Walther, ends my story.

Walther, bidding good-night, incidentally supplied to
Bertha the forgotten name of the dog.   He said:

"Many thanks, noble lady.   I can well figure you beside your singing
bird, and how you fed poor little *Strohmian*."

The rest of Tieck's story of *The Fair-haired Eckbert* we
force into brief condensation:

. . . From that day Walther visited the castle of his friend but seldom. . . . Eckbert was exceedingly distressed by this demeanor. . . .
. . . One morning Bertha sent for her husband to her bedside. . . .
"Dear Eckbert," she began, "I must disclose a secret to thee. . . .
That night, on taking leave, Walther all at once said to me: 'I can well
figure you, how you fed poor little *Strohmian*.' . . . I felt a shudder that
a stranger should help me to recall the memory of my secrets.   What
sayest thou, Eckbert?"

Eckbert . . spoke some words of comfort to her, and went out. . . .
Walther for many years had been his sole companion, and now this
person was the only mortal in the world whose existence pained and oppressed him. . . . He took his bow, to dissipate these thoughts, and went
to hunt. . . . He found no game, and this embittered his ill-humor; all

at once he saw an object moving in the distance; it was Walther gathering moss from the trunks of trees. Scarce knowing what he did, he bent his bow; Walther looked around and gave a threatening gesture, but the arrow was already flying, and he sank transfixed by it.

Eckbert felt relieved, calmed, yet a certain horror drove him home to his castle. It was a good way distant; he had wandered far into the woods. On arriving, he found Bertha dead; before her death she had spoken much of Walther and the old woman.

For a great while after this occurrence Eckbert lived in the deepest solitude. . . . The murder of his friend arose incessantly before his mind; he lived in the anguish of continued remorse.

To dissipate his feelings . . he mingled in society and its amusements. He longed for a friend to fill the void in his soul. . . .

A young knight named Hugo made advances to the silent, melancholy Eckbert, and appeared to have a true affection for him. Eckbert . . met the knight's friendship with the greater readiness, the less he had anticipated it. The two . . in all companies got together. In a word, they seemed inseparable.

. . . On a solitary ride Eckbert disclosed his whole history to Hugo, and asked if he could love a murderer. Hugo seemed touched, and tried to comfort him. Eckbert returned to town with a lighter heart.

But . . scarcely had they entered the public hall when, in the glitter of the many lights, Hugo's looks ceased to satisfy him. He thought he noticed a malicious smile; he remarked that Hugo did not speak to him as usual. . . . In the party was an old knight who had always shown himself the enemy of Eckbert, had often asked about his riches and his wife in a peculiar style. With this man Hugo was conversing; they were speaking privately, and casting looks at Eckbert. . . . As he continued gazing, on a sudden he . . . felt convinced that it was none but Walther who was talking to the knight. . . . He returned to his castle. Here . . . sleep never visited his eyes. . . . He resolved to take a journey. . . .

He set out, without prescribing to himself any certain route. . . . At length he met an old peasant who took him by a path leading past a waterfall. . . . "What use is it?" said Eckbert. "I could believe that this man, too, was none but Walther." He looked round once more, and it was none but Walther. Eckbert spurred his horse as fast as it could gallop over meads and forests, till it sank exhausted to the earth. Regardless of this, he hastened forward on foot.

In a dreamy mood he mounted a hill; he fancied he caught the sound of lively barking at a little distance; the birch-trees whispered in the intervals, and in the strangest notes he heard this song:

> Alone in wood so gay
> Once more I stay;

None dare me slay,
The evil far away:
Ah! here I stay,
Alone in wood so gay.

The sense, the consciousness of Eckbert had departed. . . .

A crooked, bent old woman crawled coughing up the hill with a crutch. " Art thou bringing me my bird, my pearls, my dog ? " cried she to him. " See how injustice punishes itself. No one but I was Walther, was Hugo."

" God of heaven ! " said Eckbert, muttering to himself; " in what frightful solitude have I passed my life ! "

" And Bertha was thy sister."

Eckbert sank to the ground.

" Why did she leave me deceitfully ? All would have been fair and well; her time of trial was already finished. She was the daughter of a knight, who had her nursed in a shepherd's house, the daughter of thy father."

" Why have I always had a forecast of this dreadful thought ? " cried Eckbert.

" Because in early youth thy father told thee he could not keep this daughter with him on account of his second wife, her stepmother."

Eckbert lay distracted and dying on the ground. Faint and bewildered he heard the old woman speaking, the dog barking, and the bird repeating its song.

And thus, seeming still unfinished, the story ends.

There is always felt by English or American readers a lack of what we might call substance in Tieck's stories—that is, a ground of reality, of probability. Hawthorne, in his eeriest fiction, feels laid upon him the obligation to suggest some sort of rational account or explanation of the supernatural element which he introduces. Tieck is perfectly free to leave all that for his reader to arrange as best he can. His reader, if he be a German, experiences no difficulty in the case. If his reader be an Englishman or an American, difficulty, indeed, is experienced, but the difficulty is soon disposed of ; the Englishman or the American ceases to read Tieck, and turns to Charles Dickens.

Tieck was not simply a romanticist in his own practice; he waged war on the classicists. From one of his productions directed against classicism, a kind of drama, we take a few generous lines on Goethe, to show as a good specimen of Tieck's poetry :

> We have made ready here a mead of flowers
> For that great artist of the latter days,
> With whose name wakes the art of Germany,
> Who sings you still full many a noble lay,
> And bids you from this time for evermore
> Know true poetic light—him Shakespeare hopes
> Erelong to clasp ;   Cervantes longs for him,
> And Dante muses welcome with his verse;
> And then these holy four shall ever walk,
> Masters of latest art, about my fields of calm.

We began our treatment of this writer with what we may call Goethe's tribute to Tieck. With Tieck's tribute to Goethe, let us account the subject closed.

If, among the German Romanticists, Tieck was by quantity the weightiest, the one most · ethereal in quality was Novalis. The bearer of this name is, indeed, scarcely more than an unfixed wandering odor in the flower-garden of German literature.

Friedrich von Hardenberg (1772–1801)—for " Novalis " is a pseudonym—exhaled himself away in an earthly life of only twenty-nine fleet and beautiful years, leaving, as we have said, behind him little but a rare and exquisite perfume. This, however—unsubstantial and volatile as it is—is precious, and we must try to catch and imprison at least a breath of it here to sweeten our pages withal.

Tieck, as biographer of him, paints the character and genius of Novalis with colors dipped in heaven. Sober criticism may abate much from the glow of the picture, and still leave Novalis a truly charming tradition of loveliness in character and brilliancy in genius.

The works of Novalis are few in number, and in form fragmentary. There is an unfinished romance entitled (from its hero, a conjectured author of the *Nibelungen Lied,* in the existing form of that poem) *Heinrich von Ofterdingen.* This we pass with the mere mention thus made, and give, in specimen of Novalis, a few " Thoughts " from his *Fragments,* a posthumous publication. In our first selection, the reader will find Novalis anticipating that recent definition of "matter" which identifies it with " force : "

All manifestation of power is transitional; stationary power is matter.

Let our readers consider whether in the second of the following " Thoughts " they have not an adumbration, on Novalis's part, of Hahnemann's principle in therapeutics, *Similia similibus curantur* (like diseases are cured by like), that foundation of homeopathy:

As only spirit is truly free, so only spirit can be forced.

Might it not be possible to cure diseases by diseases?

A character is a completely formed will.

Where children are, there is a golden age.

The Bible begins gloriously with Paradise, the symbol of youth, and ends with the everlasting kingdom, with the Holy City. . . . The history of every man should be a Bible.

Every sickness is a musical problem: the cure is the musical solution.

A space-filling individual is a body, a time-filling individual is a soul.

Life is the beginning of death; life is for death; death is an ending and a beginning at once.

In order to be able rightly to learn a truth, one needs also to have combatted it.

Many men are contemporary rather with the past and with the future than with the present.

Philosophy is, properly speaking, homesickness, a desire to be everywhere at home.

Water is a wet flame.

Every object beloved is the centre of a paradise.

The foregoing bits of wisdom, or of paradox, remarkable in themselves, but very remarkable for so young a thinker, we must submit without criticism to our readers. Some of them Novalis might have quite outgrown had he lived. They were, probably, mere jottings of thought to be further dwelt on and inquired about. They hint a great loss to literature, in the premature death of the author.

To Novalis is credited that memorable word, or "expression," as may be most convenient, about Spinoza: "Spinoza is a God-intoxicated man." This is to be understood as a favorable interpretation of Spinoza's pantheism. Spinoza—so Novalis would have it—far from finding God nowhere, which would have made him an atheist, was a pantheist because he found God everywhere; he was as one drunk with the idea of God.

Adding two stanzas from a Christian hymn by Novalis, we bid this gracious spirit farewell:

> What had I been if thou wert not?
>   What were I now if thou wert gone?
> Anguish and fear were then my lot,
>   In this wide world I stood alone;
> Whate'er I loved were safe no more,
>   The future were a dark abyss;
> To whom could I my sorrows pour,
>   If thee my laden heart should miss?
>
> But when thou mak'st thy presence felt,
>   And when the soul has grasped thee right,
> How fast the dreary shadows melt
>   Beneath thy warm and living light!
> In thee I find a nobler birth,
>   A glory o'er the world I see,
> And paradise returns to earth,
>   And blooms again for us in thee.

A literary movement like Romanticism, become perfectly self-conscious and meaning to be iconoclastic, innovative, belligerent, needs to have a kind of court of judicature, a source of authority, a resort for appeal. This the German Romantic movement found in the two brothers Schlegel, men well qualified in every way to carry the requisite weight of influence, both with the members of their school itself, and with the general public. These brothers possessed in eminence that curious, that indefinable, personal character by virtue of which its possessor, without disturbing sense of

imposture practiced, and without wavering in interior conviction of right, may all his life go on being looked up to
and addressed as "Sir Oracle;" in other words, may con-
tentedly, comfortably, and, moreover, perhaps not discredit-
ably, sustain the life-long part of one wiser than any human
being ever was.

But the pretensions of the Schlegels, overweening as they
were, had grounds, solid, at least, if not sufficient, to rest
upon. They were both men of great ability, and of acquire-
ments still greater. They were prodigies of learning. Their
self-complacency—but this is especially true of the elder—was
an exhaustless resource to them, supported as it was by dignified personal presence, courtly manners, and, at last, high
worldly position. The elder brother, August Wilhelm von
Schlegel (1767–1845), translated Shakespeare, producing the
version which was destined to be accepted as final, and which
as matter of fact has completely domesticated the prince
of English dramatists among the Germans. He also translated Dante and Calderon. He wrote original poetry of his
own. Upon that poetical form known as the sonnet, he bestowed the highest distinction within his power—by writing
in it a lyric of eulogy upon himself! His own claim therein
preferred, is not quite that he was first to write sonnets in
German—as it is sometimes said that he was; but only that
he was "conqueror, exemplar, master," in this kind. The
whole absurd travesty, by Schlegel in this sonnet, of the
calmly Olympian manner in self-appreciation, may be represented as follows in prose:

In the manners of peoples, in many a foreign clime, and in their language,
long since by experience versed—that which antiquity, that which modern
times, have produced, uniting in the chain of one knowledge—whether
standing still, moving, walking, lying in bed, even on a journey as if under
the roof of home, forever poetizing, of all things that are, and that were—
conqueror, exemplar, master in the sonnet. The first to dare on German
soil wrestle with Shakespeare's shade and with Dante, at once the creator
and the mold of law: how the mouth of the future will name him is
unknown, but this generation recognized him by the name of AUGUST
WILHELM SCHLEGEL.

The self-complacent author of the foregoing sonnet probably saw no reason why he should not do ample justice to a great name in letters simply because that great name happened to be his own.

This man was an erudite Orientalist, when Orientalism was a comparatively new department of learning among Europeans. Critic, too, as well as philologist, was August Wilhelm Schlegel; after Lessing, perhaps among Germans none wiser, none more accomplished, than he. Such, at least, was for some time at first the estimation in which he was held. But Schlegel's credit as critic has since suffered loss. A single brief critical expression of his, relating to Shakespeare (foremost with Schlegel of poets, and mighty model of romanticists), must suffice to indicate his quality as critic. The critic here appears engaged in setting forth the contrast between the distinctively antique and the distinctively modern in literature and in art. That contrast he makes substantially the same as the contrast between the classic and the romantic. He says :

The Parthenon is not more different from Westminster Abbey or from the Church of St. Stephen at Vienna than the structure of a tragedy of Sophocles from a drama of Shakespeare. The comparison between these wonderful productions of poetry and architecture might be carried still further. But does our admiration of the one compel us to depreciate the other? . . . We will quarrel with no one for his predilection, either for the Grecian or the Gothic; the world is wide, and affords room for a great diversity of objects.

We ought perhaps to apprise our readers that they would by no means find Schlegel as intelligible throughout as he appears in the brief citations from him here presented.

Friedrich Karl Wilhelm von Schlegel (1772–1829), the brother, five years younger, was, beyond even August Wilhelm, a determined and vigorous fighting romanticist. Friedrich felt a vocation to begin a new era in literature. Wieland was, for him, no poet ; Schiller, none. Goethe, the two Schlegels praised. He indeed was a god to them. This particular idolatry was probably in part a deep trick with the two Schlegels ; a trick, the conception of which is credited to the cunning of Friedrich. The plot was to separate Goethe and Schiller, attach Goethe, nominally, at least, to the romantic school, and so secure at the same time the triumph of romanticism and the downfall of Schiller. But Schiller was an unsurpassed diplomatist, and he easily succeeded in holding Goethe fast to himself; while, as for Goethe, this supremely fortunate man had nothing to do but sit still and tranquilly let the wind from either quarter fill his sails.

A certain brilliant haze of indistinctness envelops Friedrich Schlegel's writing. He seems to promise much to his reader ; but his reader vexes himself vainly to find it, and ends by bringing little away. The following passage, in which the writer glorifies his beloved middle ages, is a good and a sufficient specimen of his quality. Our critic has just previously been setting forth the claims of Ossian's poetry— a romantic product which he was unwilling to surrender as a spurious antique forged by Macpherson; and he mentions, in connection, the Icelandic Edda, the cycles of Norman song (*chansons de geste*), the works of Firdusi, the Persian poet, the Spanish epic of the *Cid,* and the German *Nibelungen Lied ;* he then says (our translations from the Schlegels' prose, Dr. Hedge's later book supplies us) :

> All these works appeared in the very heart of that long period of time usually designated the night of the Middle Ages—a term, perhaps, well fitted to express the isolated existence of nations and individuals, and the interruption of that universal active intercourse which prevailed in the later period of the Roman dominion. . . . In this view, and because the business and occupations of the time were not then prosecuted with the skill and dexterity of modern ages, that remarkable period in the civilization of mankind may, indeed, be termed a night. But how starlit, how radiant was that night! Now, on the contrary, we are wrapt in the gloom and confusion of a lingering twilight. The stars which shone upon that night are dim, many of them sunk even below the horizon, and yet no day has risen upon us. More than once, indeed, we have been summoned to hail the dawn of a new sun which was to bring universal knowledge, happiness, prosperity. But the results have by no means justified the rash anticipation ; and if some promise seems still to herald

the approach of a new day, it is but the chill breath of the morning air which ever precedes the breaking light.

The Oriental studies of the elder brother were shared, were perhaps pushed farther, by the younger. Friedrich Schlegel may be considered the original source of that western interest in Hindu philosophy and Hindu literature, of which we have seen so remarkable a growth and development in our own day. The joint services of the two brothers to the science of comparative philology were great. The elder Schlegel, who survived the younger, survived also his own commanding authority in literature. His relation as traveling tutor in the German language and literature to Madame de Staël could not but have considerable influence in carrying over the romantic literary movement from Germany to France.

Of the simply and strictly popular tale—the popular tale, that is, unmodified by the personal taste or whim or fancy of the writer—the best, as well as for us the most practicable, representative specimen is undoubtedly to be found in the collection by the brothers Grimm. These authors, if they are to be ranked as romanticists at all, are the classicists among them. That is, they seem less perhaps than any other of those who romanced in this vein, to have humored themselves, and more to have obeyed that rule of " Not too much " which is at once the awe of the classicist, and of the romanticist the scorn.

The brothers Grimm were not the inventors in Germany of the species of literature in which they so excelled. The lead was given by one Musæus, a writer of a time somewhat earlier than that of Herder. Musæus, though a meritorious writer, is not a writer of the first class in importance. Carlyle, however, in his *Specimens of German Romance*, translated several of Musæus's stories.

The brothers Grimm (Jacob Ludwig Karl, 1785–1863 ; Wilhelm Karl, 1786–1859) were seriously learned scholars as well as popular writers. Their stories, from which alone we here draw, may be regarded as mere leisure-hour recreations on their part, interposed in the midst of the most arduous philological labors. Their monumental undertaking—achievement it can hardly be called, since they did not themselves bring it to completion—is a dictionary, encyclopædic for comprehensiveness, of the German language.

There is a peculiar household cosiness about the conception and the style of the stories of these brothers, well adapted to make them, as they are, popular favorites. They are stories pure and simple. No attempt was made by the authors to moralize or sentimentalize their narratives. The personal equation in them is nothing. It is as if there were no author. The stories seem to tell themselves. Of course this is art, and, in its humble kind, it is art of high degree. The English or American taste does not so naturally as does the German take to narratives of the sort about to be exemplified. Still the stories of the brothers Grimm have had no small currency in English translation.

We shall expect our readers to throw off their dignity and heartily laugh at the whimsical grotesqueness of the following story, which must stand single, and retrenched of its beginning at that, in example of what the brothers Grimm offer their readers in this line of production. The story is entitled, *The Musicians of Bremen.*

The chief personages of the story are four—an ass, a dog, a cat, and a cock—who agree to go to Bremen, and there set up as musicians together. On their way to the city they are overtaken by night in a forest. Prospecting for accommodations, they find a house occupied by robbers. Through a lighted window was to be seen a table temptingly set out with food. The "musicians" put their heads together to contrive a plan for dispossessing the robbers. They at length hit upon an idea. Now the brothers Grimm:

The ass had to place his forefeet upon the window ledge, the hound got on his back, the cat climbed up upon the dog, and lastly, the cock flew up and perched upon the head of the cat. When this was accomplished, at a given signal they commenced together to perform their music: the ass brayed, the dog barked, the cat mewed, and the cock crew! and they made such a tremendous noise, and so loud, that the panes of the window were shivered! Terrified at these unearthly sounds, the robbers got up with great precipitation, thinking nothing less than that some spirits had come, and fled off into the forest. The four companions immediately sat down at the table and quickly ate up all that was left, as if they had been fasting for six weeks.

As soon as the four players had finished they extinguished the light, and each sought for himself a sleeping-place, according to his nature and custom. The ass laid himself down upon the straw, the hound behind the door, the cat upon the hearth near the warm ashes, and the cock flew up upon a beam which ran across the room. Weary with their long walk, they soon went to sleep.

At midnight the robbers perceived, from their retreat, that no light was burning in their house, and all appeared quiet; so the captain said, "We need not to have been frightened into fits;" and calling one of the band, he sent him forward to reconnoitre. The messenger, finding all still, went into the kitchen to strike a light, and, taking the glistening fiery eyes of the cat for live coals, he held a lucifer match to them, expecting it to take fire. But the cat, not understanding the joke, flew in his face, spitting and scratching, which dreadfully frightened him, so that he made for the back door; but the dog, who lay there, sprung up and bit his leg; and as soon as he limped upon the straw, whereupon lay the ass, it gave him a powerful kick with its hind foot. This was not all, for the cock, awakening at the noise, stretched himself, and cried from the beam, "Cock-a-doodle-doo, cock-a-doodle-doo!"

Then the robber ran back as well as he could to his captain, and said, "Ah, my master, there dwells a horrible witch in the house, who spat on me and scratched my face with her long nails; and then before the door stands a man with a knife, who chopped at my leg; and in the yard there lies a black monster, who beat me with a great wooden club; and, besides all, upon the roof sits a judge, who called out, 'Bring the knave up, do,' so I ran away as fast as I could."

After this the robbers dared not again go near their house; but every thing prospered so well with the four town-musicians of Bremen that they did not forsake their situation! And there they are to this day for any thing I know!

The interest of the Grimms' stories is undoubtedly, to the average sense of us English-speakers, often very pale. Thoroughly to enjoy your true German household or popular tale needs the spacious leisure of childhood, with childhood's vacant mind ready indifferently for any thing that offers;

and then, besides, not least, that happy unwondering credulity which we all of us leave irrecoverably behind us when we cease to be children.

ANOTHER species of composition, to be distinguished from the household story proper, is that romantic tale in which the individual imagination or reflection of the writer supplies an important element—additional to whatever basis may have existed ready to his hand from some current popular myth. Besides Tieck already spoken of, we need mention no more than three authors in this kind. Of these the first in order of time is Hoffman (Ernst Theodor Wilhelm Amadeus, 1776–1822).

Of the life of this man we need not stay to tell much ; but the circumstances and the manner of his death must be told; they were extraordinary — perhaps, taken together, quite without a parallel. He died slowly of a paralysis which, beginning at his feet, crept stealthily up by inches to his vital organs. His brain and his will, rebelling to the last, defied disease and death. He died, indeed, despite his defiance ; but who ever more defiantly died? To his physician, standing baffled by his bedside, Hoffman said, "I am almost through now, am I not?" The sufferer had noted, but had not recognized, a mortal symptom, the ceasing of pain. "Yes, almost through," said the physician, in a sense his patient did not understand. "I will go on to-night with my writing," Hoffman said next day. He had been engaged upon a romance, destined never to be finished. The dying man desired his wife to read to him what he had dictated last. With difficulty she dissuaded him. At his request he was then turned, his face to the wall, when he immediately expired. What weirdest fiction, forged by Hoffman's fancy, could equal the power of a reality like that?

From Hoffman's romance, *The Golden Pot,* divided into "vigils" (taking the place of chapters), we sever and condense, using Carlyle's translation, a "vigil," almost at random. The wayward fantastic play of fancy and the vivid pictorial power characteristic of this writer, together with also that flavor of humor which it was his way to dash his fictions withal, will be found here sufficiently exemplified. If you should read the romance throughout you would simply get more of the same sort of thing. The student Anselmus, of Dresden, is the hero, or, if the reader prefer, the victim, of the story. This young man has had the bad luck, on a walk he was taking, to run into the basket of a cake-and-apple woman, exciting her enmity—a formidable enmity, for she is a witch. By some hocus-pocus, easy to Hoffman, the student Anselmus has been got snugly packed away alive in a glass bottle. Now Hoffman :

> Justly may I doubt whether thou, favorable reader, wert ever sealed up in a glass bottle. . . . Thou art drowned in dazzling splendor ; all objects about thee appear illuminated and begirt with beaming rainbow hues ; all quivers and wavers, and clangs and drones in the sheen; thou art swimming, motionless and powerless, as in a firmly congealed ether, which so presses thee together that the spirit in vain gives orders to the dead and stiffened body. Weightier and weightier the mountain burden lies on thee ; more and more does every breath exhaust the little handful of air that still played up and down in the narrow space ; thy pulse throbs madly ; and, cut through with horrid anguish, every nerve is quivering and bleeding in this deadly agony. Have pity, favorable reader, on the student Anselmus ! . . . He could move no limbs, but his thoughts struck against the glass, stupefying him with discordant clang. . . . Then he exclaimed, in his despair: " O Serpentina ! Serpentina ! save me from this misery of hell ! " And it was as if faint sighs breathed around him, which spread like green transparent elder-leaves over the glass. The clanging ceased, the dazzling, perplexing glitter was gone, and he breathed more freely.

We need to explain that " Serpentina " is the lovely, mysterious daughter of that learned and potent master for whom our student Anselmus is working as copyist.

The bottled student had, too, a bodiless vocal message from Serpentina, which kept him in heart through much distress. But soon an old broken-nosed coffee-pot near underwent a Hoffmanian transformation, and became the hated witch before his very eyes. An altercation ensued, and then a hideous struggle, between the witch and "the Archivarius," Serpentina's father, and employer to the student Anselmus,

The witch had designs against Serpentina which the father appeared in the nick of time to foil. The "golden pot," filled with a magic earth, was the witch's resource of evil power. She had a black cat to help her. A parrot, on the other hand, was pitted against the cat. Now let Hoffman describe the struggle and the event. The witch first speaks, egging on the cat against Serpentina:

"To her, my lad!" creaked the crone; then the black cat darted through the air, and soused over the Archivarius's head toward the door; but the gray parrot fluttered out against him, caught him with his crooked bill by the nape, till red, fiery blood burst down over his neck, and Serpentina's voice cried, "Saved! saved!" Then the crone, foaming with rage and desperation, darted out upon the Archivarius; she threw the golden pot behind her, and, holding up the long talons of skinny fists, was for clutching the Archivarius by the throat; but he instantly doffed his nightgown and hurled it against her. Then, hissing and spluttering and bursting, shot blue flames from the parchment leaves, and the crone rolled round in howling agony, and strove to get fresh earth from the pot, fresh parchment leaves from the books, that she might stifle the blazing flames; and whenever any earth or leaves came down on her the flames went out. But now, from the interior of the Archivarius, issued fiery, crackling beams, and darted on the crone.

"Hey, hey! To it again! Salamander! Victory!" clanged the Archivarius's voice through the chamber; and a hundred bolts whirled forth in fiery circles round the shrieking crone. Whizzing and buzzing flew cat and parrot in their furious battle.

The end of this strange strife was foregone. The wicked witch was vanquished, and both Anselmus and Serpentina were saved. A potent voice said aloud to the imprisoned student, "Be free and happy." The sequel is thus related by Hoffman:

A bright flash quivered through the spirit of Anselmus; the royal triphony of the crystal bells sounded stronger and louder than he had ever heard it; his nerves and fibres thrilled; but swelling higher and higher, the melodious tones rang through the room; the glass which inclosed Anselmus broke, and he rushed into the arms of his dear and gentle Serpentina.

Some likeness of character and of life seems to emphasize the literary likeness in Hoffman to our American Poe,

The two are occasionally spoken of together as kindred in genius.

CHAMISSO is an instance of that rare phenomenon, a man achieving in a language to which he was not born literary success signal enough to rank him among the classics of his adopted tongue. This writer was a pleasing poet, but his popular literary fame rests chiefly on a single romance of his, *The Wonderful History of Peter Schlemihl*. Chamisso's work in botany, it should be said in passing, fairly entitles him to a distinguished place among men of science.

Adalbert von Chamisso (1781–1838) was born a Frenchman in noble rank. Till nine years of age he lived in France, and, of course, spoke French. He was twenty years old before he could be said to have taken full possession of his adopted vernacular. His masterpiece, *Peter Schlemihl*, has a world-wide celebrity. It is an original in literature. Hoffman repeated the idea of it in a characteristically different treatment of his own, entitled, *The Lost Looking-glass Image*. The idea of Peter Schlemihl is that of a man who, for a valuable consideration—nothing less, in short, than the bottomless purse of Fortunatus—has parted with the seemingly needless appendage of his own shadow. The bargain proves a sinister one, and the business of the story is to tell how. Of course, it was none but the devil himself that could be the customer to purchase, at such a price, an article like a human shadow. There is little introduction of supernaturalism in the story beyond what is necessarily involved in this its very idea. The interest, indeed, and the power of the production lie precisely in the verisimilar, realistic way in which the natural consequences of a supernatural transaction are worked out and presented.

The story divides itself into two parts—not named and apparently not recognized by the author himself as constituting two parts, but in fact quite distinctly such. In the first part the writer really exhausted the development of his original idea. In the second part, Chamisso accordingly

19

takes up a new and different piece of supernaturalism. He has his hero buy himself a pair of boots—which, for no cause whatever that appears, turn out to be seven-leaguers. With these, shadowless still, and therefore still cut off from his fellow-men, but without the purse, renounced, of Fortunatus, the solitary man becomes a wanderer from continent to continent, devoted to preparing a great and final work on geography in the largest sense of that term. There might almost seem to be here a tacit anonymous allusion to Chamisso's contemporary, Humboldt, that famous geographical philosopher who made the circuit of the globe, traveling as with seven-league boots, to write his stupendous work, *Cosmos,* so-called. But it is rather Chamisso himself that supplied to Chamisso the idea of such a world-wandering man. He circumnavigated the earth on his botanical quests.

Peter Schlemihl is introduced—or rather is made to introduce himself, for the story is autobiographical in form—as a poor fellow out of money, calling, a stranger, on a rich man to sue for his patronage. This rich man he finds out walking with a company, among whom is one person that on call produces from his pocket successively at intervals a pocket-book with plaster in it for a wound from a thorn, at the moment received by a lady on her hand, a telescope, a large Turkey carpet, a tent (canvas, poles, cordage, iron-work, and all), and, finally, three horses—"I tell thee three beautiful great black horses, with saddle and caparison," Peter Schlemihl says, with firmness, to overawe incredulity, writing to his friend Chamisso. This necromantic personage, making an approach to Peter, obsequiously begs to buy that gentleman's shadow. Now let Chamisso make Peter Schlemihl take up the word. Peter first speaks, replying to the devil:

"But, sir, pardon your most humble servant, I do not understand your meaning. How, indeed, could my shadow—" He interrupted me—- . . .

"I give you the choice of all the treasures which I carry in my pocket— . . . Fortunatus's wishing-cap, newly and stoutly repaired, and a lucky-bag, such as he had—"

"The luck-purse of Fortunatus!" I exclaimed, interrupting him; and great as my anxiety was, with that one word he had taken my whole mind captive. A dizziness seized me, and double ducats seemed to glitter before my eyes.

"Honored sir, will you do me the favor to view, and to make trial of this purse?" . . . I plunged my hand into it, and drew out ten gold pieces, and again ten, and again ten, and again ten. . . . "Agreed! . . . For the purse you have my shadow!"

He . . . kneeled instantly down before me, and I beheld him, with an admirable dexterity, gently loosen my shadow from top to toe from the grass, lift it up, roll it together, fold it, and, finally, pocket it.

The consequences follow promptly. Chamisso:

. . . I hastened to quit the place where I had nothing more to expect. In the first place I filled my pockets with gold; then I secured the strings of the purse fast round my neck, and concealed the purse itself in my bosom. I passed unobserved out of the park, reached the highway, and took the road to the city. As, sunk in thought, I approached the gate I heard a cry behind me:

"Young gentleman! eh! young gentleman! hear you!"

I looked round; an old woman called after me:

"Do take care, sir; you have lost your shadow!"

"Thank you, good mother!" I threw her a gold piece for her well-meant intelligence, and stopped under the trees.

At the city gate I was compelled to hear again from the sentinel, "Where has the gentleman left his shadow?" And immediately again from some woman, "Jesus Maria; the poor fellow has no shadow!" That began to irritate me, and I became especially careful not to walk in the sun. This could not, however, be accomplished everywhere—for instance, over the broad street which I next must approach, actually, as mischief would have it, at the very moment that the boys came out of school. A cursed, hunch-backed rogue—I see him yet—spied out instantly that I had no shadow. He proclaimed the fact with a loud outcry to the whole assembled literary street youth of the suburb, who began forthwith to criticise me, and to pelt me with mud. "Decent people are accustomed to take their shadow with them, when they go into the sunshine." To defend myself from them I threw whole handfuls of gold amongst them and sprang into a hackney-coach, which some compassionate soul procured for me.

As soon as I found myself alone in the rolling carriage I began to weep bitterly. The presentiment must already have arisen in me, that far as gold on earth transcends in estimation merit and virtue, so much higher than gold itself is the shadow valued; and as I had earlier sacrificed wealth to conscience, I had now thrown away the shadow for more gold. What in the world could and would become of me? I ordered the coachman to drive to the most fashionable hotel. The house faced the north, and I had not the sun to fear. I dismissed the driver with gold; caused the best front rooms to be assigned me, and shut myself up in them as quickly as I could!

What thinkest thou, I now began? O, my dear Chamisso, to confess it even to thee makes me blush. I drew the unlucky purse from my bosom, and with a kind of desperation which, like a rushing conflagration, grew in me with self-increasing growth, I extracted gold, and gold, and gold, and ever more gold, and strewed it on the floor, and strode amongst it, and made it ring again, and, feeding my poor heart on the splendor and the sound, flung continually more metal to metal, till in my weariness I sank down on the rich heap, and, rioting thereon, rolled and reveled amongst it. So passed the day, the evening. I opened not my door; night and day found me lying on my gold, and then sleep overcame me.

Chamisso's idea, though novel, certainly, and interesting, was not a very fruitful one. There was really little or nothing for the author to do with it but go on telling with variations the same thing over and over, namely, how a man observed not to cast a natural shadow became at once an object of the most embarrassing suspicion among his fellows, wherever he might go. Skillful, however, the conduct of the story is throughout, and the reader's interest is kept alive. Openly humorous conception appears in one passage, that in which the distracted shadowless man, attended by an attached faithful servant, approaches a retired residence previously secured by the latter for his master's retreat. The good people of the vicinage thought they recognized in Peter a most illustrious person—no other, in short, than the King of Prussia in disguise. The shadowless man has for once in the world a royal welcome.

With the experiences of Peter after buying his seven-league boots, we need not concern ourselves. The really distinctive idea in the story has already been, perhaps, sufficiently exemplfied.

There is no little resemblance in kind between *Peter Schlemihl*, and such realistic, impossible fiction as that of which Mr. Edward Everett Hale has shown himself a consummate master, in, for instance, his tales of *My Double and How He Undid Me,* and *Philip Nolan, or the Man without a Country.*

A TITLE as familiar perhaps to English-speakers as that of any other book in German literature—excepting only a few titles associated with Goethe or with Schiller as author, is *Undine.* This is the name of the lovely heroine in the romantic masterpiece of the romanticist Fouqué.

Friedrich Heinrich Karl, Baron de la Motte Fouqué (1777–1843) was, as his name indicates, of French extraction. He was not, however, himself, like Chamisso, an immigrant from France. He descended from a Huguenot family, one of those families whom Louis XIV., blind with bigotry, impoverished his realm by driving into exile through his revocation of the Edict of Nantes. Fouqué became a productive and a successful author, one to be reckoned strictly in the school of the Romanticists. His work has shared the fortune of his school, and become for the most part a fashion of the past. He rose to popularity under the patronage of the Schlegels, and he fell with the fall of his patrons. His *Undine,* however, still stands, floats, rather, high in heaven—for its quality is ethereal—and securely bears up its author's name. The fairest "little classic" in all German literature, to us English and American, is the *Undine* of Fouqué.

The idea of *Undine* is that of a water-spirit in human form issuing from her proper haunt in the water-world, to move among men and to become at length, through union to the human race in marriage, endowed with a soul. The romance is a pure and charming creation of fancy—but it is emphatically of fancy all compact. Not every one will thoroughly enjoy it, it is so destitute of ground in truth or likelihood. You have, in reading it, to give yourself up to the sway of sheer caprice. But a sweet and gracious caprice is *Undine,* and, to spirits ready for the lesson, not without hint of moral purifying sense in its fable. The soul received by Undine at marriage with one of the sons of men is a sinless soul, no taint in it derived from Adam's lapse, and apparently no taint possible from lapses of its own. This impeccable quality is not insisted upon by the author; nay, it is not even expressly attributed by him. But in effect it is, and the sequel is exquisite in a unique and painless pathos reached at last.

A fisherman and his wife, living lonely by the shore, with a haunted forest lying between them and the great world, lose an infant daughter through death (or supposed death) by drowning—who is afterward replaced by a foundling child mysteriously brought to their door. This is Undine, a bright, gay, sparkling creature, innocently full of pranks played especially in connection with water. A knight, having wandered with much adventure through the forest to the cot of the fisherman, becomes enamored of Undine and marries her. The morning after, she rises a different being. The frolic, incalculable maid has become a sweetly serious woman, dutiful wife and daughter. But let Fouqué himself describe her, first as she had been, and then as she became. The priest has joined the pair in wedlock, and the bride, as yet not transformed, behaves before him according to her first thoughtless nature. The holy man reproves her:

"My dear young lady, . . . it is your duty to keep watch over your soul." . . .

"Soul!" cried Undine, laughing; . . . "but if one has no soul at all, pray how is one to keep watch over it? And that is my case."

The priest was deeply hurt, and turned away his face in mingled sorrow and anger. . . .

At length . . . she looked at the priest earnestly and said, "There must be much to love in a soul, but much that is awful too. For God's sake, holy father, tell me, were it not better to be still without one? . . . Heavy must be the burden of a soul. . . . Heavy indeed! for the mere approach of mine overshadows me with anxious melancholy. And, ah! how light-hearted, how joyous I used to be!"

The change apparent next morning is thus described. The fisherman and his wife, with the priest and the husband, are waiting for Undine to enter. At last she appears. Now Fouqué:

They could not help rising to meet her, and stood still, astonished; the young creature was the same, yet so different. The priest was the first to address her, with an air of paternal kindness, and, when he raised his hands in benediction, the fair woman sank on her knees, trembling with pious awe. In a few meek and humble words she begged him to forgive the folly of the day before, and besought him, with great emotion, to pray for the salvation of her soul. Then rising, she kissed her foster parents, and, thanking them for all their kindness, she said: "O, now I feel from the bottom of my heart how much you have done for me; how deeply grateful I ought to be, dear, dear people!" She seemed as if she could not caress them enough; but soon, observing the dame glance toward the breakfast, she went toward the hearth, busied herself arranging and preparing the meal, and would not suffer the good woman to take the least trouble herself.

So she went on all day; at once a young matron and a bashful, tender, delicate bride. The three who knew her best were every moment expecting this mood to change and give place to one of her crazy fits, but they watched her in vain. There was still the same angelic mildness and sweetness.

Undine explains to her husband about the wonder of herself and of her kind, as follows:

"You must know, my own love, that in each element exists a race of beings whose form scarcely differs from yours, but who very seldom appear to mortal sight. In the flames the wondrous salamanders glitter and disport themselves; in the depths of earth dwell the dry, spiteful race of gnomes; the forests are peopled by wood-nymphs, who are also spirits of air; and the seas, the rivers, and brooks contain the numberless tribes of water-sprites. Their echoing halls of crystal, where the light of heaven pours in, with its sun and stars, are glorious to dwell in; the gardens contain beautiful coral plants, with blue and red fruits; they wander over bright sea-sands and gay-colored shells, among the hidden treasures of the old world, too precious to be bestowed on these latter days, and long since covered by the silver mantle of the deep: many a noble monument still gleams there below, bedewed by the tears of Ocean, who garlands it with flowery sea-weeds and wreaths of shells. Those that dwell there below are noble and lovely to behold, far more so than mankind. Many a fisherman has had a passing glimpse of some fair water-nymph rising out of the sea with her song; he would then spread the report of her apparition, and these wonderful beings came to be called *Undines;* and you now see before you, my love, an Undine."

And further, Undine:

> "We have no souls; the elements move us, obey us while we live, close over us when we die; and we light spirits live as free from care as the nightingale, the gold-fish, and all such bright children of nature. But no creatures rest content in their appointed place. My father, who is a mighty prince in the Mediterranean Sea, determined that his only child should be endowed with a soul, even at the cost of much suffering, which is ever the lot of souls. But a soul can be infused into one of our race only by being united in the closest bands of love to one of yours. And now I have obtained a soul; to thee I owe it, O best beloved! and for that gift I shall ever bless thee, unless thou dost devote my whole futurity to misery."

After such a frank disclosure of the truth concerning herself and her relations to a world not human, she offers to leave her husband, if he will have her, though her own cost in doing so will be unimaginably great. Say but the word, she exclaims, and—now Undine once more:

> "I will plunge into this brook; it is my uncle, who leads a wonderful, sequestered life in this forest, away from all his friends. But he is powerful, and allied to many great rivers; and as he brought me here to the fisherman a gay and laughing child, so he is ready to take me back to my parents, a loving, suffering, forsaken woman."

This same uncle of Undine's is a character, and he plays a great part in the sequel of the story. He takes upon himself to linger near Undine in her wedded estate, with a view to seeing that she suffers no wrong. Wrong, however, she suffers, for her husband's heart is won away from his beautiful wife by a woman who had loved him before he married Undine. Bertalda is the woman's name. Bertalda is in fact —this the uncle reveals to Undine—the fisherman's own daughter, rescued by the water-spirits from drowning, and fallen into the hands of a noble family who adopt her. Undine brings about the meeting of Bertalda with her true parents; but, to her deep chagrin, Bertalda scorns and spurns them. The result is that, cast off by her adoptive parents, and not desired by her true, Bertalda is welcomed by Undine to a home with herself. The uncle makes ominous appearances from time to time in defense of his niece, until she herself, in self-renouncing love, shuts him away from access to the castle by having a vast stone laid over the fountain in the court by which he used to come. Nothing, however, is strong enough to overcome fate. Fate ruled that Undine and her knight untrue should be parted. She has conjured him never to indulge his anger at his wife—anger was indeed a passion which even in that display, so she effaced herself to acknowledge, ennobled his beauty—but never to indulge it when they were on the water; for there they were under the power of her kindred. This very thing he of course at last does. It occurs when the three, husband, wife, and Bertalda, are sailing together down the Danube to visit Vienna. What impended for Undine fell. She was drawn back to her home among her kindred.

Her husband and Bertalda at length, against solemn forewarnings, marry. Upon Undine then devolves a dreadful duty which she cannot evade. She must, returning to the castle, execute doom upon her faithless lord. Her way to do this was made easy by Bertalda, unawares. This lady, in the pride of her joy at power acquired in the castle, had had that stone removed which, for self-sacrificing love of her, the gentle Undine had placed over the fountain in the courtyard. The workmen were astonished at the ease with which the great weight suffered itself to be lifted. Now our last from "Undine:"

More and more did the stone heave, till, without any impulse from the men, it rolled heavily along the pavement with a hollow sound. But, from the mouth of the spring arose, slowly and solemnly, what looked like a column of water. At first they thought so, but presently saw that it was no waterspout, but the figure of a pale woman, veiled in white. She was weeping abundantly, wringing her hands and clasping them over her head, while she proceeded with slow and measured step toward the castle. The crowd of servants fell back from the spot; while, pale and aghast, the bride and her women looked on from the window.

The knight had now dismissed his train; half undressed, and in a dejected mood, he was standing near a large mirror, by the light of a dim taper. He heard the door tapped by a soft, soft touch. It was thus Undine had been wont to knock when she meant to steal upon him playfully.

"It is all fancy!" thought he. "The bridal bed awaits me."

"Yes, but it is a cold one," said a weeping voice from without; and the mirror then showed him the door opening slowly, and the white form coming in, and closing the door gently behind her.

. . . .

Trembling at once with love and awe, the knight approached her; she received him with a tender embrace; but instead of relaxing her hold, she pressed him more closely to her heart, and wept as if her soul would pour itself out. Drowned in her tears and his own, Huldbrand felt his heart sink within him, and at last he fell lifeless from the fond arms of Undine upon his pillow.

"I have wept him to death!" said she to the pages, whom she passed in the antechamber; and she glided slowly through the crowd, and went back to the fountain.

There is, in the lightness, the brightness, the delicacy, the grace, the Attic measure, of this charming romance of Fouqué's, something that suggests the French strain in the author's blood. But it has in it the German quality too of mystic marvel. Of course the starting-point of a conception seeming, at first blush, to be so utterly new and strange, so out of imaginative reach, as that of the *Undine,* might have been supplied to Fouqué by the mythology of the ancient pagan world which peopled spring and stream and sea with various "gay creatures of the element." Fouqué had only to give to this fancy of the elder time a turn, and, as it were, a meaning, of his own—"the fair humanities of old religion" receiving thus through him an unexpected interpretation to the modern imaginative sense. In truth, however, there was a whole system of imaginary animated nature ready made to Fouqué's hand in the fairy lore of his adopted fatherland.

Coleridge testified that the *Undine* of Fouqué furnished to him what was rare, almost unique, in his experience of literature—an absolutely new and original idea.

THE Romanticists of Germany had, of course, their poets. Among these there is one entitled, perhaps, to the dignity of being called by eminence their poet. This is Uhland. Nearly all the romanticist brethren poetized ; but Uhland, by merit or by fortune, or, it may be, rather by that happy choice of his genius which made him, in a time of national exigency, a voice in verse of the national spirit, became the most popular and most powerful German poet, not only of his own school, but of his generation. Of the romantic school in literature we thus assume that Uhland must be reckoned. It is true, however, that a saving influence from without, exerted probably by Goethe—to which a felicity of his own temperament responded—kept Uhland from going extravagant lengths in the romantic direction.

Johann Ludwig Uhland (1787–1862), born at Tübingen, lived a life in which there was little outward event of general interest to commemorate. An ardent patriot, he chanted with youthful enthusiasm the high strains of freedom for his country. But the soul of the poet, as poet, was after all more in meditative and imaginative themes. He was a deep student in the manuscript lore of the middle ages, and he drew thence matter and inspiration for poetry. But he was not a mere mystic dreamer. The cloudy vagueness that the German romanticists before him had loved, Uhland dispelled from his verse with the bright shining of a cheerful intellect in him, which lived in the present though it visited the past. The dimness of twilight became in him the clearness of day ; and with the clearness of day Romanticism blinked like an owl, and disappeared. Uhland may be considered the last of the German romanticists.

The period of Uhland's chief poetic productiveness was comparatively short. Like Béranger in France, Uhland in Germany sang his songs early, as birds sing their matins, and ceased. The singer ceased ; but Uhland's songs, caught up in the mouths of the people, filled Europe about the silent singer, still living, with the echoes of his melody.

We must, of course, in showing Uhland, begin with that little poem of his, doubtless to English and American fame the dearest of all his songs, *The Passage.* The *Edinburgh*

Review, of old date, thus translates it; the translation is every thing that could be desired for congenial pensive spirit and delicate melody of rhythm:

> Many a year is in its grave
> Since I crossed this restless wave;
> And the evening, fair as ever,
> Shines on ruin, rock, and river.
>
> Then in this same boat beside
> Sat two comrades old and tried—
> One with all a father's truth,
> One with all the fire of youth.
>
> One on earth in silence wrought,
> And his grave in silence sought;
> But the younger, brighter form
> Passed in battle and in storm.
>
> So, whene'er I turn my eye
> Back upon the days gone by,
> Saddening thoughts of friends come o'er me,
> Friends that closed their course before me.
>
> But what binds us, friend to friend,
> But that soul with soul can blend?
> Soul-like were those days of yore;
> Let us walk in soul once more.
>
> Take, O boatman, thrice thy fee—
> Take, I give it willingly;
> For, invisible to thee,
> Spirits twain have crossed with me.

We know of nothing to surpass the foregoing in sweetness of sentiment and perfect fit felicity of form. What a happy bit of drama the closing stanza! How luckily it finishes the poem, with that touchingly simple suggestion of softened feeling, from remembrance, converted into generosity! It would be pathetically interesting to know, if one could know, that the two—" one with all a father's truth " and " one with all the fire of youth "—were to be identified as the elder and the younger Körner. The allusion seems to fit, for Körner, the father, did his work quietly in civic action, and Theodor Körner, as has been noted, having but just written his famous *Sword-Song*, died on the field of battle fighting for the freedom of Germany.

Our next specimen from Uhland is a translation by Longfellow. It is entitled *The Castle by the Sea:*

" Hast thou seen that lordly castle,
   That castle by the sea?
Golden and red above it,
   The clouds float gorgeously.

"And fain it would stoop downward,
   To the mirrored wave below;
And fain it would soar upward,
   In the evening's crimson glow."

" Well have I seen that castle,
   That castle by the sea,
And the moon above it standing,
   And the mist rise solemnly."

" The winds and the waves of the ocean,
   Had they a merry chime?
Didst thou hear, from those lofty chambers,
   The harp and the minstrel's rhyme?"

" The winds and the waves of the ocean,
   They rested quietly;
But I heard on the gale a sound of wail,
   And tears came to mine eye."

"And sawest thou on the turrets
   The king and his royal bride,
And the wave of their crimson mantles,
   And the golden crown of pride?"

" Led they not forth, in rapture,
   A beauteous maiden there,
Resplendent as the morning sun,
   Beaming with golden hair?"

" Well saw I the ancient parents,
   Without the crown of pride;
They were moving slow, in weeds of woe;
   No maiden was by their side!"

Longfellow's is, on the whole, a successful version of Uhland's poem. It by no means, however, perfectly reproduces the effect of the original. The German stanzas are fully equipped with rhymes. The English translation, by omitting a rhyme for the first line of each stanza, loses not a little in melodious impression on the ear. One is surprised, too, that the translator should, in the second stanza, have said "mirrored" to express the "mirror-clear" of the original.

A poem of more energy, love no longer making gentle the poet, but indignation making him fierce, is *The Minstrel's Curse.* For our translation of this we go to *Blackwood's Magazine* of forty years ago. The poem is a ballad, not very long, but too long to be here given entire. The story of the "curse" we tell in plain prose of our own, to give the *Curse* itself in Uhland's ringing rhyme. An aged minstrel with a fair youth visits a kingly court to make music and song. The ruthless monarch, vexed at the purport and effect of their singing, strikes the youth dead, and the aged minstrel strikes back with his "curse of poesy" on the king:

"Woe! woe! proud towers—dire House of blood! thy guilty courts among
Ne'er may the chords of harmony be waked—the voice of song;
The tread of silent slaves alone shall echo 'mid the gloom;
Till ruin waits, and hovering fiends of vengeance shriek thy doom!

"Woe! woe! ye blooming gardens fair—decked in the pride of May,
Behold this flower untimely cropped—look—and no more be gay!
The sight should wither every leaf—make all your fountains dry,
And bid the bright enchantment round in wasteful horror lie!

"And thou, fell Tyrant, curst for aye, of all the tuneful train—
May blighted bays and bitter scorn mock thy inglorious reign!
Perish thy hated name with thee—from songs and annals fade
Thy race, thy power, thy very crimes—lost in oblivion's shade!"

The aged Bard has spoken, and Heaven has heard the prayer;
The haughty towers are crumbling low—no regal dome is there!
A single column soars on high, to tell of splendors past—
And, see! *'tis cracked, it nods the head*—this hour may be its last!

Where once the fairy garden smiled, a mournful desert lies—
No rills refresh the barren sand, no graceful stems arise—
From storied page and legend strain, this King has vanished long;
His race is dead—his power forgot—such is the might of Song!

The gentle genius of Uhland must not take his farewell of us in such a strain of prophetic doom denounced as the foregoing. Let our last specimen of him rather be that soft, sweet melody of his entitled *The Serenade.* A child, dying, speaks with the watching mother:

"What sounds so sweet awake me?
 What fills me with delight?
O, mother, look! who sings thus
 So sweetly through the night?"

"I hear not, child, I see not;
 O, sleep thou softly on!
Comes now to serenade thee,
 Thou poor, sick maiden, none!"

"It is not earthly music,
 That fills me with delight;
I hear the angels call me:
 O, mother, dear, good night!"

German Romanticism may be said to have come in, half-unconsciously, with Bürger, a poet. It was fit that with a poet, Uhland, it should vanish away.

XII.

HEINE.

1799–1856.

GENIUS, with wit amounting to genius, joined to unhappy fortune in life, makes of Heinrich Heine quite the most interesting and most striking literary figure that has risen among Germans since Goethe and Schiller. Among Germans, we say; but this phrase seems almost to class Heine amiss, for Heine was the least German of Germans. By quality of mind and quality of heart, by style of literary expression, and, finally, by long Parisian residence, he half failed of his proper native national character, and was less German than French.

And, indeed, German in blood Heine was not. His parentage on his father's side—on his mother's side, too, we believe, though this seems to be uncertain—was Jewish. At twenty-five years of age Heine himself became a nominal Lutheran; but it was strictly a nominal Lutheran that he became. "Paris is well worth a mass," said Henry of Navarre, as, for the sake of thus winning that city to be his capital, he lightly went over to the Catholic from the Protestant side. It was in a like spirit—so Heine himself expressly says, quoting the words of King Henry—that our German jester made the change from Judaism to Christianity; he might get on in the world better as a Lutheran than he could as a Jew. The simple truth is that, in religion as in every thing else, Heine, to the end of his days, yes, literally to his parting breath, was a mocker. "God will forgive me; that is his business," was one of his last gasps of speech.

Scarce in all literary history is there a picture more depressing than the picture of this man dying, years long, in agony, that endless death of his, in his little chamber in Paris. For Heine—perhaps in retributive result from a duel in which he was wounded, a duel occasioned by his own wanton indulgence in ribald reviling regardless of truth—became, in 1848, a helpless, bedridden man, almost paralytic and almost blind. In this miserable plight he lingered, suffering frequent paroxysms of exquisite pain, nearly eight years, during which he never went out of doors—until he died. So much is sad enough, but so much is not all; and what remains is sadder still. You have to imagine Heine's features fixed, all the while, in that set sardonic grin, grown the unalterable habit of his face; or, to use a truer figure, galvanically twitching without rest in a play of expression that changed, indeed, forever, but forever meant a jeer. Take, now, one of the characteristic grim fancies that, on his death-bed, this thinking skeleton pleased himself horribly with forging in verse, and pity, pity the half-crazed brain which apparently could not but entertain, as it were automatically, such hobgoblin conceits. The genius, the character, the misfortune, of Heine are all present haunting the German lines. Our translation, which we transfer from an old number of the *Athenæum* (London), is very good, but it inevitably allows the volatile spirit of the original in some part to escape:

> How wearily time crawls along—
> That hideous snail that hastens not—
> While I, without the power to move,
> Am ever fixed to one dull spot.
>
> Upon my dreary chamber-wall
> No gleam of sunshine can I trace;
> I know that only for the grave
> Shall I exchange this hopeless place.
>
> Perhaps already I am dead,
> And these perhaps are phantoms vain—
> These motley phantasies that pass
> At night through my disordered brain.
>
> Perhaps with ancient heathen shapes,
> Old faded gods, this brain is full;
> Who, for their most unholy rites,
> Have chosen a dead poet's skull;—
>
> And charming, frightful orgies hold—
> The madcap phantoms!—all the night,
> That in the morning this dead hand
> About their revelries may write.

Heine's birthday was the thirteenth of December, 1799; but he himself jocularly set it forward to January 1, 1800, in order, as he said, that he might be one of the first men of the century. (Curiously enough, Heine thus, instead of making himself one of the first men of an opening century, succeeded only in making himself a little more emphatically one of the last men of the century preceding. For, in point

20

of fact, the eighteenth century was of course not complete until its hundredth year was finished, and that hundredth year was the year 1800.)

That he was born in Düsseldorf, that he died in Paris, and that between his birth and his death his activity was that of a student and writer, sums up Heine's biography. He went to Paris to live, because Paris was the true home of his soul. He acquired in Paris the fame of being the wittiest Frenchman since Voltaire. But his wit made him almost friendless, for he exercised it both recklessly and maliciously. It is saying little to say that always he would rather lose a friend than a jest. Whole nations he made his butt. He jested constantly at Germans and at Germany; but Englishmen he especially scorned. He verily believed, he said, that God was any day better pleased with a cursing Frenchmen than with a praying Englishman.

Heine wrote in both prose and verse. The first prose production of his to make its author famous was his *Pictures of Travel*. This work is still popularly reckoned Heine's prose masterpiece. Its contents are highly miscellaneous. It is even mixed of prose and verse, for it contains a considerable number of Heine's best-known songs. The book, in fact, is a kind of scrap-book, into which the author emptied all the accumulated treasures of his genius and his wit, and, we must add, a full equivalent too of his ribaldry and his gall. It is very unequal in its different parts, as to interest and as to merit. We may, of course, conscientiously give our readers only of the best—provided we, at the same time, faithfully apprise them that they would find the book as a whole somewhat less entertaining than are the specimen pages shown them here.

One of the parts into which the *Pictures of Travel* is divided bears the title of *Book Le Grand*. "Le Grand" is the name of a Frenchman, one of Napoleon's veterans, to whom Heine in his boyhood appears to have become genuinely attached. Le Grand is a very important figure in the "book," which, in honor to his memory, is thus inscribed with his name. Let us begin at once with this book, opening it at the sixth chapter.

The author has previously mentioned his being born at Düsseldorf. "Yes, madam," he resumes and repeats — idiosyncratically thus addressing himself to an indefinite, mythical lady, who stands to him here in place of the conventional " dear reader " of authors in general—as he thus proceeds :

> Yes, madam, there was I born, and I am particular in calling attention to this fact, lest after my death seven cities . . . should contend for the honor of having witnessed my birth. Düsseldorf is a town on the Rhine, where about sixteen thousand mortals live, and where many hundred thousands are buried. . . . Little William lies there—and that is my fault. We were schoolmates in the Franciscan cloister, and were one day playing on that side of the building where the Düssel flows between stone walls, and I said, " William, do get the kitten out, which has just fallen in!" and he cheerfully climbed out on the board which stretched over the brook, and pulled the cat out of the water, but fell in himself, and when they took him out he was dripping and dead. The kitten lived to a good old age.
>
> The town of Düsseldorf is very beautiful, and if you think of it when in foreign lands, and happen at the same time to have been born there, strange feelings come over the soul. I was born there, and feel as if I must go directly home. And when I say home I mean the Volkerstrasse and the house where I was born. This house will be some day very remarkable, and I have sent word to the old lady who owns it that she must not for her life sell it. For the whole house she would now hardly get as much as the present which the green-veiled English ladies will give the servant girl when she shows them the room where I was born, and the hen-house wherein my father generally imprisoned me for stealing grapes, and also the brown door on which my mother taught me to write with chalk. Ah, madam, should I ever become a famous author, it has cost my poor mother trouble enough.

The passage which we are here transferring is as clear as any thing in Heine of what needs to be " edited " out of his text. But even here we have to be vigilant, and suppress occasionally. We take likewise the liberty to touch here and there the translation which we use—that of C. G. Leland, the chief introducer of Heine to the English-speaking audience now commanded by this writer, especially for America.

The vein of autobiographic allusion and disclosure, observable in what precedes, runs through the entire work. The element of personal " confession " qualifies every thing that is said. Sterne's *Sentimental Journey* is no doubt responsible for the cast of Heine's *Pictures of Travel.* There follows now an unlooked-for contrast. Against himself, with his humorous-earnest expectation of fame as yet unearned, he satirically offsets a certain obscure Prince Elector who is substantially honored with a bronze statue standing in the great square of Düsseldorf. Heine says :

> But my renown as yet slumbers in the marble quarries of Carrara ; the waste paper laurel with which they have bedecked my brow has not spread its perfume through the wide world, and the green-veiled English ladies, when they visit Düsseldorf, leave the celebrated house unvisited, and go directly to the Market Place, and there gaze on the colossal black equestrian statue which stands in the midst. This represents the Prince Elector, Jan Wilhelm. He wears black armor, and a long, hanging wig. When a boy, I was told that the artist who made this statue observed with terror while it was being cast that he had not metal enough to fill the mold, and then all the citizens of the town came running with all their silver spoons, and threw them in to make up the deficiency ; and I often stood for hours before the statue wondering how many spoons were concealed in it, and how many apple-tarts the silver would buy. Apple-tarts were then my passion—now it is love, truth, liberty and crab soup. . . . But I was speaking of the equestrian statue which has so many silver spoons in it, and no soup, and which represents the Prince Elector, Jan Wilhelm.
>
> He was a brave gentleman, 'tis reported, and was himself a man of genius. He founded the picture gallery in Düsseldorf, and in the observatory there they show a very curiously executed piece of wooden work, consisting of one box within another, which he himself had carved in his leisure hours, of which latter he had every day four-and-twenty.

The state of things in Germany, supposed thus far in the description, is one of profound peace and somnolency. The picture already sketched of this quiescence is first emphasized by one or two additional strokes, and then a rude contrast is presented ; for the time of the French Revolution succeeds. Heine :

> In those days princes were not the persecuted wretches which they now are. Their crowns grew firmly on their heads, and at night they drew

their caps over them and slept in peace, and their people slumbered calmly at their feet, and when they awoke in the morning they said, "Good morning, father!" and he replied, "Good morning, dear children!"

But there came a sudden change over all this, for one morning when we awoke, and would say, "Good morning, father!" the father had traveled away, and in the whole town there was nothing but dumb sorrow. Everywhere there was a funeral-like expression, and people slipped silently through the market, and read the long paper placed on the door of the town-house. . . . An old invalid soldier from the Palatine read it, . . . and little by little a transparent tear ran down his white, honorable old mustache. I stood near him, and asked why he wept. And he replied: "The Prince Elector has abdicated." And then he read further, and at the words "for the long-manifested fidelity of my subjects," "and hereby release you from allegiance," he wept still more. It is a strange sight to see, when so old a man, in faded uniform, with a scarred veteran's face, suddenly bursts into tears. While we read, the Princely Electoral coat-of-arms was being taken down from the Town Hall, and every thing began to appear as miserably dreary as though we were waiting for an eclipse of the sun. The gentlemen town councilors went about at an abdicating, wearisome gait; even the omnipotent beadle looked as though he had no more commands to give. . . . But I went home, weeping and lamenting, because "the Prince Elector had *abducted!*"

By the word "abducted" here, used instead of "abdicated," Mr. Leland seeks to represent an ignorant blunder in language committed by the people, and unconsciously repeated by the boy Heine in reporting to his mother from their mouths what had happened. Mr. Leland's device is ingenious, but the effect of the humor is hardly thus reproduced for the English reader. Heine proceeds—relating a dream that he professes to have had on the occasion. This is probably, for the most part, a forgery of the waking mature brain of the writer; but at all events it forms satire as exquisite as ever was written. It is, by the way, a favorite trick of Heine's to have symbolic dreams of all sorts, both in his prose and in his verse. Heine :

My mother had trouble enough to explain the word, but I would hear nothing. I knew what I knew, and went weeping to bed, and in the night dreamed that the world had come to an end—that all the fair flower gardens and green meadows of the world were taken up and rolled up, and put away like carpets and baize from the floor; that a beadle climbed up on a high ladder and took down the sun, and that the tailor, Kilian, stood by and said to himself: "I must go home and dress myself neatly, for I am dead, and am to be buried this afternoon." And it grew darker and darker—a few stars glimmered sparely on high, and these at length fell down like yellow leaves in autumn. One by one all men vanished, and I, a poor child, wandered in anguish around, until before the willow fence of a deserted farm-house I saw a man digging up the earth with a spade, and near him an ugly, spiteful-looking woman, who held something in her apron like a human head—but it was the moon, and she laid it carefully in the open grave—and behind me stood the Palatine invalid, sighing and spelling, "The Prince Elector has abducted."

In what follows the allusion is to Murat, Napoleon's gallant marshal, made "Arch-Duke Joachim" in succession to the "abducting" Prince Elector. The mention of the "barber" will be better understood if it be borne in mind that the German custom is for the barber to visit his customers professionally at their houses. What could be more lively, and more life-like, than this description of that morning's occurrences in Düsseldorf, as seen from a boy's point of view? Heine's admiration for the French incidentally comes out:

When I awoke, the sun shone as usual through the window. There was a sound of drums in the street, and as I entered the sitting room and wished my father, who was sitting in his white dressing-gown, a good-morning, I heard the little light-footed barber, as he made up his hair, narrate very minutely that homage would that morning be offered at the Town Hall to the Arch-Duke Joachim. I heard, too, that the new ruler was of excellent family—that he had married the sister of the Emperor Napoleon, and was really a very respectable man—that he wore his beautiful black hair in flowing locks, that he would shortly enter the town, and in fine that he must please all the ladies. Meanwhile, the drumming in the streets continued, and I stood before the house-door and looked at the French troops marching in that joyful race of fame, who, singing and playing, swept over the world; the merry, serious faces of the grenadiers; the bear-skin shakos; the tricolored cockades; the glittering bayonets; the *voltigeurs* full of vivacity and *point d'honneur*, and the omnipotent, giant-like, silver-laced Tambour Major, who cast his *baton* with a gilded head as high as the second story, and his eyes to the third, where pretty girls gazed from the windows. I was so glad that soldiers were to be quartered in our house—in which my mother differed from me—and I hastened to the market-place. There every thing looked changed—somewhat as though the world had been new whitewashed. A new coat-of-arms was placed on the Town Hall; its iron balconies were hung with embroidered velvet drapery. French grenadiers stood as sentinels; the old gentlemen town councilors had put on new faces, and donned their Sunday coats, and looked at each other Frenchily, and said "*Bon jour!*"; ladies looked from every window; curious citizens and armed soldiers filled the square, and I, with other boys, climbed on the great bronze horse of the Prince Elector, and thence gazed down on the motley crowd.

In the humor of what now follows we recognize a style of representation which much use has made but too familiar in America. There must have been, one would say, a direct transplantation from this very place in Heine:

Our neighbor's Peter, and tall Jack Short, nearly broke their necks in accomplishing this feat, and it would have been better if they had been killed outright, for the one afterward ran away from his parents, enlisted as a soldier, deserted, and was finally shot in Mayence, while the other, having made geographical researches in strange pockets, was on this account elected member of a public tread-mill institute. But having broken the iron bands which bound him to his fatherland, he passed safely beyond sea, and eventually died in London, in consequence of wearing a much too long cravat, one end of which happened to be firmly attached to something, just as a royal official removed a plank from beneath his feet.

Let our readers remember, in enjoying the admirable raillery of the passage next to be submitted—we condense it from the seventh chapter of that same *Book Le Grand*— that what is taken off so wittily, and withal so sensibly, by Heine, is really not the studies themselves of which he speaks, but only the absurd lack of proportion with which these seem to have been taught. The connection of the present extract with the one preceding is immediate, except that a brief paragraph has been omitted by us at the close of chapter sixth:

The next day the world was again all in order, and we had school as before, and things were got by heart as before—the Roman emperors, chronology—the *nomina* in *im*, the *verba irregularia*—Greek, Hebrew, geography, German, mental arithmetic—ah! my head is still giddy with it!—all must be thoroughly learned. And much of it was eventually to my advantage. For had I not learned the Roman emperors by heart it would subsequently have been a matter of perfect indifference to me whether Niebuhr had or had not proved that they never really existed.

And had I not learned the numbers of the different years, how could I ever, in later years, have found out any one in Berlin, where one house is as like another as drops of water, or as grenadiers, and where it is impossible to find a friend unless you have the number of his house in your head. Therefore I associated with every friend some historical event which had happened in a year corresponding to the number of his house, so that the one recalled the other, and some curious points in history always occurred to me whenever I met any one whom I visited. For instance, when I met my tailor I at once thought of the battle of Marathon; if I saw the banker, Christian Gumpel, I remembered the destruction of Jerusalem; if a Portuguese friend, deeply in debt, of the flight of Mahomet; if the university judge, a man whose probity is well known, of the death of Haman. . . .

O, the trouble I had at school with my learning to count!—and it went even worse with the ready reckoning. I understood best of all *subtraction*, and for this I had a very practical rule—"Four can't be taken from three, therefore I must borrow one"; but I advise all, in such a case, to borrow a few extra dollars, for no one can tell what may happen.

But O! the Latin!—madam, you can really have no idea of what a mess it is. The Romans would never have found time to conquer the world if they had been obliged first to learn Latin. Lucky dogs! they already knew in their cradles the nouns ending in *im*. I, on the contrary, had to learn it by heart, in the sweat of my brow, but still it is well that I knew it. For if I, for example, when I publicly disputed in Latin, in the College hall of Göttingen, on the 20th of July, 1825—madam, it was well worth while to hear it—if I, I say, had said, *sinapem* instead of *sinapim*, the blunder would have been evident to the freshmen, and an endless shame to me. *Vis, buris, sitis, tussis, cucumis, amussis, cannabis, sinapis*—these words which have attracted so much attention in the world, effected this inasmuch as they belonged to a determined class, and yet were withal an exception. And the fact that I have them ready at my fingers' ends when I perhaps need them in a hurry, often affords me in life's darkened hours much internal tranquillity and spiritual consolation.

The topsy-turvy introduced by the revolutionary French into the political geography of Europe, and the beneficent changes, as well, that took place, or began to take place, in the condition especially of the German people, under the disturbing initiative of Napoleon, are now described with a wit and a humor, the secret of which, in their fine and their incalculable quality, perished with Heinrich Heine:

I avail myself of this opportunity to mention, madam, that it was not my fault, if I learned so little of geography that later in life I could not make my way in the world. For in those days the French made an intricate mixture of all limits and boundaries; every day lands were re-colored on the world's map; those which were once blue suddenly became green; many, indeed, were even dyed blood-red; the old established rules were so confused and confounded that the devil himself would never have remembered them. The products of the country were also changed, chicory and beets now grew where only hares, and hunters running after them, were once to be seen; even the character of different races changed, the Germans became pliant, the French paid compliments no longer, the English ceased making ducks and drakes of their money, and the Venetians were not subtle enough; there was promotion among princes, old kings obtained new uniforms, new kingdoms were cooked up and sold like hot cakes, many potentates were chased, on the other hand, from house and home, and had to find some new way of earning their bread, while others went at once at a trade, and manufactured, for instance, sealing-wax, or—madam, this paragraph must be brought to an end, or I shall be out of breath—in fine, in such times it is impossible to advance far in geography. I succeeded better in natural history, for there we find fewer changes, and we always have standard engravings of apes, kangaroos, zebras, rhinoceroses, etc., etc. And having many such pictures in my memory, it often happens that at first sight many mortals appear to me like old acquaintances.

Monsieur Le Grand, the Frenchman, after whom the present "book" is named, gets painted, "drum" and all, into Heine's picture:

How much do I not owe to the French drummer who was so long quartered in our house, who looked like the devil, and yet had the good heart of an angel, and who above all this drummed so divinely. He was a little nervous figure, with a terrible black mustache, beneath which red lips came bounding suddenly outward, while his wild eyes shot fiery glances all round. I, a young shaver, stuck to him like a bur, and helped him to clean his military buttons till they shone like mirrors, and to pipe-clay his vest—for Monsieur Le Grand liked to look well—and I followed him to the watch, to the roll-call, to the parade—in those times there was nothing but the gleam of weapons and merriment—*les jours de fête sont passés!* [the holidays are over!] Monsieur Le Grand knew but a little broken German, only the three principal words in every tongue—"bread" "kiss," "honor"—but he could make himself very intelligible with his drum. For instance, if I knew not what the word *liberté* meant, he drummed the *Marseillaise*—amd I understood him. . . . He once wanted to explain to me the word *l'Allemagne* [look out now for one of Heine's slants at Germany], and he drummed the all too *simple* melody, which on

market days is played to dancing dogs, namely, *dum—dum—dumb!* I was
vexed—but I understood him, for all that.

Napoleon Bonaparte is the great hero of Heine. We cannot blame the hero-worshiper in this case, cannot wonder
that he worshiped. We must remember that Heine was a
German Jew, and that the German Jew before Napoleon was
little better treated than a hunted wild beast. Napoleon
changed all that. Let us then bear cheerfully with Heine, while
he chants his pæan to the emancipator of his race. Once,
barely once, the boy Heinrich saw his demigod with his own
eyes ; his chief early impression of Napoleon he got through
Monsieur Le Grand and his "drum"—that hermeneutic
drum ! Shall we even let Heine build for us now his dithyrambics in "The Emperor's" praise, till he rears them almost
to the height of impious audacity ? It will be but a very
slight hint that we shall thus give of the blasphemy of
which Heine was capable—and capable, alas! upon occasions
not affording, as this occasion affords, extenuation of his sin.
Heine (and now we give him here his course unchecked, save
by omissions, to the end of two short chapters more of *Book
Le Grand*):

When I think of the great emperor all in my memory again becomes
summer-green and golden. . . . I often lay upon the bank, and piously
listened there when Monsieur Le Grand told of the warlike feats of the
great emperor, beating meanwhile the marches which were drummed
during the deeds, so that I saw and heard all to the life. I saw the
passage over the Simplon, the emperor in advance, and his brave grenadiers climbing on behind him, while the scream of frightened birds of
prey sounded around, and avalanches thundered in the distance; I saw
the emperor with flag in hand on the bridge of Lodi; I saw the emperor
in his gray cloak at Marengo; I saw the emperor mounted in the battle
of the Pyramids, naught around save powder, smoke, and Mamelukes; I
saw the emperor in the battle of Austerlitz—ha ! how the bullets whistled
over the smooth, icy road ! I saw, I heard the battle of Jena—*dum, dum,
dum ;* I saw, I heard the battles of Eylau, of Wagram—no, I could hardly
stand it ! Monsieur Le Grand drummed so that I nearly burst my own
sheepskin.

But what were my feelings when I first saw with highly blest, and with
my own, eyes, *him*—hosannah !—the emperor ! . . . The trembling trees

bowed toward him as he advanced; the sun-rays quivered, frightened, yet curiously, through the green leaves, and in the blue heaven above there swam visibly a golden star. The emperor wore his invisible-green uniform and the little world-renowned hat. He rode a white palfrey which stepped with such calm pride, so confidently, so nobly, had I then been Crown Prince of Prussia I should have envied that horse. The emperor sat carelessly, almost lazily, holding with one hand his rein and with the other good-naturedly patting the neck of the horse. It was a sunny, marble hand, a mighty hand—one of the pair which bound fast the many-headed monster of anarchy, and reduced to order the war of races, and it good-naturedly patted the neck of the horse. Even the face had that hue which we find in the marble Greek and Roman busts, the traits were as nobly proportioned as in the antiques, and on that countenance was plainly written, "Thou shalt have no gods before me!" . . . It was an eye clear as heaven; it could read the hearts of men; it saw at a glance all things at once, and as they were, in this world, while we, ordinary mortals, see them only one by one, and by their shaded hues. The brow was not so clear, the phantoms of future battles were nestling there, and there was a quiver which swept over the brow, and those were the creative thoughts, the great seven-mile-boots thoughts, wherewith the spirit of the emperor strode invisibly over the world; and I believe that every one of those thoughts would have given to a German author full material wherewith to write all the days of his life.

The emperor is dead. On a waste island in the Indian Sea lies his lonely grave; and he for whom the world was too narrow lies silently under a little hillock, where five weeping willows hang their green heads, and a gentle little brook, murmuring sorrowfully, ripples by. There is no inscription on his tomb; but Clio, with unerring pen, has written thereon invisible words, which will resound, like spirit-tones, through thousands of years. . . . Strange! A terrible destiny has already overtaken the three greatest enemies of the emperor. Londonderry [Lord Castlereagh, British foreign secretary during the final struggle with Napoleon] has cut his throat, Louis XVIII. has rotted away on his throne, and Professor Saalfeld is still, as before, Professor in Göttingen.

That last stroke about the Göttingen professor! What concentration is there of Heine's memorable contempt for his own university!

A very important feature of the *Pictures of Travel*, as of most of Heine's works, is the ribaldry, now blasphemous, now lewd, which it contains. Another unhappy thing in the book is the inconceivably venomous personal vituperation vented in it by Heine. Von Platen, a brother-poet of the author, is, through page after page, elaborately jeered at with a witty bitterness of vulgar malice probably not paralleled in literature, or, if paralleled, paralleled only elsewhere in Heine's own works. From this spiteful tirade a specimen extract or two must suffice the present purpose. Heine says :

> Everywhere in Platen's poems we see the ostrich, which only hides its head; the vain, weak bird, which has the most beautiful plumage, and yet cannot fly; and which, ever quarrelsome, stumbles along over the polemic sandy desert of literature. With his fine feathers, without the power to soar, with his fine verse, without poetic flight, he is the very opposite to that eagle of song who, with less brilliant wings, still rises to the sun. I must turn to my old refrain : Count Platen is no poet. . . .

> I cannot avoid mentioning that Count Platen has often assured the public that in days as yet to come he will compose the most remarkable poetry of which no one has as yet even a presentiment; yes, and that he will publish Iliads and Odysseys and classic tragedies, and similar immortally colossal poems, after he has toiled so or so many lustrums. Reader, you have, perhaps, read some of these outpourings of self-consciousness in his laboriously filed verses, and the promise of such a glorious future was probably the pleasanter to you, when the count, at the same time, represented all the contemporary German poets, with the exception of the aged Goethe, as a set of nasty wretches who only stood in his way on the path to immortality, and who were so devoid of shame as to pluck the laurels and the praise which of right belonged to him alone.

Heine taunts Platen with his poverty, and is, besides, foul in his scurrility beyond belief. The man whom he thus bespattered with filth was true poet enough to write the following very striking verses on the abdication of Charles V. of Spain and his retirement to a monastery. Our translation is kindly furnished by Miss Elizabeth Sihler, of Fort Wayne, Indiana :

> 'Tis night, the tempest rages more and more;
> Ye Spanish monks, now ope to me your door.

> Here let me rest till sounds the convent bell
> That frightens you to church, your beads to tell.

> Prepare for me all that your house affords,
> The order's garb, a coffin—without words.

Grant me a cell, nor do my vow decline,
More than one half of all this world was mine.

The head that meekly boweth to be shorn,
Full many a kingly diadem hath worn.

The shoulders that the cowl would humbly bear
Were wont imperial ermine once to wear.

To be as are the dead is my desire—
A crumbling ruin, like the old empire.

What beauty could dwell with what deformity, in a single human breast, the contrast of Heine's attack on Platen with the following strain of pensive sentiment from the same source may serve to show. Heine, the youth, is looking forward to Heine, the old man. The vision that he sees is not the vision that will be. Heine's locks, we believe, never whitened; his beard is by observers described as having flowed, large and long, in raven black, over the clothes that covered him in his bed of suffering at Paris. All, in short, was to be very different from the dream that he dreamed ; but here is the dream :

But a day must come when the fire of youth will be quenched in my veins, when winter will dwell in my heart, when his snow-flakes will whiten my locks, and his mists will dim my eyes. Then my friends will lie in their lonely graves, and I alone shall remain like a solitary stalk forgotten by the reaper. A new race will have sprung up with new desires and new ideas, full of wonder. I hear new names and listen to new songs, for the old names are forgotten, and I myself am forgotten, perhaps honored by but few, scorned by many and loved by none! And then the rosy-cheeked boys will spring around me and place the old harp in my trembling hand and say, laughing, "Thou indolent, gray-headed old man, sing us again songs of the dreams of thy youth."

Then I will grasp the harp, and my old joys and sorrows will awake, tears will again gleam on my pale cheeks. Spring will bloom once more in my breast, sweet tones of woe will tremble on the harp-strings. I shall see once more the blue flood and the marble palaces, and the lovely faces of ladies and young girls—and I will sing a song of the flowers of Brenta [a little stream of Italy].

It will be my last song, the stars will gaze on me as in the nights of my youth, the loving moonlight will once more kiss my cheeks, the spirit chorus of nightingales long dead will sound from afar, my eyes intoxicated with sleep will softly close, my soul will re-echo with the notes of my harp—perfume breaths from the flowers of the Brenta.

A tree will shadow my grave. I would gladly have it a palm, but that tree will not grow in the North. It will be a linden, and of a summer evening lovers will sit there caressing; the green finches will be listening silently, and my linden will rustle protectingly over the heads of the happy ones, who will be so happy that they will have no time to read what is written on the white tombstone. But when, at a later day, the lover has lost his love, then he will come again to the well-known linden, and sigh and weep, and gaze long and oft upon the stone until he reads the inscription: "He loved the flowers of the Brenta."

Those who know Bryant's exquisite little poem entitled *June* will think of the parallel between one stanza of that and the last lovely imagining of Heine's young dream, dream never to be realized, of his own end of life.

If the ill taste from that vile passage about Platen has not yet yielded quite on the palate of the reader, let him take the following. The scene is, no matter where; the time, no matter when—only it is still youth :

From my heart poured out the feeling of love; it poured forth with wild longing into the broad night. The flowers in the garden beneath my window breathed a stronger perfume. Perfumes are the feelings of flowers, and as the human heart feels most powerful emotions in the night, when it believes itself to be alone and unperceived, so, also, do the flowers, soft-minded, yet ashamed, appear to wait for concealing darkness, that they may give themselves wholly up to their feelings, and breathe them out in sweet odors. Pour forth, ye perfumes of my heart, and seek beyond yon blue mountain for the loved one of my dreams! *Now* she lies in slumber, at her feet kneel angels, and if she smiles in sleep it is a prayer which angels repeat; in her breast is heaven with all its raptures, and as she breathes, my heart, though afar, throbs responsively. Behind the silken lids of her eyes the sun has gone down, and when they are raised the sun rises, and birds sing and the bells of the flock tinkle, and I strap on my knapsack and depart.

This dreamer, more deliciously sentimental than Rousseau, than Chateaubriand, far more so than the author of the *Sorrows of Young Werther*, can strike with quite equal power a quite other string. What exquisite satire on blind admiration of genius—perhaps, too, on the genius itself blindly admired—is conveyed in the following account of a conversation about Goethe and Schiller, in which four persons were engaged, two youths, a lady, and himself, the veracious reporter :

> . . . One of them, a long, lean youth, full of quicksilver, and who looked like a barometer, praised the virtue and purity of Schiller, while the other, also a long, up-sprouted young man, lisped verses from the "Dignity of Woman," smiling meanwhile as sweetly as a donkey who has stuck his head into a pitcher of molasses and delightedly licks his lips.

> Both of the youths confirmed their assertions with the refrain, " But he is still greater. He is really greater, in fact. He is the greater, I assure you upon my honor he is greater." The lady was so amiable as to bring me, too, into this æsthetic conversation and inquire, " Doctor, what do *you* think of Goethe ? " I, however, crossed my arms on my breast, bowed my head as a believer, and said, *La illah ill allah wamohammed rasul allah !*

For bewildering effect of raillery, doubtful whether more against Goethe himself or more against Goethe's deifying admirers, what could possibly surpass that unintelligible final jargon, with its murmur of " Allah," muttered with the gesture, and as if in the dialect, of a Mohammedan devotee ?

But we must not forget that Heine was a poet as well as a prose writer—and a poet, too, even in the *Pictures of Travel.* Here is a song of his from that book, a song which every one already knows by heart, but which, for that very reason, no one would wish to miss from these pages. It is " The Lorelei." Its pretended legend—so we have seen it stated as if by one who knew—is the fabrication of a modern poet's brain. But Heine adopted it, and he has fairly sung it, and forever, into the folk-lore of the Rhine. They show you the eddy, the rapid, in the current of the river, where Heine's "maiden wondrous fair " still sits, as truly as ever she did, singing her "wonderful melody." The reader must not lose the peculiar Heine-like turn into lightness from pathos with which the song closes. Mr. C. P. Cranch is the translator we choose. Many hands have tried their cunning on this piece to produce it in an English form, but no one else, in our opinion, has succeeded quite as Mr. Cranch has done :

> I know not what it presages,
>   This heart with sadness fraught;
> 'Tis a tale of the olden ages
>   That will not from my thought.
>
> The air grows cool and darkles;
>   The Rhine flows calmly on;
> The mountain summit sparkles
>   In the light of the setting sun.
>
> There sits, in soft reclining,
>   A maiden wondrous fair,
> With golden raiment shining
>   And combing her golden hair.
>
> With a comb of gold she combs it,
>   And combing, low singeth she—
> A song of a strange, sweet sadness,
>   A wonderful melody.
>
> The sailor shudders as o'er him
>   The strain comes floating by;
> He sees not the cliffs before him—
>   He only looks on high.
>
> Ah! round him the dark waves, flinging
>   Their arms, draw him slowly down—
> And this, with her wild, sweet singing,
>   The Lorelei has done.

Mr. C. G. Leland has done his cleverest and best with this that follows, but you might as well seek to translate a violet into verse as seek to render in language other than its own the delicate sentiment, the exquisite rhythm, of the German original.   It bears no title:

> Thou'rt like a lovely floweret,
>   So void of guile or art;
> I gaze upon thy beauty,
>   And grief steals o'er my heart.
>
> I fain would lay, devoutly,
>   My hands upon thy brow,
> And pray that God will keep thee
>   As good and fair as now.

Longfellow as translator has laid the magic of his touch on some of Heine's songs. The following is a version by Longfellow :

> The sea it hath its pearls,
>   The heaven hath its stars,
> But my heart, my heart,
>   My heart hath its love.
>
> Great are the sea and the heaven,
>   Yet greater is my heart,
> And fairer than pearls and stars
>   Flashes and beams my love.
>
> Thou little, youthful maiden,
>   Come unto my great heart;
> My heart, and the sea, and the heaven
>   Are melting away with love.

This, next to be given, is not unlike in motive. There is a remarkable monotony in change—like the moan of the sea unseen heard ceaselessly underneath all the other noises of nature—prevailing through Heine's songs. Longing not satisfied, and never to be satisfied, sad presentiment and sad reminiscence, love and loss, make up the burden of the best of them all. Bitter mockery not seldom breaks the sweetness into discord. The following translation is a specimen of Mr. Leland's workmanship in its finest felicity:

> Thou gentle ferry maiden,
>   Come, draw thy boat to land,
> And sit thee down beside me,
>   We'll talk with hand in hand.
>
> Lay thy head against my bosom,
>   And have no fear of me;
> Dost thou not venture boldly
>   Each day on the roaring sea?
>
> My heart is like the ocean,
>   It hath storm, and ebb, and flow;
> And many a pearl is hidden
>   In its silent depths below.

21

One more song and the singer shall be still. We find our translation in the *North American Review* for July, 1849:

> A lonely fir-tree standeth
>   On a chilly northern height;
> The snow and the ice, while it sleepeth,
>   Weave round it a garment white.
>
> It dreameth of a palm-tree
>   That, far in the eastern land,
> Alone and silent mourneth
>   On its plain of burning sand.

Did not Heine, on his death-bed, at last become religious? Our own answer we have already implied; but let us have testimony furnished from the pen of Heine himself. He did make a quasi-religious confession; but he spoke, making it, in his old character, that of mocker—a character held by him, say rather holding him, to the last. What a cruel, inevitable clutch, as of the cat that may play with her captive but that will by no means let him go! Here, then, is what Heine, prefacing a publication of his, says of his own final religious state. We find our translation in the *Fortnightly Review*, 1869. The translator makes silent omissions at points. These we indicate, or else restore the matter omitted. We also make a few changes for better expression of the author's meaning:

> When we lie on our death-bed we become very gentle and tender-hearted, and would willingly make peace with God and man. I confess I have scratched many, and bitten many, and been no lamb. But believe me, those bepraised lambs of mildness would behave themselves less piously if they possessed the teeth and the claws of the tiger. I can glory that I have only seldom used such native weapons. . . . But since I have stood in need of God's mercy I have made a truce with all my foes; many beautiful poems, which were directed against very high and very low persons, are for that reason excluded from the present collection. Poems which contained half-way personalities against the dear God I have committed to the flames with the zeal of fear. It is better that the verses should burn than the versifier. Yes, I have made peace with the Creator as well as with the creature—to the great displeasure of my enlightened friends, who reproach me for my relapse into the old su-

perstition, as they are pleased to call my return to God. Others express themselves with still bitterer intolerance. Atheism's Convocation has pronounced its anathema over me, and there are certain fanatical priests of unbelief who would willingly place me on the rack to make me renounce my heterodoxy. Happily, they have no instruments of torture at command except their writings. But I will confess every thing without torture. I have really returned to God, like the prodigal son, after feeding swine with the Hegelians for many years. The divine home-sickness came upon me, and drove me forth, through woods and vales, over the dizziest mountain pathways of dialectic. On my way I found the god of the pantheists, but I could make nothing of him. This poor visionary creature is interwoven with and grown into the world. Indeed, he is almost imprisoned in it, and yawns at you, without voice, without power. To have will one must have personality, and to manifest one's self one must have elbow-room. . . .

In theology I admit my backsliding, . . . but I must expressly contradict the report that it has brought me to the bosom or the threshold of any Church whatever. . . . I have abjured nothing, not even my pagan gods, from whom it is true I have parted, but only in friendship and love.

How this man cajoles you with the play of his mockery! But be gentle toward him, for not less he also cajoled himself. If, however, lighting, for instance, upon some such charming utterance from Heine as is, in part, the one about to be given, you are tempted for a moment to think that perhaps this writer is cruelly misjudged to have been only a mocker, you may justly then set yourself right again by recalling the mocking ambiguous tenor of that religious confession of the dying man's of which you have just now had a taste. You might almost, when you read the first part of the following, think it was Renan making his Galilæan idyll of Jesus:

How beautiful, how serenely fair, how unutterably sweet was the Christianity of the early centuries, while it still resembled its divine founder in the heroism of suffering! There lingered yet the beautiful story of an undeclared divinity, who wandered in the fair form of youth under the palms of Palestine, who preached love, and revealed the doctrines of freedom and equality which the reason of the greatest thinkers has since recognized as true. Compare with that religion of Christ the several Christianities that have been established in the several countries as state religions—the Roman Catholic Church, or that Catholicism without poetry which we see prevailing in England as High Church—that decaying skeleton of belief from which all bloom and life have passed away.

How far off after all Heine was from truly appreciating the serious, the religious, spirit of Luther, whom he praised, and of Protestantism, let the following expressions of his show. This shallow brain, this shallower heart, thought that lascivious painting was a better protest against the Roman Catholic Church than were the theses of Luther! Heine:

> The painters of Italy engaged in far more effective polemics than did the Saxon theologians. The blooming flesh-tints upon the paintings of Titian are all Protestantism. The graces of his Venus are more real theses than those which the German monk fixed on the church door of Wittenberg.

Heine wrote as if afraid to be candid—lest for one dreadful moment he might possibly be dull. He was as inevitably, as unalterably, a jester as was Lucian. He was even more incapable of seriousness than was Voltaire. It thus seems quite impossible to judge him at all in any other capacity than that of a wit and a mocker, whether in his prose or in his verse. He sentimentalized indeed, but this was chiefly that he might finish by mocking at his own sentiment, and also at you for having been cheated into taking him seriously. He called himself a "soldier in the war for the liberation of humanity," and the merit of being this has been somewhat too gravely accorded to him by Mr. Matthew Arnold. But Heine is hardly in any sense to be reckoned a beneficent power in literature. Such a spirit as his is a blight rather than a blessing to whatever it touches. Sorrowfully we say this, confessing ourselves susceptible, exquisitely susceptible, to the charm of his genius and his wit, and remembering also the heavy lot that so long was his of helplessness and of pain. Nothing perhaps could better, as with a concentrated solar ray, imprint on the imagination of the reader a final image, at once faithful and pathetic, of Heine—the whole man, his genius, his wit, his character, and his misfortune— than the following expression of his concerning himself :

> The great author of the universe, the Aristophanes of heaven, has resolved that the little author on earth, the so-styled "Aristophanes of Germany," shall feel, to his inmost soul, what insignificant needle-pricks his most brilliant sarcasms have been, compared with the awful thunderbolts which his divine humor can hurl against weak mortals.

After the audacity and the pathos of words like those, one feels like being "dumb with silence." Indeed, what could possibly be said that would not rather harm than help the sentiment inspired of mingling admiration, horror, and pity ?

XIII.

EPILOGUE.

THE author's preface is usually in effect the author's epilogue. But in the present case the preface going before seems not quite to make unnecessary something following after, to say a few things still left unsaid, such as the author, in retrospect of his labor accomplished, would naturally feel like saying to a kindly interested friend at his side.

We shall hardly, we presume, in the opinion of any, have made the mistake of admitting German literary names not worthy to be included in a book like this. We may further, with some confidence, assume that the proportion of space here allotted to one name and another will generally be allowed as approximately true to their comparative importance taken in connection with their adaptedness to interest a popular audience of readers. Yet again. We cannot have gone widely astray in choosing from among the various productions of each several author the one, or the ones, best deserving to be shown to our readers. Of course, in seeking to strike the right critical tone for appreciation of different authors and different masterpieces there is more chance of failure. At this point we cannot suppose ourselves fortunate enough so to have hit the mark as to unite all qualified suffrages in our favor. What we do hope is that all judges will agree in clearing us of intentional unfairness. If we have anywhere through ignorance made false statements as of fact, we shall on conviction confess ourselves blameworthy; though no writer is bound to know every thing, every writer is at least bound to know what he undertakes to tell as of knowledge.

The present writer profoundly believes that for the interests of literature, quite apart from the interests of life, nothing is more fatal than to attempt the divorce, in thought and in judgment, of character from genius, of morality from literary production. He has criticised constantly in view of this principle. His ethical judgments may thus properly be regarded as pronounced less in the behoof of ethics than in the behoof of letters. Bad men have sometimes been good writers, and, alas, on the other hand, too, good men have sometimes been bad writers; there is no certain inference possible in either direction—from character to production or from production to character. Still, for ourselves, we freely confess, we consider it—and this purely as a matter of literary criticism—of the two courses, safer to infer from a man's known evil life and character that there must be flaw in his literary performance than, inversely, to infer from the apparent excellence of his literary work that his life and character, though apparently evil, must really be good. That which is in character will generally come out in production, whether the production be of art or of literature. Such correspondence—often latent, but seldom lacking, especially where the question is of poetry—between what an author is and what that author does, it is, in each case, within the just province of literary criticism to divine and discover. The danger to the critic of undue personal bias, adverse or favorable, existing on his own part, as to the man whom he criticises, is always great. One criticising must task one's self to be fair—alike to the author considered and to the cause of good literature.

There are many German writers absent even in name from the preceding pages, whom, if this were a history of German literature, it would be an unpardonable deficiency not at least to have mentioned and characterized. We should need, for instance, to have told how Kotzebue, the playwright—what with talent and what with impudence—pushed himself to the front, alongside of Goethe and of Schiller, in the public attention, and, with his century or more of successful plays, renewed on German soil that tradition of fecundity in production for dramatists which is among the wonders of Greek literary history. Kotzebue, to be sure—worked over and adapted in our own language by Sheridan—is known among us to spectators of the drama, by some plays of his remarkable for effective situation and eloquent dialogue ; witness his *Incas in Peru,* more recognizable under its English alias of *Pizarro.* But Kotzebue was more nearly a charlatan than a classic in German literature. The same may be said of Werner, who may be described as a kind of exaggeration, a reduction to absurdity, of Schiller.

The philosophers, likewise, one would wish to have shown something of ; all the more from the fact that metaphysic speculation in Germany has so vitally affected German literary development—Kant, for instance, having imposed the mold of his system on Schiller's later production, and Fichte and Schelling having, through their idealism in philosophy, prepared the way for romanticism in literature. Jacobi, indeed, among German philosophers, unites a literary, with his philosophical, claim to attention, which well-nigh persuaded us to give him place in the company of our select German immortals. The like thing might be said of Schleiermacher among theologians ; for Schleiermacher translated Plato into German. Among preachers, Krummacher appealed to us for inclusion ; and more strongly still, Theremin, a writer on sacred eloquence, who most felicitously joined a delightful lucidity in exposition, inherited, with his blood, from France, to a singular philosophical depth and suggestiveness, communicated, perhaps, by some commingling of German in his nearer ancestry. The name of Krummacher as preacher recalls that preacher's father. The elder Krummacher was author of many "parables," over which the present writer long affectionately delayed before he could bring himself to give up showing them in specimen to the readers of this book.

Some glance at more recent German literature might appear to be natural here. But the truth is, interests other than literary have, since Goethe's death, for the most part absorbed the intellectual energies of Germany. Revolutionary upheaval, beginning about 1848, soon subsided, or was soon suppressed, into a stagnation and torpor unfriendly to literary achievement. Political, philosophical, and scientific activity, predominating later, left literature proper to languish. Materialism, too—a spirit naturally enough engendered under the incubus of heavy military establishments, which made peace itself seem like war—invaded the land of ideas. As a consequence of these things, and as a consequence too—so, at least, the present writer ventures to think—of a sterilizing influence exerted by Goethe, who in literature added nothing, unless it were the idea of self-culture as the great thing in life, to the stock of human ideas, and who set the example of endlessly elaborating the old, in place of fruitfully originating new—at any rate, for some reason or reasons, within the last fifty years, no distinctively literary name, except Heine, stands out with a prominence at all comparable to his. Schopenhauer is not a distinctively literary name, though he did write his oppressive philosophy in almost a literary style; but Schopenhauer, whose pessimistic speculation has registered so deep a score in modern human thought, and whose fame and influence seem in origin only of to-day, in fact wrote his chief work before Goethe died. Germans have indeed continued to think, all the time that they have been with long patience schooling themselves to be the chief military power in Europe; but they have not meantime produced any recognized masterpieces of literature. In history, however—not only in political history, but in history of philosophy, of letters, of art, and of culture—they have achieved praiseworthy things.

German fiction, also, has of late been illustrated with some noteworthy names.

We could hardly hope to make even approximately apprehensible to our readers the self-denials which the necessary limits of space imposed upon us as to the authors to be here included. As to the things to be included from the authors finally chosen, the case was yet more trying. We can truthfully testify that merely to select and condense the translated extracts that appear in the foregoing pages has cost much more labor and thought than to write the original text that introduces or accompanies them.

The effort has constantly been to treat and to show the authors selected, not in such a manner that readers testing our results by the current criticism of the day would find us in accord with prevailing opinion; but in such a manner that readers subsequently pushing, however far, their study of any particular author himself should at no time have just occasion to say that we had seriously misled them.

INDEX.

———•———

We undertake here simply to furnish a few practical suggestions, such as may help those entirely unacquainted with German to make some tolerable approach to the true pronunciation of the proper names with which they will meet in reading this book.

The sounds of the simple vowels in German are easy to learn, because they are consistently uniform. The *quantity* may be long or short, but the *quality* remains the same. *A* has the sound of *a* in *ah*, *e* the sound of *a* in *ale*, *i* (and *ie*) of *e* in *eel*, *o* of *o* in *no*, *u* of *u* in *sure*. The obscure sound of *e*, in unaccented syllables, is nearly like English *ĕ* in *ebb*, given very lightly. Of the diphthongs, *ai* and *ei* have very nearly the sound of English long *i*, *au* has the sound of *ow* in *now*, *eu* very nearly the sound of *oi* in *oil*. *A*, *o*, and *u* are severally combined with *e* to produce what are called *umlauts* (oomlowts). The umlauts are oftenest noted by two dots over the principal vowel, thus : *ae*＝*ä*, *oe*＝*ö*, *ue*＝*ü*. *Ae*, or *ä*, sounds like the German vowel *e* ; *ö* is sounded by making up the mouth to say *o*, and then saying *a* (as in *ale*) ; *ü* by making up the mouth to say *u* (as in *sure*), and then saying *ee*. The combination *äu* sounds like *eu*. Doubling a vowel, as *aa*, *ee*, *oo*, merely lengthens the proper sound of that vowel ; the same is true of *h* following a vowel.

There are no silent vowels in German. (*Ie*＝*i* is an apparent exception.) Each *vowel* (or diphthong) makes a syllable. For example, *Undine* would in German be pronounced *Oondeé nĕh*.

The consonants *b* and *d* are, when final, generally sharpened into *p* and *t* respectively. *G*, beginning a word or a syllable, is always hard, as in *gun*. *J* has the sound of *y* beginning a syllable. *W*, beginning a word or a syllable, is sounded by making up the mouth to say *w* (as in *we*), and then saying *v* ; in other words, a German *w* is an English *v* pronounced with the *lips* without the aid of the teeth. *V* is sounded like *f*. *Ch* initial is sounded like *k* ; elsewhere like *k* gently roughened in utterance, as if you were clearing your throat. The combination *ng* never in German is separated in pronunciation, as sometimes it is in English ; for example, *finger*, in German, rhymes strictly with *singer*, *anger* with *hanger*. *Sch* has the sound of *sh*. *Th* has the sound of *t*.

The full name of the greatest literary man of Germany will serve to exemplify many of the foregoing hints. Johann Wilhelm von Goethe is pronounced *Yo'han Vil'helm fone Goe'tĕh*. (The syllable *Goe* has very nearly the sound of the first syllable in the English word *guerdon*, with the *r* left unpronounced.)

The names of authors treated in the preceding pages with a greater or less degree of fullness are here distinguished from those of authors but incidentally mentioned, by being printed with capital letters and in a heavier type.

5487